A CONCISE
ENCYCLOPEDIA
of
JUDAISM

A CONCISE
ENCYCLOPEDIA
of
JUDAISM

DAN COHN-SHERBOK

ONEWORLD

OXFORD

A CONCISE ENCYCLOPEDIA OF JUDAISM

Oneworld Publications
(Sales and Editorial)
185 Banbury Road
Oxford OX2 7AR
England
http://www.oneworld-publications.com

Oneworld Publications
(US Marketing Office)
160 N. Washington St.
4th floor, Boston
MA 02114
USA

ISBN 1–85168–176–0

Cover design by Design Deluxe
Typeset by Saxon Graphics Ltd, Derby
Printed and bound in England by Clays Ltd, St Ives plc

Contents

Acknowledgements

The author and publishers wish to thank the following for permission to reproduce material in this volume:

Ancient Civilizations and Historical Persons (p. 163); British Israel Public Affairs Centre and the Zionist Federation of Great Britain and Ireland (pp. 39, 47, 155, 168, 173, 179, 194 and cover); Circa Photo Library (pp. 88, 126, 131); Israeli Press and Photo Agency (p. 51); Italian Cultural Institute (pp. 22, 70); Moojan Momen (p. 106); PA News (pp. 41, 128, 161); Robert Harding Picture Library (cover); Sonia Halliday Photographs (pp. 33, 78, 89, 114, 134, 150, 201).

Every effort has been made to trace and acknowledge ownership of copyright. If any credits have been omitted or any rights overlooked, it is completely unintentional.

Preface

For more than twenty years I have taught courses dealing with Jewish life and thought in secondary schools and universities. During this time I have frequently directed students to such multi-volume encyclopedias of Judaism as the *Jewish Encyclopedia* and the *Encyclopedia Judaica*. These vast repositories of material provide a wealth of information about all aspects of Judaism. Nonetheless, very often students find these works overwhelming as well as difficult to use if they are much in demand in the library.

Aware of this problem, I suggested they look at a number of single-volume encyclopedias and dictionaries of Judaism; yet many of these works failed to meet their needs since they are often highly selective in their choice of entries. Increasingly I came to see that what was needed was a concise encyclopedia of Judaism containing basic information on a wide variety of subjects. Such a handy reference book could not be expected to take the place of standard multi-volume or even single-volume comprehensive works, but it could serve as a first point of entry into the fascinating richness of the Jewish tradition.

This volume was thus designed to fill a gap in the types of reference books available to students, teachers and more general readers. It contains over a thousand entries. Although all aspects of Jewish civilization are covered – including people, places, theology, liturgy, ritual, literature, institutions, ethics, history, beliefs – the main criterion for inclusion has been reference-worthiness. My intention is that this encyclopedia should provide the type of information most commonly sought by students of the Jewish heritage.

Any scholar working in Jewish studies owes an enormous debt to those excellent lexicographers who have already published reference works in the field. All the following have been consulted in checking and cross-checking the information contained in this encyclopedia: Geoffrey

Wigoder, *The New Standard Jewish Encyclopedia* (London, W. H. Allen, 1977); *Jewish Encyclopedia* (New York, Funk and Wagnalls, 1901–5); *Encyclopedia Judaica* (Jerusalem, Keter, 1972–); Yacov Newman and Gavriel Sivan, *Judaism A–Z: Lexicon of Terms and Concepts* (Jerusalem, Department for Torah Education and Culture in the Diaspora of the World Zionist Organization, 1980); Raphael Judah Zwi Werblowsky and Geoffrey Wigoder, eds, *The Encyclopedia of the Jewish Religion* (London, Phoenix House, 1967); Glenda Abramson, ed., *The Blackwell Companion to Jewish Culture* (Oxford, Blackwell, 1989); Geoffrey Wigoder, ed., *The Encyclopedia of Judaism* (New York, Macmillan, 1989); David Bridger and Samuel Wolk, eds, *The New Jewish Encyclopedia* (New York, Behrman House, 1976); Louis Jacobs, *The Jewish Religion* (Oxford, Oxford University Press, 1995).

Using the Encyclopedia

Cross-references within the entries are intended to provide fuller information by directing the reader to similar or related matters. Cross-references are indicated by text in small capitals, e.g. RABBI. For readers wishing to explore Judaism from a thematic viewpoint, the Thematic Index on pp. 217–37 will refer them to the appropriate entries. The Chronology on pp. 209–11 gives a full picture of the major events through the life of the faith. Readers should note that Hebrew words have generally been transliterated according to the Sephardi pronunciation. In general I have followed the most commonly used spelling of Hebrew terms. In common with other volumes in this series, dates are given as BCE (Before the Common Era) and CE (the Common Era).

Historical Introduction

For thousands of years, Jews have formed a tiny percentage of the population of the world. Nonetheless, their influence has been incalculable. Nearly twenty centuries ago, Christianity emerged out of Judaism. Through the Hebrew Bible, the Jewish people gave the world ethical monotheism. In addition, the Jewish nation produced intellectual giants who profoundly influenced the course of Western civilization. Despite these contributions, the Jewish community was often viewed as strange and alien; as a consequence, Jews were frequently persecuted and massacred. Yet Jewry survived; and now, on the threshold of the twenty-first century, the Jewish people continue to play an important role on the world stage.

Jews in the Ancient World

The origins of this remarkable people go back nearly four millennia to a time when major empires struggled for dominance in the Middle East. At the end of the fourth millennium BCE the Sumerians created city-states in southern Mesopotamia, and during the third millennium BCE waves of Semitic peoples settled amid the Sumerians, adopting their writing and other cultural practices. The culture of these Mesopotamian civilizations had a profound impact on the Jewish faith: ancient Near Eastern myths were refashioned to serve the needs of the Hebrews. It appears that the Jewish nation emerged in this milieu between the nineteenth and sixteenth centuries BCE. According to the Jewish scriptures, Abraham was the father of the nation. Initially known as Abram, he came from Ur of the Chaldees; at God's command he went to Canaan (modern Syria), later settling in the plain near Hebron.

Abraham was followed by his son Isaac and grandson Jacob, whose son Joseph was sold into slavery in Egypt. There he prospered, and eventually the entire Hebrew clan moved to Egypt, where they flourished for centuries until a new Pharaoh decreed in the thirteenth century BCE that all first-born Hebrews should be put to death. To persuade Pharaoh to release the Jewish people, God sent a series of plagues on the Egyptians; eventually, Moses – the leader of the Hebrews – was allowed to lead his kinsfolk out of Egypt. After wandering in the desert for forty years, the Hebrews finally entered the promised land of Canaan.

Under the leadership of Joshua, an Israelite commander appointed by Moses as his successor, the Hebrews conquered the inhabitants of the land; later they began to form into separate groups. At first there were twelve tribes, named after the sons of Jacob: Joseph, Benjamin, Levi, Simeon, Reuben, Judah, Issachar, Zebulun, Dan, Naphtali, Gad and Asher. When the Levites became a special priestly group, the tribe of Joseph was divided into two parts, named after his sons: Ephraim and Manasseh. During this period, the Hebrews were ruled by twelve national heroes who served successively as judges.

Frequently the covenant between God and his chosen people was proclaimed at gatherings in national shrines. This emphasis on covenantal obligation reinforced the belief that the Jews were the recipients of God's loving-kindness. As the Jewish people established a more settled existence, the covenant expanded to include additional legislation, such as the measures necessary to regulate an agricultural community. During this period it became clear that the God of the covenant directed human history: the Exodus and the entry into the promised land were perceived as the unfolding of a divine providential plan.

In the time of the judges (*c.*1200–1000 BCE), God was viewed as the supreme monarch of the Jewish people. When some tribes suggested to Gideon that he should occupy a formal position of power, he stated that it was impossible for the nation to be ruled by both God and a human king. Nonetheless, Saul (fl. eleventh century BCE) was elected as king despite the prophet Samuel's warnings against the dangers of monarchy. Later, around 930 BCE, the Israelite nation divided into two kingdoms. The northern tribes, led by Ephraim, and the southern tribes, led by Judah, had been united only by allegiance to King David; when his successor King Solomon, and Solomon's son Rehoboam, violated many of the ancient traditions, the northern tribes revolted.

The ostensible reason for this rebellion was the injustice of the monarchy, but in fact the northern tribes sought to recapture the simple ways of the Hebrews who had fled from Egypt. Then there had been no monarch, and leadership was exercised on the basis of charisma. What the north looked for was allegiance and loyalty to the King of Kings who had delivered them from the Egyptian bondage. It was against this background that the pre-exilic prophets (Elijah, Elisha, Amos, Hosea, Micah and Isaiah) sought to bring the nation back to true worship of God. In their view, righteousness served as the standard by which all people were to be judged.

During the first millennium BCE the Jews watched their nation emerge as two powerful states, only to see its influence wane due to spiritual and moral decay. Following the Babylonian conquest in 586 BCE, the Temple was destroyed and Jerusalem laid waste. This was God's punishment for their iniquity, predicted by the prophets. Yet despite defeat and exile, the nation rose from the ashes of the old kingdoms. In the centuries which followed, the Jewish people maintained their religious traditions. Though they had lost their independence, their devotion to God's law sustained them through suffering and hardship and inspired them to new heights of creativity.

In Babylonia the exiles prospered, keeping their religion alive in the synagogues. These institutions were founded so that Jews could meet together for worship and study; no sacrifices were offered since that was the prerogative of the Temple in Jerusalem. In 538 BCE King Cyrus of Persia, having conquered Babylonia, allowed the Jews to return to their former home, and the nation underwent a transformation. The Temple was rebuilt, and religious reforms were enacted. This return to the land of their forebears led to national restoration and a renaissance of Jewish life which was to last until the first century CE, when the former southern kingdom, known as Judea, came under Roman overlordship.

The period following the death of King Herod in 4 BCE was a time of intense anti-Roman feeling among Jews in Judea as well as in the diaspora. In time such hostility led to war, which brought defeat and the destruction of the Second Temple in 70 CE; thousands of Jews were deported. Such devastation, however, did not extinguish Jewish hopes of ridding the Holy Land of its Roman oppressors. In the second century a messianic rebellion led by Simeon bar Kokhba was crushed by Roman forces who killed multitudes of Jews and ravaged Judea. Yet despite this defeat, the Pharisees carried on Jewish learning in the academy at Javneh near Jerusalem.

Rabbinic Judaism

From the first century BCE scholars (rabbis) in Palestine engaged in the interpretation of the Jewish scriptures. The most important sage of this period was Judah Ha-Nasi, the head of the scholarly and legal body known as the Sanhedrin; his main achievement was the redaction of the Mishnah, a compendium of the oral Torah, in the second century. This volume consists of the teachings and rulings of rabbinic scholars whose teachings had been passed on orally. According to rabbinic Judaism, the law recorded in the Mishnah was given orally to Moses along with the written law: 'Moses received the Torah from Sinai, and handed it down to Joshua, and Joshua to the elders, and elders to the prophets, to the men of the Great Assembly.'

The Mishnah, which is almost entirely legal in character, consists of six sections. The first section – Seeds – begins with a discussion of benedictions and required prayers and continues with other matters such as the tithes of the harvest to be given to priests, Levites and the poor. The second section – Set Feasts – contains twelve subdivisions, called tractates, dealing with the Sabbath, Passover, the Day of Atonement and other festivals as well as shekel dues (Temple taxes) and the proclamation of the New Year. In the third section – Women – seven tractates consider matters affecting women such as betrothal, marriage, contracts and divorce. The fourth section – Damages – contains ten tractates concerning civil law: property rights, legal procedures, compensation for damage, ownership of lost objects, treatment of employees, sale and purchase of land, Jewish courts, punishments and criminal proceedings. In addition, a tractate of rabbinic moral maxims (Sayings of the Fathers) is included in this section. In the fifth section – Holy Things – there are eleven tractates dealing with sacrifical offerings and other Temple matters. The final section – Purifications – treats various types of ritual uncleanliness and methods of legal purification.

In addition to the Mishnah, the rabbis composed scriptural commentaries; this 'midrashic literature' was written over a period of centuries and is divided into works connected directly with books of the Bible and those dealing with readings for special festivals and other topics.

The Sanhedrin met in several cities in Galilee, but subsequently moved to the Roman district of Tiberias. At the same time other scholars created their own schools in other parts of the country where they applied mishnaic teaching to everyday life, together with old rabbinic teachings which had not been included in the Mishnah. During the third century CE, the Roman Empire experienced numerous difficulties, including inflation, population decline and a lack of technological development to support the army. Rival generals engaged in a struggle for power, and the government became increasingly inefficient. Throughout this period the Jewish community underwent a similar decline as a result of famine, epidemics and plunder. At the end of the century the Emperor Diocletian inaugurated reforms that strengthened the Empire. In addition, he introduced measures to repress the spread of Christianity, which had become a serious challenge to the imperial religion. However, Diocletian's successor Constantine the Great reversed these policies and extended official toleration to the Christian community. By this stage Christianity had succeeded in gaining a substantial following among the urban population. Eventually Constantine himself became increasingly involved in Church affairs and just before his death he was baptized. By the early 400s the Christian faith was established as the state religion of the Roman Empire.

During the first half of the fourth century Jewish scholars in Palestine had collected together the teachings of generations of rabbis in the academies of Tiberias, Caesarea and Sepphoris. These extended discussions of the Mishnah became the Palestinian Talmud. The text of this work included four sections of the Mishnah (Seeds, Set Feasts, Women and Damages), but here and there certain tractates were omitted. The views of these Palestinian teachers had an important impact on scholars in Babylonia, even though this work never attained the same prominence as that of the Babylonian Talmud.

Paralleling the development of rabbinic Judaism in Palestine, Babylonian scholars founded their own centres of learning. The third-century teacher Rav established an academy at Sura in central Mesopotamia, while his contemporary Samuel was head of another Babylonian academy at Nehardea. After Nehardea was devastated by an invasion in 259 CE, the academy at Pumbedita became a dominant centre of Jewish learning. The Babylonian sages carried on and developed the Galilean tradition of disputation, and the fourth century produced two of the most distinguished scholars of the talmudic period, Abbaye and Rava, both of whom were teachers at Pumbedita. With the decline of Jewish institutions in Palestine, Babylonia became the predominant centre of Jewish scholarship.

By the sixth century Babylonian scholars had completed the redaction of the Babylonian Talmud, an editorial task begun by Rav Ashi in the fourth to fifth century at Sura. This work parallels the Palestinian Talmud, and is largely a summary of the rabbinic discussions that occurred in the Babylonian academies. Both Talmuds are elaborations of the Mishnah, though neither commentary contains material on every passage. The texts themselves consist largely of summaries of rabbinic discussions in the course of which a phrase of the Mishnah is interpreted, discrepancies resolved and redundancies explained. In this compilation, conflicting opinions of the early scholars are contrasted, unusual words explained and anonymous opinions identified. Frequently individual teachers cite specific cases to support their views, and hypothetical eventualities are examined to enable a resolution of the discussion. Debates between outstanding scholars in one generation are often cited, as are differences of opinion between contemporary members of an academy or between a teacher and his students. The range of talmudic exploration is much broader than that of the Mishnah, and includes a wide range of rabbinic teachings about such subjects as theology, philosophy and ethics.

Judaism in the Middle Ages

By the sixth century the Jews had become largely a diaspora people. Despite the loss of their homeland, the Jewish nation was united by a common background: law, liturgy and shared tradition bound together the various communities stretching from Spain to Persia and from Poland to Africa. Though subcultures did emerge during the middle ages which could have divided the Jewish world, Jews remained united in their hope for messianic redemption, the restoration of the Holy Land and an ingathering of the exiles. Living among Christians and Muslims, the Jewish community was everywhere a minority group, and its marginal status resulted in repeated persecution.

Within the Islamic world, Jews together with Christians were viewed as 'Peoples of the Book' and were guaranteed religious toleration, judicial autonomy and exemption from military service. In return, they were compelled to accept the supremacy of the Islamic state. Such an arrangement was formally established by the Pact of Omar, dating from about 800CE. According to this treaty, Jews were restricted in various ways: they were not allowed to build new houses of worship, make converts, carry weapons or ride horses. In addition, they were compelled to wear distinctive clothing and pay a yearly poll tax. Jewish farmers were also obliged to pay a land tax consisting of part of their produce. Despite such conditions, Jewish life prospered; in many urban centres Jews engaged in various crafts, including tanning, dyeing, weaving, silk manufacture and metal work. Other Jews participated in inter-regional trade, establishing networks of agents and representatives.

During the first 200 years of Islamic rule (seventh and eighth centuries) under the Ummayad and Abbasid caliphates, Muslim rulers confirmed the authority of Babylonian Jewish institutions. When the Arabs conquered Babylonia and, under the new ruling dynasty of the Abbasids, moved the capital from Damascus to Baghdad, they officially recognized the exilarch, who for centuries had been the ruler of Babylonian Jewry. By the Abbasid period, the exilarch had come to share his power with the heads of the rabbinical academies, the major centres of rabbinic learning. The head of each academy, known as the *gaon*, delivered lectures as well as issuing learned opinions on legal matters.

In the eighth century various messianic Jewish movements appeared in Persia, leading to a series of armed uprisings against the Muslim authorities. Such revolts were quickly subdued; however, a more serious threat to traditional Judaism was posed later in the century by the creation of an anti-rabbinic sect, the Karaites. This group was founded in Babylonia by Anan ben David in the early eighth century. The guiding principle formulated by Anan, 'Search thoroughly in Scripture and do not rely on my opinion,' was intended to highlight the authority of the scriptures as the source of law. After the death of the founder, new parties within Karaism soon emerged, and by the tenth century Karaite communities were established in Israel, Babylonia and Persia. These groups rejected rabbinic law and promulgated their own laws, provoking the rabbis to attack Karaism as a heretical sect.

By the eighth century the Muslim empire was disintegrating. This process was accompanied by a decentralization of rabbinic Judaism. The Babylonia academies began to lose their hold on the Jewish scholarly world; rabbinic schools in which rabbinic texts were studied were created in many places. The growth of these local centres of scholarship enabled teachers to exert their influence on Jewish learning independently of the academies of Sura and Pumbedita. In the Holy Land, Tiberias became the location of a rabbinic academy as well as a centre for the masoretic scholars who produced the standard text of the Bible. In Egypt, Kairouan and Fez were centres of scholarship. But it was in Spain that the Jewish community attained the highest level of achievement in literature, philosophy, theology and mysticism.

The Muslims were not able to conquer all of Europe, and many countries remained under Christian rule, as did much of the Byzantine Empire. In Christian Europe, Jewish study took place in towns such as Mainz and Worms in the Rhineland, and Troyes and Sens in northern France. In such an environment talmudic study reached great heights: in Germany and northern France scholars known as tosafists employed new methods of talmudic interpretation. In addition, Ashkenazic Jews of this period composed religious poetry based on the liturgical compositions of fifth- and sixth-century Israel.

Despite such developments, the expulsion of the Jews from countries in which they lived became a widespread policy of Christian European rulers. In 1182 the King of France expelled all Jews from the royal domains near Paris, cancelled nearly all debts to Jewish moneylenders and confiscated Jewish property. Though the Jews were recalled in 1198, they were compelled to pay an additional royal tax, and in the next century they increasingly became the property of the king. In thirteenth-century England the Jewish population was continuously taxed; it was eventually expelled in 1290, as were French Jews some years later. By the end of the thirteenth century the German Jewish community had suffered similar attack. In the next century Jews were blamed for the Black Death, and from 1348–9 Jews in France, Switzerland, Germany and Belgium suffered at the hands of their Christian neighbours. In the following two centuries massacre and expulsion of Jews became a frequent occurrence. Prominent Spanish Jewish thinkers of this period were Solomon ibn Gabirol, Bahya ibn Pakuda, Judah Halevi, Maimonides (Moses ben Maimon), Hasdai Crescas and Joseph Albo. During this period, too, the major mystical work of Spanish Jewry, the Zohar, was composed by Moses de Leon.

Jewry in the Early Modern Period

By the end of the fourteenth century political instability in Christian Europe had encouraged the massacre of many Jewish communities, notably in Castile and Aragon. In 1391, fearing for their lives, thousands of Jews converted to Christianity. Two decades later, the Castilian laws were introduced which separated Jews from their Christian neighbours. In the next year, 1413, a public debate was held in Tortosa about the doctrine of the messiah. As a consequence, increased pressure was applied to the Jewish population to convert. Those who became apostates (marranos) found life much easier. Yet during the fifteenth century, anti-Jewish sentiment again became a serious problem. In 1480 King Ferdinand and Queen Isabella established the Inquisition to ascertain whether former Jews practised Judaism in secret. In the late 1480s inquisitors used torture to extract confessions. In 1492 the entire Jewish community was expelled from Spain, and in the next century the Inquisition was established in Portugal.

To escape such persecution, many Spanish and Portuguese marranos sought refuge in various parts of the Ottoman Empire. Some of these Sephardic immigrants prospered and became part of the Ottoman court. Prominent among rabbinic scholars of this period was Joseph

Caro, who emigrated from Spain to tne Balkans. In the 1520s he commenced a study of Jewish law, *The House of Joseph*, based on previous
codes of Jewish law. In addition, he composed a shorter work, the
Shulḥan Arukh, which became the authoritative code of law in the
Jewish world.

While working on the *Shulḥan Arukh*, Caro emigrated to Safed in
Israel, which had become a major centre of Jewish life and mystical
activity. Over the sixteenth century Safed's Jewish population grew from
a small community to over 10,000. Here talmudic academies were created, and small groups engaged in the study of kabbalistic literature as
they awaited the advent of the messianic age. One of the greatest mystics
of Safed, Moses Cordovero, collected, organized and interpreted the
teachings of early mystical authors. Here too, later in the sixteenth century, kabbalistic speculation was transformed by Isaac Luria.

By the beginning of the seventeenth century Lurianic mysticism had
made an important impact on Sephardi Jewry, and messianic speculation
became a central feature of Jewish life. The arrival in this milieu of
Shabbetai Zevi brought about a transformation of Jewish life and
thought. After living in various cities, he travelled to Gaza where he
encountered Nathan Benjamin Levi; Levi believed Shabbetai to be the
long-awaited messiah, and in 1665 announced Shabbetai's messiahship,
sending letters to Jews in the diaspora asking them to recognize
Shabbetai Zevi as their redeemer. In the following year Shabbetai journeyed to Constantinople, but on the order of the grand vizier he was
arrested and imprisoned. Eventually he was given the choice between
conversion and death; in the face of this alternative, he converted to
Islam. Such an act of apostasy scandalized most of his followers, but others continued to regard him as the messiah. In the following century, the
most important Shabbetaian sect was led by Jacob Frank, who believed
himself to be the incarnation of Shabbetai.

During this period Poland had become a great centre of scholarship.
In Polish academies scholars collected together the legal interpretations
of previous authorities and composed commentaries on the *Shulḥan
Arukh*. To regulate Jewish life, Polish Jews established regional federa-
tions that administered Jewish affairs. However, in the midst of this general prosperity, the Polish Jewish community was subjected to a series of
massacres carried out by Cossacks, Crimean Tartars and Ukrainian peas-
ants. In 1648 Bogdan Chmielnicki was elected hetman of the Cossacks,
and instigated an insurrection against the Polish gentry; as administra-
tors of noblemen's estates, Jews were killed in these revolts.

As the seventeenth century progressed, Jewish life in Poland became increasingly unstable; nonetheless, the Jewish community increased in size during the eighteenth century. In the 1730s and 1740s Cossacks known as Haidemaks invaded the Ukraine, robbing and murdering Jewish inhabitants. In Lithuania, Jewish life flourished and Vilna became an important centre of Jewish scholarship. Here Elijah ben Solomon Zalman, the Vilna Gaon, lectured to disciples on a wide range of subjects and composed commentaries on rabbinic sources.

Elsewhere in Europe this period witnessed persecution and oppression of Jews. Despite the positive contact between Italian humanists and Jews, Christian anti-Semitism frequently led to persecution and suffering. In the sixteenth century the Counter-Reformation Church sought to isolate the Jewish community. The Talmud was burned in 1553, and two years later Pope Paul IV reinstated the segregationist edict of the Fourth Lateran Council; this decree forced Jews to live in ghettos and barred them from most spheres of economic activity. Further, marranos who took up the Jewish tradition were burned at the stake, and Jews were expelled from most Church domains.

In Germany the growth of Protestantism led to adverse conditions for the Jewish population. Although Martin Luther was initially well disposed towards the Jewish community, he soon came to realize that Jews were intent on remaining true to their faith. Some Jews, known as Court Jews, attained positions of great importance among the German nobility. A number of these favoured individuals were appointed by the rulers as chief elders of the Jewish community and acted as spokesmen for and defenders of German Jewry.

In Holland some Jews had come to exercise an important influence on trade and finance. By the mid-seventeenth century both marranos and Ashkenazi Jews had come to Amsterdam and engaged in economic activity, and by the end of the century there were nearly 10,000 Jews in the city port. Here the Jewish community was employed on the stock exchange, in the sugar, tobacco and diamond trades, and in insurance, manufacturing, printing and banking. In this milieu Jewish cultural activity also flourished. Although Jews in Holland were not granted full rights as citizens, they nevertheless enjoyed religious freedom, personal protection and the liberty of participating in a range of economic affairs.

Judaism in the Modern World

By the middle of the eighteenth century the Jewish community had suffered numerous waves of persecution and was deeply dispirited by

Shabbetai Zevi's conversion to Islam. Against this background the Hasidic movement sought to revitalize Jewish life. The founder of this new denomination was Israel ben Eleazer, known as the Baal Shem Tov. Born in southern Poland, in the 1730s he went to Medziobzh in Polodia, Russia. There he performed various miracles and taught kabbalistic lore to his disciples. After his death in 1760, Dov Baer became the leader of his sect and Hasidism spread to southern Poland, the Ukraine and Lithuania. The growth of this movement engendered considerable hostility from rabbinic authorities, and at the end of the century the Jewish establishment of Vilna denounced Hasidism to the Russian government.

During the latter part of the eighteenth century the treatment of Jews in Central Europe improved due to the influence of Christian polemicists who pressed for the amelioration of the conditions of Jewish life. The Holy Roman Emperor Joseph II embraced such attitudes, abolishing the Jewish badge as well as taxes imposed on Jewish travellers, and issuing an edict of toleration which granted Jewry numerous rights. As in Germany, reformers in France during the 1770s and 1780s sought to improve the situation of the Jewish population. In 1789 the National Assembly declared that all human beings are born and remain free and equal and that no person should be persecuted for his opinions as long as they do not subvert civil law. In 1791 a resolution was passed which bestowed citizenship rights on all Jews. This alteration in Jewish status occurred elsewhere in Europe as well – in 1796 the Dutch Jews of the Batavian Republic were granted full citizenship rights, and in 1797 the ghettos of Padua and Rome were abolished.

In 1799 Napoleon became First Consul of France and five years later was proclaimed Emperor. Napoleon's Code of Civil Law was propounded in 1804, establishing the right of all individuals to follow any trade. After 1806 a number of German principalities were united in the French kingdom of Westphalia, where Jews were granted equal rights. Also in 1806 Napoleon called an assembly of Jewish notables to consider a series of religious issues, and in the following year he summoned a Great Sanhedrin consisting of rabbis and laity to confirm the views of the assembly. This body pledged its allegiance to the emperor and nullified any aspects of the Jewish tradition that conflicted with the requirements of citizenship.

After Napoleon's abdication, the map of Europe was redrawn by the Congress of Vienna in 1814–15. The diplomats at the Congress issued a resolution that instructed the German confederation to improve the status of Jewry. Despite this decree, the German governments disowned the rights of equality that had previously been granted to Jews by the French. However, in 1830 a more liberal attitude prevailed, and several nations advocated a more tolerant approach. The French revolution of 1848, which led to disturbances in Prussia, Austria, Hungary, Italy and Bohemia, forced rulers to grant constitutions which guaranteed freedom of speech, assembly and religion.

In this environment Jewish emancipation gathered force. At the end of the eighteenth century the Jewish philosopher Moses Mendelssohn advocated the modernization of Jewish life. In pursuit of this end he translated the Pentateuch into German so that Jews would be able to speak the language of the country in which they lived. Following Mendelssohn's example, a number of his Prussian followers (*maskilim*) fostered a Jewish Enlightenment – the Haskalah – encouraging Jews to abandon medieval forms of life and thought. By the 1820s the centre of this movement shifted to the Austrian Empire, where journals advancing the ideas of the Enlightenment were published. In the 1840s the Haskalah spread to Russia, where writers made contributions to Hebrew literature and translated textbooks and fiction into Hebrew.

Paralleling this development, reformers encouraged the modernization of the Jewish liturgy and the overhaul of Jewish education. At the beginning of the nineteenth century the Jewish financier and communal leader Israel Jacobson initiated a programme of reform. In 1801 he established a boarding school for boys in Seesen, Westphalia; later he created other schools throughout the kingdom. In these new educational establishments general subjects were taught by Christian teachers while a Jewish instructor gave lessons about the Jewish faith. Subsequently, Jacobson built a Reform Temple next to the school and another in Hamburg. Although such reforms were denounced by the Orthodox, Reform Judaism spread throughout Europe. In 1844 the first Reform synod was held in Brunswick; this consultation was followed by another conference in 1845 in Frankfurt. At this meeting one of the more conservative rabbis, Zecharias Frankel, expressed dissatisfaction with progressive reforms to the worship service, and resigned from the assembly. He later established a Jewish theological seminary in Breslau; the revolution of 1848 and its aftermath led to the cessation of the reformers' activities until 1868, when another synod was held at Cassel.

In the United States, Reform Judaism became an important movement. The most prominent of the early reformer was Isaac Mayer Wise, who settled in Cincinnati, Ohio, where he published a new Reform prayer book as well as several Jewish newspapers. In addition, he attempted to convene a Reform synod. In 1869 the first meeting of the Central Conference of American Rabbis was held in Philadelphia; this was followed in 1873 by the creation of the Union of American Hebrew Congregations. Two years later the Hebrew Union College was established to train rabbinical students for Reform congregations. In 1885 a Conference of Reform Rabbis, meeting in Pittsburgh, issued a formal list of principles, the Pittsburgh Platform.

In Eastern Europe and Russia conditions were less conducive to emancipation. In 1804 Tsar Alexander I specified territory in western Poland as an area in which Jews would be permitted to live (the Pale of Settlement). After several attempts to expel Jews from the countryside, the tsar in 1817 initiated a new policy of integrating the Jewish community into the population by founding a society of Israelite Christians which extended legal and financial concessions to baptized Jews. In 1824 the deportation of Jews from villages began. In the same year Alexander I died and was succeeded by Nicholas I, who adopted a severe attitude to the Jews in his realm. In 1827 he initiated a policy of inducting Jewish boys into the Russian army for a twenty-five-year period to increase the number of Christian converts. Nicholas I also deported Jews from villages in certain areas. In 1844 he abolished the *kehillot* (Jewish communal bodies) and placed Jewry under the authority of the police and municipal government. Between 1850 and 1851 the government sought to forbid Jewish dress, men's sidecurls and the ritual shaving of women's hair. After the Crimean War of 1853–6 Alexander II emancipated the serfs, modernized the judiciary and created a system of local self-government. Further, he permitted certain groups to reside outside the Pale of Settlement. As a consequence, Jewish communities appeared in St Petersburg and Moscow. A limited number of Jews were allowed to become lawyers and participate in local government.

Jews in the Twentieth Century

After the Russian pogroms of 1881–2 large numbers of Jews emigrated to the United States; in addition, a significant number went to Palestine. By the late 1880s the idea of a Jewish homeland had spread throughout Europe. At the First Zionist Congress, held at Basle in 1897, Theodor Herzl called for the creation of a Jewish national home. After founding the basic institutions of the Zionist movement, he then embarked on a range of diplomatic negotiations. By the beginning of the twentieth century a sizeable number of Jews had settled in Palestine. After the First World War Jews in Palestine organized a National Assembly and

Executive Council. By 1929 the Jewish community numbered 160,000, with 110 agricultural settlements. In the next ten years the population increased to 500,000, with 223 agricultural communities. Fearful of the future of the country, the Arab community rioted in 1927 following a dispute concerning Jewish access to the Western Wall of the ancient Temple. This conflict caused the British to curtail Jewish immigration as well as the purchase of Arab land.

During the 1920s Labour Zionism became the dominant force in Palestinian Jewish life, and by 1930 various socialist and Labour groups had joined together in the Israel Labour Party. Within the Zionist movement a right-wing section criticized Chaim Weizmann, the President of the World Zionist Organization, who was committed to co-operation with the British, governors of Palestine under a League of Nations mandate. Under the leadership of Vladimir Jabotinsky, these Zionist Revisionists stressed that the aim of the Zionist movement was to create an independent Jewish state in the whole of Palestine. At several Zionist Congresses, the Revisionists established their own organization and in 1931 withdrew from the underground military organization, the Haganah, to form their own military force. In 1936, Arab riots broke out in Jaffa, and the Arabs proclaimed a general strike, with the aim of stopping Jewish immigration, prohibiting the transfer of land to Jewish owners, and establishing a national government. After the outbreak of the strike, a campaign of terror was initiated. The next year a British Royal Commission proposed that Palestine be partitioned into a Jewish and an Arab state with a British zone. Although this recommendation was accepted by the Zionists, it was rejected by the Arabs. Eventually the British government produced a White Paper in 1939 which rejected the concept of partition, limited Jewish immigration to 75,000 and stated that Palestine would become independent in ten years.

As these events took place in the Middle East, German Jewry was confronted by increasing hostility. Once the Nazis gained control of the government they curtailed civil liberties. In 1935 the Nuremberg Laws made Jews into second-class citizens, and all intermarriage and sexual liaisons between Jews and non-Jews were depicted as crimes against the state. In 1938 Jewish community leaders were put under control of the Gestapo, and Jews were compelled to register their property. On 9–10 November that year, the Nazi party organized an onslaught against the Jewish populace in which Jews were killed and their property destroyed. This event, Kristallnacht, was a prelude to the Holocaust.

The first stage of the Nazis' plan for European Jewry commenced with the invasion of Poland. In September 1939 Hitler sought to incorporate much of Poland into Germany, and more than 60,000 Jews were gathered into a large area in Poland. When the Jewish population was ghettoized into what Hitler referred to as a huge Polish labour camp, a massive work programme was begun. Jews worked all day, seven days a week, dressed in rags and fed on bread, soup and potatoes. Officially these workers had no names, only numbers tattooed on their bodies; if one died, a replacement was sought without any inquiry into the cause of death.

With the invasion of Russia in 1941 the Nazis used mobile killing battalions (*Einsatzgruppen*) to destroy Russian Jewry. These units moved into Russian towns, sought out the rabbi or Jewish court and obtained a list of all Jewish residents. The Jews were then rounded up in marketplaces, crowded into trains, buses and trucks and taken to woods where graves had been dug. They were then machine-gunned. Other methods were also used by the Nazis. Mobile gas units were supplied to the *Einsatzgruppen*. Meanwhile these mobile killing operations were being supplanted by the development of fixed centres – the death camps of Auschwitz, Majdanek, Treblinka, Belzec, Chelmno and Sobibor.

Despite acts of resistance against the Nazis such as took place in 1942 in Warsaw, six million Jews were murdered by the Germans. In Poland more than ninety per cent of Jews (3,300,000) were killed. The same percentage of the Jewish population died in the Baltic states, Germany and Austria. More than seventy per cent were killed in the Bohemian protectorate, Slovakia, Greece and the Netherlands; more than fifty per cent in White Russia, the Ukraine, Belgium, Yugoslavia and Norway.

During the Second World War and afterwards, the British prevented illegal immigrants from entering the Holy Land. Campaigning against this policy, in 1946 the Haganah blew up the King David Hotel in Jerusalem, where part of the British administration was housed. Later in the same year Ernest Bevin, the British Foreign Secretary, handed over the Palestinian problem to the United Nations. On 29 November 1947 the General Assembly of the United Nations endorsed a plan of partition, whereupon the Arabs attacked Jewish settlements. In March 1948 David Ben-Gurion read out the Scroll of Independence of the Jewish State; a government was formed, and immediately the Arabs stepped up their campaign. Following the War of Independence, peace talks were held and later an armistice was signed with Egypt, the Lebanon, Transjordan and Syria.

In 1956 President Gamal Abdel Nasser of Egypt refused Israeli ships access to the Gulf of Aqaba, seized the Suez Canal and formed a pact with Saudi Arabia and other Arab states. In response Israel launched an attack, conquering Sinai and opening the sea route to Aqaba. In 1967 Nasser began another offensive against Israel; this resulted in the Six Day War, from which Israel emerged victorious. This conflict was followed by the Yom Kippur War in 1973, and by an Israeli offensive against Lebanon in 1982. Although the invasion of Lebanon provoked discord between Israel and its allies, as well as controversy within Israel, the Jewish state has held fast to its aim of providing a refuge for all Jews. In recent years various steps have been taken to resolving the conflict between Jews and Palestinian Arabs; despite the actions of those on both sides who seek to undermine a peace agreement, there are signs that Jews and Arabs may at long last be able to live together in harmony.

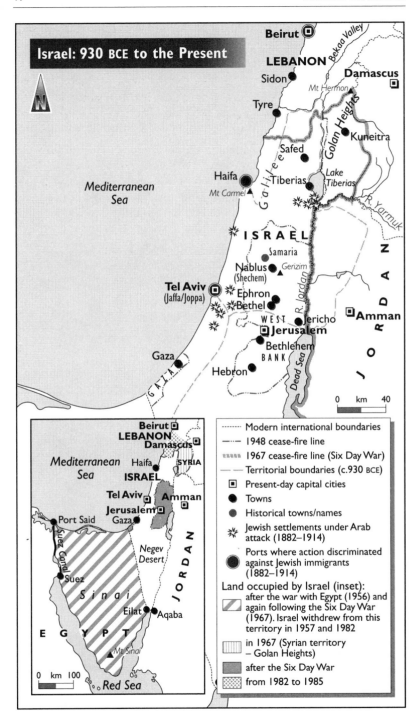

Israel: 930 BCE to the Present

Beirut
LEBANON
Sidon
Tyre
Damascus
Mt Hermon
Safed
Kuneitra
Golan Heights
Haifa
Mt Carmel
Tiberias
Lake Tiberias
R. Yarmuk
Mediterranean Sea
Galilee
ISRAEL
Samaria
Nablus (Shechem)
Gerizim
R. Jordan
Tel Aviv (Jaffa/Joppa)
Ephron
Bethel
Jericho
WEST
Jerusalem
Amman
Bethlehem
BANK
Gaza
GAZA
Dead Sea
Hebron
JORDAN
Bekaa Valley

0   km   40

Legend (inset key):
- ------- Modern international boundaries
- —·—·— 1948 cease-fire line
- ····· 1967 cease-fire line (Six Day War)
- ~~~~~ Territorial boundaries (c.930 BCE)
- ▣ Present-day capital cities
- ● Towns
- ● Historical towns/names
- ⁂ Jewish settlements under Arab attack (1882–1914)
- ◉ Ports where action discriminated against Jewish immigrants (1882–1914)

Land occupied by Israel (inset):
- ▨ after the war with Egypt (1956) and again following the Six Day War (1967). Israel withdrew from this territory in 1957 and 1982
- ▥ in 1967 (Syrian territory – Golan Heights)
- ▦ after the Six Day War
- ▨ from 1982 to 1985

Inset map:
Beirut
LEBANON
Damascus
Mediterranean Sea
Haifa
SYRIA
ISRAEL
Tel Aviv
Amman
Jerusalem
Port Said
Gaza
Negev Desert
JORDAN
Suez Canal
Suez
Sinai
Eilat
Aqaba
EGYPT
Mt Sinai
Red Sea

0   km   100

A

Aaron (?13th century BCE)

Brother of MOSES, as whose spokesman he served in Moses' confrontation with Pharaoh. Nonetheless, when Moses ascended MOUNT SINAI and failed to return, Aaron was induced to make a GOLDEN CALF to mollify the people. Once the TEMPLE was constructed, Aaron and his sons were installed as PRIESTS and charged to oversee the cult. At the age of 123 Aaron died on Mount Hor, situated on the border of Edom. According to rabbinic sources, he is the personification of piety and peace. (*See also* AARONIDES.)

Aaronides

Hereditary PRIESTS. According to Numbers 18:7, the descendants of AARON 'shall attend to your priesthood for all that concerns the ALTAR and that which is in the veil'. In Scripture a distinction is made between the Aaronides and the LEVITES, even though it is sometimes implied that all the Levites were priests. Some scholars argue that the Aaronides were Egyptian in origin, since Egyptian names are found among their records. (*See also* COHEN; LEVITE.)

Abbaye (278–338 CE)

Babylonian AMORA and head of the ACADEMY at PUMBEDITA. He contributed to the development of talmudic dialectic, and his debates with his colleague RAVA had an important impact on the BABYLONIAN TALMUD. In all cases (except six) where he differed with Rava, Rava's opinions were regarded as authoritative. Abbaye's contributions to rabbinic study include the distinction between the literal meaning of the biblical text (PESHAT) and the figurative interpretation (DERASH).

ablution

Ritual washing to remove impurities before the performance of religious observances or after contact with unclean objects. According to biblical and rabbinic legislation, there are three types of ablution: (1) Complete immersion. This must occur either in a natural water source or in a ritual bath (MIKVEH). During the biblical period, this took place in the TEMPLE; subsequently, rabbinic law prescribed complete immersion for PROSELYTES and for married women following menstruation and childbirth. Among pious Jews, particularly HASIDIM, complete immersion has also been carried out as an act of spiritual purification. (2) Washing the feet and hands. This was limited to PRIESTS in the Temple service. (3) Washing the hands. Rabbinic law prescribes washing of the hands prior to a meal, before prayer, on rising from sleep, after proximity to a corpse and after going to the lavatory. (*See also* NIDDAH; PURITY.)

abortion

Termination of a pregnancy. According to Jewish law, abortion is generally prohibited. Rabbinic legislation stipulates, however, that if the foetus is less than 41 days old an abortion may take place under special circumstances. The main reason for terminating a pregnancy is if the mother's life or health is in danger. In modern times the interpretation of this ruling has been extended to include cases in which the mother's mental health might be jeopardized either by the continuation of the pregnancy or by the likelihood that the child will be malformed or suffer from a genetic disease.

Abrabanel, Isaac (1437–1508)

Portuguese statesman, philosopher and exegete. Initially serving as treasurer to Alfonso V of Portugal, he fled to Spain in 1483 to escape from the charge of conspiracy levelled by Alfonso's son against his father's ministers. During his sojourn in TOLEDO he served under Ferdinand and Isabella, but was compelled to leave Spain for Italy when the Jews were expelled in 1492. Initially he was employed in the court in Naples, eventually settling in VENICE where he attempted to negotiate a treaty with Portugal. His writings include a commentary on Scripture, philosophical studies of an anti-rationalist character and theological treatises stressing the primacy of the Jewish faith.

Abraham (fl.?16th century BCE)

Father of the Jewish people. According to Scripture, he was the son of Terah and the father of ISAAC (by SARAH) and of Ishmael (by Hagar). After leaving Ur of the Chaldees, Abraham travelled to CANAAN, visited Egypt and returned to HEBRON. God appeared to him in a vision and promised that his descendants would inherit the land. The Lord tested Abraham's faith by asking him to sacrifice his son Isaac (Gen. 11:26–25:10).

When Sarah died, Abraham purchased the cave of MACHPELAH as a burial place. He died at the age of 175.

Abraham, Apocalypse of

Jewish PSEUDEPIGRAPHIC work dating from the late first or second century CE. Originally written in HEBREW or ARAMAIC, the only extant version is a Slavonic translation. The work depicts ABRAHAM's conversion to monotheism, his destiny in heaven and the fate of all the nations of the earth. (*See also* APOCALYPSE.)

Abraham, Testament of

Jewish PSEUDEPIGRAPHIC work from probably the second century CE. It was revised by the Christian Church and is extant in Greek versions. It portrays ABRAHAM's initation into the divine mysteries before his death and his ascent to heaven.

Abraham bar Ḥiyya
(fl. 12th century)

Spanish scholar. Known also as Abraham Judaeus and Abraham Savasorda, he established the foundation of HEBREW scientific terminology; in addition, he transmitted Greco-Arab science to the Christian world. His *Meditation of the Sad Soul* is a study of ethics influenced by Neoplatonism.

Abrahamites

Christian sect influenced by Judaism. Living in Bohemia, the Abrahamites practised CIRCUMCISION, kept Saturday as the SABBATH, refrained from eating pork and rejected the doctrine of the Trinity. Their leader Jan Pita was executed in 1748, but the sect survived until the end of the 18th century.

Abrahams, Israel (1858–1924)

English scholar. A reader in rabbinics at Cambridge University, together with Claude MONTEFIORE he founded the

Jewish Quarterly in 1888, and served as its editor. His writings include *Jewish Life in the Middle Ages, Studies in Pharisaism and the Gospels*, and *Hebrew Ethical Wills*.

Abulafia, Abraham ben (1240–c.1291)

Spanish kabbalist and pseudo-MESSIAH. He travelled extensively in Palestine, Greece and Italy; eventually he returned to Spain, where he proclaimed he was a PROPHET. In 1280 he went to ROME in order to persuade Pope Nicholas III to improve the condition of the Jewish people. He was saved from being burned at the stake by the Pope's death. Subsequently he announced that the onset of the messianic era would take place in 1290; many were persuaded by this prediction and prepared to emigrate to Palestine. Because of his views, he was regarded with hostility by the rabbinic establishment, particularly by Solomon ibn ADRET. His mystical activity was characterized by a quest for the prophetic spirit through combining the letters of the divine names. (*See also* KABBALAH.)

academy (Hebrew: *yeshivah*)

Name of rabbinic institution of higher learning in PALESTINE and BABYLONIA. After the destruction of the Second TEMPLE, Palestinian academies gained increasing importance. The first Palestinian academy founded after 70 CE was established by JOHANAN BEN ZAKKAI at JABNEH. Subsequently others were created under the leadership of such scholars as Eliezer ben Hyrcanus and Joshua ben Hananiah. After the BAR KOKHBA rebellion in the second century, other academies were set up in GALILEE. The major academy was initially located at USHA, later moving to Shepharam, Bet Shearim and Sepphoris. After the death of JUDAH HA-NASI, the academy was located at TIBERIAS. In Babylonia during the tannaitic period (*c.*100 BCE–200 CE; see TANNA) the main

academies were at Nisbis and Hehar Pekod. In the third century SAMUEL presided over the academy at NEHARDEA and RAV headed the academy at SURA. After the destruction of Nehardea in 259, a new academy was established at PUMBEDITA. Throughout the period of the SAVORAIM and the GEONIM, these two academies were the pre-eminent rabbinic institutions in the Jewish world. Subsequently other rabbinic academies were established elsewhere. (*See also* BET HA-MIDRASH; PUMBEDITA; RABBINICAL SEMINARIES; YESHIVAH.)

Acosta, Uriel (c.1585–1640)

Spanish heretic. Born in Oporto of MARRANO parents, he fled with his family to AMSTERDAM, where he lived openly as a Jew. However, he was troubled that Jewish practice did not conform with the literal interpretation of Scripture. In 1616, while living in Hamburg, he sent to VENICE his eleven theses critical of the Jewish tradition. As a result, he was EXCOMMUNICATED by the rabbis of Hamburg and Venice in 1618, and later by the rabbinic establishment in Amsterdam. On returning to Amsterdam, he composed works attacking the ORAL LAW as well as the doctrines of IMMORTALITY, RESURRECTION and REWARD AND PUNISHMENT. These writings were confiscated by the Dutch courts since they were viewed as containing HERESIES against the Christian faith. Eventually Acosta recanted; however, he was excommunicated for heresy a second time in 1633. Again, he recanted and underwent the penance of flogging and other humiliations. Late in his life he wrote his autobiography, *Exemplar Humanae Vitae*. In 1640 he committed suicide.

Adam

First man. Created in the image of God, Adam was formed of the dust of the earth on the sixth day of creation. He was given dominion over the earth.

Adam, from Michelangelo's painting on the ceiling of the Sistine Chapel: Adam and Eve are shown eating the forbidden fruit, and being expelled from the Garden of Eden.

Subsequently EVE was formed out of one of his ribs. Adam and Eve were then placed in the GARDEN OF EDEN and permitted to eat the fruit of all the trees except for the tree of the knowledge of good and evil. Seduced by the serpent, both Adam and Eve ate the forbidden fruit; because of this act of disobedience, God expelled them from the Garden. Adam was condemned to a life of labour and Eve to the travail of childbirth (Gen. 1–3). (*See also* PRIMORDIAL MAN.)

Adam, Book of

PSEUDEPIGRAPHIC work possibly composed originally in HEBREW or ARAMAIC, but extant in Greek, Latin and Slavonic versions. It depicts the lives of ADAM and EVE after their expulsion from the GARDEN OF EDEN, as well as their repentance, death and promised RESURRECTION. (*See also* APOCALYPSE.)

Adam Kadmon

See PRIMORDIAL MAN.

additional service

(Hebrew: *musaf*)

Extra service for SABBATH and FESTIVALS. It is usually recited after the TORAH and HAFTARAH readings. It corresponds to the additional sacrifices that were made in the TEMPLE on Sabbaths and festivals.

additional soul

(Hebrew: *neshamah yeterah*)

Belief that an additional soul is given for the SABBATH. This notion is found in the TALMUD and KABBALISTIC sources. The use of spices in the HAVDALAH service is probably connected with the need to revive the original soul after the departure of the NESHAMAH YETERAH.

Adloyada

Hebrew term for PURIM celebration. According to the rabbis, one should rejoice on Purim 'until one no longer knows' the difference between 'Blessed be Mordecai' and 'Cursed by HAMAN'. In Israel, Adloyada involves a carnival parade. (*See also* ESTHER, BOOK OF.)

Adon Olam

(Hebrew, 'Lord of the World')

Liturgical hymn depicting the unity and providence of God. It is usually recited at the beginning of the morning liturgy or at the close of the MORNING SERVICE (in some cases both at the beginning and at the end of the worship service). It is also recited in the night prayers and at one's deathbed. Although its authorship and date of composition are not known, it has been traditionally ascribed to Solomon ibn GABIROL.

Adonai (Hebrew, 'My Lord')

Name of God. When the TETRAGRAMMA-TON (JHWH) appears in Scripture, it is read out loud either as Adonai or as Ha-Shem ('The Name'). (*See also* GOD, NAMES OF.)

adoption

Establishment of a parental relationship with an individual who is not one's biological offspring. The legal conception of adoption is not found in the BIBLE or the TALMUD. Nonetheless Jewish law provides for circumstances similar to those brought about by adoption. A guardian may be appointed to care for the welfare and property of the child. If the child is not of Jewish origin, various provisions are stipulated for his or her inclusion into the Jewish people.

Adret, Solomon ibn (1235–1310)

Spanish rabbi, theologian and KABBALIST. Known as Rashba, he was one of the most important scholars of the medieval period. Initially he studied under NAHMANIDES, subsequently becoming the leader of Spanish Jewry. His legal decisions constitute a primary source of information about the history of the Jews of this time. In the debates about the study of philosophy, he adopted a middle course: he discouraged philosophical study, yet he declared it forbidden only to those under the age of 25. He also defended Judaism from Christian and Muslim detractors, and disputed the messianic claims of Abraham ben ABULAFIA.

adultery

Sexual relationship between a betrothed or married woman and a man who is not her husband; Jewish LAW does not regard a sexual relationship between a married man and an unmarried woman as technically adulterous. Adultery is prohibited in the Decalogue (Exod. 20:13; Deut. 5:17). The punishment for adultery is death (Lev. 20:10), although in practice the adulterer seems to have been able to pay compensation instead. According to rabbinic law, a woman who commits adultery is prohibited from having sexual relations with either her husband or the adulterer. If she is the wife of a PRIEST, she is so prohibited even if the sexual act was committed against her will. Jewish law prescribes an elaborate procedure to determine whether a woman who is suspected of committing adultery is guilty. The children of adulterous relationships are regarded as MAMZERIM and as a consequence suffer a particular handicap in Jewish law.

afikoman (Hebrew, 'desert')

A piece of matzah (UNLEAVENED BREAD) which is set aside during the PASSOVER meal to be eaten at the conclusion of the SEDER. Among ASHKENAZI Jews it is customary for the children to hide the *afikoman* during the course of the meal and return it only after a forfeit has been paid.

afterlife

The Jewish belief in the hereafter has undergone considerable development from biblical times. According to Scripture, the dead were thought to live in SHEOL, a shadowy place under the earth. During the time of the Second TEMPLE, the PHARISEES taught that with the advent of the MESSIAH the dead would be resurrected and there would be eternal reward for the righteous and everlasting punishment for the wicked. The medieval Jewish philosopher Moses MAIMONIDES maintained that the belief in the resurrection of the dead was a fundamental tenet of the Jewish faith. In modern times the notion of bodily RESURRECTION remains a belief for the ORTHODOX, even though most now reject the idea of everlasting punishment. Non-Orthodox Jews have generally substituted the doctrine of the IMMORTALITY of the soul for the concept of bodily resurrection. (*See also* HEAVEN; HELL.)

afternoon service
(Hebrew: *minḥah*)

A substitute for the TEMPLE afternoon sacrifice. The service includes the ASHREI, AMIDAH and *taḥanun* prayers and the ALENU. Traditionally the service dates back to the time of the PATRIARCHS when, according to Gen. 24:26, ISAAC meditated in the field in the evening. In modern times the *maariv* (EVENING SERVICE) is recited immediately afterwards.

aggadah (Hebrew, 'narrative')

Rabbinic teaching which is an amplification of biblical narrative, history, ethics and prophecy. The *aggadah* developed in PALESTINE during the Second TEMPLE period up to approximately 500 CE. It includes parables, allegories, prayers, laments, polemics, stories, homilies, theology, ethics and letter symbolism. This material is found in MIDRASHIC LITERATURE and is scattered throughout the PALESTINIAN and BABYLONIAN TALMUDS. Traditionally *aggadah* does not have the same authority as HALAKHAH (Jewish LAW).

Aggadat Bereshit (Hebrew, 'Narrative on "In the Beginning"' [Genesis])

MIDRASH on Genesis dating from about the 12th century. It is based on other *midrashim*, particularly the TANḤUMA. Explanations of verses from Genesis are combined with interpretations of verses from the PSALMS or PROPHETS on similar topics.

Agnon, Shmuel Yosef
(1888–1970)

Galician HEBREW writer. He settled in PALESTINE and wrote novels and short stories depicting life in Galicia and Palestine. One of the greatest epic writers of modern Hebrew literature, he was awarded the Nobel Prize. His writings include *The Bridal Canopy* and *A Guest for the Night*.

agunah

See TIED WOMAN.

Ahab (fl. ninth century BCE)

King of Israel who ruled *c.*876–853 BCE. He was reproved by the PROPHET ELIJAH for seizing Naboth's vineyard. When his wife JEZEBEL, the daughter of the King of Sidon, introduced BAAL worship, a struggle took place between Elijah and the royal house. In battle Ahab defeated Ben-Hadad of Damascus, regaining several districts which the Syrians had previously captured. Subsequently the two kings formed an alliance against the Assyrians (1 Kgs. 16:29–22:40).

Aḥad Ha-Am (1856–1927)

Essayist and philosopher. Aḥad Ha-Am (Asher Ginsberg) was born in Ukraine and receieved a traditional Jewish education. After attending the universities of VIENNA, BERLIN and Breslau, he settled in Odessa where he joined the ḤOVEVEI ZION (Lovers of Zion) and founded the Bene Mosheh League, of which he served as president. In addition he was a founder of the Aḥiasaph publishing society. He wrote numerous articles about PALESTINE, becoming a spokesman for spiritual ZIONISM. Eventually he settled in TEL AVIV, where he published his correspondence and memoirs.

Ahaz (fl. eighth century BCE)

King of JUDAH who ruled *c.*735–720 BCE. As the Edomites and Philistines attacked his southern territory, Judah was attacked by Israel and Syria. Despite the opposition of the PROPHET Isaiah, he sought help from the Assyrian king,

Tiglath-Pileser, who invaded Syria and Israel in 733 BCE. Subsequently Judah became an Assyrian vassal and its religious cult was influenced by Assyrian religious practices.

Ahaziah (1) (fl. ninth century BCE)

King of Israel from *c.*853 BCE. He was denounced by ELIJAH as an idolator (1 Kgs. 22).

Ahaziah (2) (fl. ninth century BCE)

King of JUDAH *c.*844–843 BCE. Like his mother Athaliah, he was a worshipper of BAAL. He joined Jehoram of Israel in battle against Hazael of Syria (2 Kgs. 8–9). When Jehoram was wounded, Ahaziah visited him in Jezreel where they were both killed by JEHU.

Aharonim (Hebrew, 'latter ones')

Later rabbinic authorities, as distinguished from the RISHONIM (early authorities). The dividing line between these two groups of scholars is placed between the 11th and 12th centuries.

Ahikar, Book of

Book of folklore composed in ARAMAIC. Ahikar was a cup-bearer, keeper of the royal signet, and chief administrator during the reigns of the Assyrian rulers Sennacherib and Esarhaddon (eighth to seventh century BCE). The book tells the story of Ahikar (who is also mentioned in the Book of TOBIT) and his advice to his adopted son Nadan.

Akdamut

ARAMAIC acrostic poem. Composed by Meir ben Isaac of Worms in the eleventh century, it is recited by ASHKENAZI Jews in the SYNAGOGUE before the reading on SHAVUOT. It consists of 90 lines containing a double alphabet and the poet's name.

akeda

See BINDING.

Akiva (50–135 CE)

Palestinian scholar, patriot and MARTYR. Little is known of his early life; according to tradition he was of humble origin and remained uneducated until the age of 40. With the help of his wife, Rachel, the daughter of Kalba Sabbua, he devoted himself to study. Akiva developed a method of biblical exegesis, systematized the ORAL LAW, and established an ACADEMY at Bene Brak. In his view, Simeon BAR KOKHBA was the MESSIAH. He was imprisoned by the Romans for teaching TORAH and was tortured to death.

al het (Hebrew, 'For the sin')

Opening words of a confession of SIN. It is recited on YOM KIPPUR.

Albo, Joseph (*c.*1380–1435)

Spanish philosopher. A pupil of Hasdai CRESCAS, he took part in the DISPUTATION of TORTOSA in 1413–14. He was the author of *Sefer ha-Ikkarim* (*Book of Dogmas*), in which he reduced the principles of the Jewish faith to three: divine existence, divine revelation, and reward and punishment. From these three tenets he derived secondary dogmas.

Alenu
(Hebrew, 'It is our duty to praise')

Prayer declaring the sovereignty and unity of God. In all likelihood it was composed by RAV in BABYLONIA in the third century for the NEW YEAR. It is now recited at the end of every SYNAGOGUE service. During the middle ages it was the prayer recited by MARTYRS. Due to its uncompromising assertion of MONOTHEISM, it became the object of attack by those who perceived it as critical of the Christan faith; its recitation was prohibited in Aragon in 1336, and PRAGUE in 1399. In 1703 the cancellation of one passage – which is currently omitted in the ASHKENAZI rite – was formally authorized. In Ashkenazi synagogues it is chanted during the additional service on the HIGH HOLY DAYS.

Alexandria

Egyptian port. During the Roman period, the Jewish community constituted a significant part of the population. When Alexandrian Jews sought to obtain civil rights, riots broke out. Under the influence of the revolt in JUDEA in 66 CE, further disturbances occurred which were suppressed by the Roman governor, Tiberius Julius Alexander.

Alfasi, Isaac ben Jacob (1013–1103)

TALMUDIC scholar. Known as Rif, he lived and taught in FEZ, North Africa. Late in his life, he became the victim of slander and was compelled to escape to Spain. In Africa as well as in Spain, he attracted a wide circle of followers and composed important RESPONSA. His compendium of the legal discussions in the Babylonian TALMUD, *Sefer ha-Halakhot* (*Book of Legal Decisions*), is a classic Jewish legal source.

aliyah (Hebrew, 'going up')

Calling up of a member of the congregation to read the TORAH in the SYNAGOGUE service. Originally each person was called up to read a section of the weekly portion. Subsequently a special reader took over this function. Those who are called up read blessings instead. The term is also used to refer to the immigration of the Jews to Israel. The First Aliyah took place from 1882 to 1903; the Second from 1904 to 1914; and the Third from 1918 to 1923.

Alkalai, Yehuda Ḥai (1798–1878)

Bosnian ZIONIST. Born in Sarajevo, he grew up in JERUSALEM. In 1825 he became RABBI of the SEPHARDI community at Zemun, near Belgrade. Following the DAMASCUS AFFAIR in 1840, he urged that Jews settle in PALESTINE. Initially he attempted to gain support for this plan among the Jews of Western Europe. In 1874 he settled in Jersualem where he continued to work for the colonization of the land. In his writings, he argued that Jewish pioneers must settle in the land in anticipation of messianic redemption.

allegory

Extended metaphor. Allegory is found in both the BIBLE and the APOCRYPHA. Subsequently, it was used by ALEXANDRIAN Jews such as the first-century philosopher PHILO. In addition, it was employed by rabbinic sages in MIDRASHIC sources who sought to draw out what they believed to be implicit in Scripture. In the middle ages Jewish philosophers such as Moses MAIMONIDES and Solomon ibn GABIROL interpreted the Bible allegorically. However, other scholars such as SAADIAH GAON and Joseph ALBO issued warnings against its employment. Later KABBALISTS alleged that the Bible contains an inner reality and utilized allegory to uncover its true meaning. In modern Hebrew literature, allegory is frequently used.

almemar (Aramaic, 'dais')

Platform in the SYNAGOGUE on which the reading desk stands. The TORAH is read from here. In ASHKENAZI congregations it is called the BIMAH, and *tebah* in SEPHARDI synagogues.

alphabet

The HEBREW alphabet consists of 22 consonants (see opposite), derived from the CANAANITE alphabet. Until the exile in the sixth century BCE, it was identical with that of the Phoenicians, but subsequently it was gradually replaced by the letter forms based on ARAMAIC. The square script now used developed during the first two centuries CE. Originally vowels were not indicated by Hebrew script, but in time certain letters (*yod, vav, he*) came to serve as vowel indicators. From the seventh to the ninth centuries various systems were developed to indicate the vowels by means of new signs placed above and below the consonants.

Alroy, David (fl. 12th century)

Leader of a messianic movement in Kurdistan. Among Jews living in the mountains of the north-east Caucasus, he was proclaimed the long-awaited MESSIAH. Subsequently he was murdered. He was the subject of *The Wondrous Tale of David Alroy* by Benjamin Disraeli.

altar

Place where offerings are made to God. According to the Five Books of Moses (the PENTATEUCH) there should be only one central altar: this was initially located in the TABERNACLE and later in the TEMPLE in JERUSALEM, where it took the form of a bronze table. After the return of the EXILES from BABYLONIA, an altar of stone was set up before the Temple was rebuilt. In addition to the altar for burnt offerings, an incense altar overlaid with gold stood before the veil of the inner sanctum. In the SYNAGOGUE the place of the altar has been taken by the ark which contains the TORAH scroll.

am ha-aretz

(Hebrew, 'people of the land')

Expression used in Scripture to refer to the Jewish masses. Later in talmudic

The Hebrew Alphabet		
Hebrew letter form	*Hebrew letter name*	*English transliteration*
א	*aleph*	silent
ב	*bet*	{ b v
ג	*gimmel*	g
ד	*dalet*	d
ה	*hey*	h
ו	*vav*	v
ז	*zayin*	z
ח	*chet*	{ ḥ kh
ט	*tet*	t
י	*yod*	y
כ	*kaf*	{ k kh
ל	*lamed*	l
ם מ	*mem*	m
ן נ	*nun*	n
ס	*sameh*	s
ע	*ayin*	silent
פ	*pey*	{ p f
ץ צ	*tsade*	ts
ק	*qof*	k
ר	*resh*	r
ש	*shin*	{ sh s
ת	*tav*	t

times it was applied to common people who did not observe rabbinic ordinances. Eventually it came to denote an ignorant person.

Amalekites

Ancient people hostile to Israel. They attacked the Israelites in the desert near Rephidim after the EXODUS, but were defeated by the Israelite army led by JOSHUA (Exod. 7:8–13; Deut. 25:17–19). Subsequently they continued to threaten the Jewish people until the time of the early monarchy. In rabbinic sources Amalek came to symbolize eternal enmity to the Jewish people.

amen (Hebrew, 'true', 'truly')

Expression of affirmation made as a part of blessings and prayers. This practice goes back to the days of the Second TEMPLE when it was said in response to the songs chanted by the LEVITES. Normally the person reciting the prayer does not say amen. According to the sages, God nods amen to the blessings offered by worshippers.

Amichai, Yehuda (b. 1924)

Israeli poet and novelist. Born in Germany, he settled in PALESTINE in 1936. His poetry reflects the changes in the HEBREW language during the second World War and the Israeli WAR OF INDEPENDENCE: aeroplanes, fuel trucks and administrative contracts all feature in his poems. His writings include *Shirim: 1948–1962* and *Not of this Time, Not of this Place*.

amidah (Hebrew, 'standing')

Major prayer (also know as *shemoneh esreh*) in the Jewish liturgy, originally consisting of 18 BENEDICTIONS (a 19th was added later). Traditionally they were decreed by the men of the GREAT ASSEMBLY; others were added after the destruction of the Second TEMPLE. In the worship service (excluding the EVENING SERVICE) they are recited by the congregation and then repeated by the leader. On the SABBATH and FESTIVALS the number of benedictions recited is far smaller. The full version consists of the following prayers:

I. First blessings. Praise:

1. commemoration of ABRAHAM, ISAAC and JACOB;
2. mightiness of God in nature;
3. sanctification.

II. Intermediate blessings. Prayers for:

4. understanding;
5. penitence;
6. forgiveness;
7. redemption;
8. healing;
9. blessing of the harvest;
10. ingathering of the EXILES;
11. restoration of the judges;
12. destruction of the sectarians;
13. reward for the righteous;
14. rebuilding JERUSALEM;
15. restoring the kingdom of DAVID.

III. Last blessings. Praise and thanksgiving:

16. acceptance of prayer;
17. restoration of the Temple;
18. thanksgiving;
19. blessing of PRIESTS, prayer for peace.

amoraim (Hebrew, 'speak')

Title of scholars in PALESTINE and BABYLONIA from the third to the sixth century. Their views are recorded in the TALMUD and various MIDRASHIM. Originally an *amora* was a teacher who expounded the views of previous sages; subsequently, he discussed the meaning of the MISHNAH text. The *amoraim* were active during the period after the completion of the Mishnah by JUDAH HA-NASI in the second century. Some *amoraim* were known for their expertise in HALAKHAH; other were noted for their AGGADIC expositions.

Amos, Book of

Biblical book of prophecy dating from the eight century BCE. The PROPHET Amos was a herdsman from Tekoa who criticized the nations of the earth as well as the kingdoms of Israel and JUDAH for their lack of righteousness. He prophesied during the reign of Jeroboam II. In his view, the Jewish nation had become corrupt because of the people's exploitation of the poor. At BETHEL he declared that the kingdom of Israel was doomed and foretold its destruction. Although Amaziah, the priest of Bethel, told him to return to Judah, Amos insisted on carrying out his mission.

Amsterdam

City in The Netherlands. During the 16th and 17th centuries Jews flourished in its climate of religious tolerance. Up until the end of the 18th century, the Jewish community in Amsterdam was the most significant in Western Europe, and the city remained one of the most important centres of Jewry throughout the 19th century. However, during the Nazi occupation the Jewish population suffered terribly and in 1942 mass deportations of Jews took place.

amulet (Hebrew: *kamia*)

Charm carried about by an individual as protection against evil. Usually it bears sacred letters or symbols including the names of ANGELS or demons which are written in geometric patterns. They were frequently worn in TALMUDIC and GAONIC times. Under the influence of later Jewish mysticism, they took the form of KABBALISTIC diagrams, biblical verses, and letter combinations inscribed on paper, parchment or metal. (*See also* MAGIC.)

Anan ben David (fl. eighth century)

BABYLONIAN biblical scholar and founder of the KARAITE movement. According to tradition, he was the eldest son of the Babylonian EXILARCH. When the heads of the ACADEMIES installed his younger brother Hananiah as the exilarch, he proclaimed himself his father's successor. Imprisoned in 767, he declared that he and his supporters advocated an interpretation of the faith different from other Jews, and therefore he was not a rival of the official exilarch. Once released, he became the leader of a separate sect initially called the Ananites; this movement was characterized by its rejection of the TALMUDIC tradition. In his *Sefer ha-mitzvot* (*Book of Precepts*), Anan declared that the Bible should serve as the sole basis for Judaism. Subsequent Karaite scholars were generally less strict in their interpretation of the faith.

angel

Divine messenger. In Scripture, there are various types of angels, such as CHERUBIM and SERAPHIM. As emissaries from God, they convey his word to human beings and perform various actions. According to post-biblical sources, they act as independent beings; in the TALMUD and MIDRASH they are portrayed as involved in human affairs. Subsequently medieval philosophers identified them with the higher intelligences. In mystical sources they occupy the seven heavenly halls. Within the liturgy, their praise for God (based on Isa. 6:1–3) is included in the *kedushah* prayer as well as in PIYYUTIM and *selihot* (*see* HOLINESS; PENITENTIAL PRAYERS).

Ani Maamin (Hebrew, 'I believe')

Prayer in most ASHKENAZI prayer books based on MAIMONIDES' THIRTEEN PRINCIPLES OF THE FAITH. It is of unknown authorship and dates back to around the 15th century.

animals

Jewish LAW prohibits cruelty to animals. (Deut. 22:4). This attitude is enshrined

in the principle *tzaar baale ḥayyim*
('pain of living creatures'). Scriptural
precepts regarding animals include the
prohibition against muzzling an ox while
threshing; the injunction that animals
must rest on the Sabbath; and the law
that an animal that falls down under its
load must be helped to rise up. In addition, animals are not to be gelded or
crossbred. Such an emphasis on kindness
to animals continued into the rabbinic
period. Thus rabbinic legislation specifies that a person may not eat until he
has first given food to his animals, nor
should he buy an animal unless he can
supply it with an adequate amount of
food. Although animals may be eaten
and used for SACRIFICE, they must not be
subject to unnecessary suffering. In this
spirit, rabbinic authorities prohibited
hunting as a sport.

anointing

Pouring oil on a person to indicate his
status. In biblical times, kings were consecrated in this way – the procedure was
connected with the pouring out of God's
spirit (1 Sam. 16:13). In addition,
PRIESTS were anointed with oil in order
to symbolize their separation from
everyday affairs (Exod. 40: 9–13).
Although the practice of anointing
appears to have died out around the seventh century BCE, the term *Mashi'aḥ*
(MESSIAH = the anointed one) was used
to designate the long-awaited king who
would usher in the messianic age.

anthropomorphism

Attribution of human characteristics to
GOD. Frequently anthropomorphic
terms were used in Scripture; yet the
desire to distance Jewish belief from
such terminology was apparent in the
biblical emendations of the SCRIBES. Such
a process also filtered into the early
translations of the Hebrew Bible into
ARAMAIC and Greek – here the concept
of the word of God was frequently
added to the text. HELLENISTIC thought,

as represented by the writings of the
first-century philosopher PHILO, was
devoid of such anthropomorphic terminology. Nonetheless, in rabbinic sources
anthropomorphic expressions were frequently employed to describe God's
nature and activity. In this connection,
the mystical text *Shiur Komah*
('Measurement of Stature') contains references to God's body. In the writings of
medieval Jewish philosophers such as
Moses MAIMONIDES, however, there was
a conscious rejection of such descriptions. According to these writers, God is
incorporeal. However, despite the influence of these thinkers, anthropomorphic
expressions were introduced into KAB-
BALISTIC texts.

Antiochus IV Epiphanes
(fl. second century BCE)

SYRIAN king who reigned from 175 to
163 BCE. On his second expedition
against EGYPT in 168 BCE, he occupied
JERUSALEM, plundered the TEMPLE and
attempted to HELLENIZE the population.
In response the Jewish masses rebelled,
causing Antiochus to suppress the people: thousands of Jews were massacred
and many were sold into slavery. In addition, Antiochus brought gentile settlers
into Jerusalem, fortified Acra as a
Hellenistic stronghold, and persecuted
the Jewish community. He prohibited
CIRCUMCISION as well as SABBATH worship, desecrated the Temple and compelled the Jews to engage in pagan
practices. Such anti-Jewish activity
brought about the HASMONEAN uprising.

anti-Semitism

Hostility towards Jews. Although the
term was used first in the 19th century,
the dislike and persecution of Jewry go
back to ancient times. In the Greco-
Roman world Jews were regarded as
alien and undesirable, and such antipathy intensified with the advent of
Christianity. The New Testament contains a strong anti-Jewish bias; such an

attitude was subsequently fostered by the Church Fathers and continued into the medieval world. Jews fared better in Muslim lands, although they were not granted full civil rights. In the modern world, anti-Semitism has been generated by factors other than religious belief. In response to such hostility, ZIONISTS were convinced that the Jewish people needed a nation of their own, and the State of ISRAEL was eventually established after the devastation of the HOLOCAUST. However, because of Arab–Israeli conflict, Muslim anti-Semitism has become particularly virulent in recent times.

anusim (Hebrew, 'compelled ones')

Jews who were forced to convert to another faith. Instances of such forced conversion have occurred throughout Christian and Muslim history. Often the *anusim* attempted to preserve Jewish customs in secret and teach them to their children. (*See also* MARRANOS.)

apikoros (Greek, 'Epicurean')

Heretic. The word is derived from the name of the Greek philosopher Epikoros (Epicurus). It refers to an individual who disobeys the divine COMMANDMENTS, derides the TORAH and defames rabbinic scholars. According to the 12th-century philosopher Moses MAIMONIDES, an *apikoros* is someone who rejects God's foreknowledge, prophecy and REVELATION. The term was first used in the MISHNAH; in the modern period it is used to describe any type of heretic.

apocalypse (Greek, 'revelation')

REVELATION of the end of time and the final judgement. Most Jewish apocalyptic literature was composed between the second century BCE and the second century CE, represented by the APOCRYPHA and PSEUDEPIGRAPHA. These works contain descriptions of the mysteries of the heavens, the secrets of world government, the functions of ANGELS and evil spirits, details of the end of the world, and the soul's existence in HEAVEN and HELL.

Apocrypha

Non-canonical Jewish writings from the Second TEMPLE period consisting largely of historical and ethical works. The Apocrypha contains I and II Esdras, Tobit, Judith, additions to Esther, the Wisdom of Solomon, Ecclesiasticus, Baruch with the Epistle of Jeremiah, the Song of Three Holy Children, the History of Susanna, Bel and the Dragon, the Prayer of Manasseh, and I and II Maccabees.

apologetics

Defensive argument or method of disputation. Jewish works of apologetics originated in response to pagan and Christian challenges to the Jewish faith. The first systematic Jewish apologetic was JOSEPHUS' *Contra Apionem*. In medieval sources Jewish apologists defended Judaism from external criticism as well as from doubts arising from comparisons with other cultural traditions. In addition, in the middle ages leading Jewish and Christian figures were bought face to face as adversaries in religious DISPUTATIONS. Later, treatises critical of Christianity began to make their appearance. From the 17th century ex-MARRANO scholars in AMSTERDAM and their RABBIS began a tradition of polemics in Spanish and Latin. In modern times, however, Jews and Christians have engaged in a more tolerant form of dialogue.

apostasy

Abandonment of a religious faith. In Judaism an apostate is called a *meshummad* or *mumar*. During the HELLENISTIC period, a number of Jews became apostates. Once Christianity became the dominant religion in the West, very few

Jews left the faith. However, during the middle ages FORCED CONVERSION brought about large-scale desertion of the tradition. According to Jewish law, a distinction is made between apostates who convert through pressure or force (ANUSIM) such as MARRANOS, and those who voluntarily leave the faith. Traditionally an apostate remains a Jew, although he is viewed as a sinner; no formal ceremony is required if such a person returns to the Jewish tradition.

Aramaic

North-Semitic language. It is divided into three principal groups: (1) ancient Aramaic, used in the Bible; (2) intermediate Aramaic, comprising western Aramaic (used in the PALESTINIAN TALMUD, AGGADIC MIDRASHIM, the Targum Jonathan, and the Samaritan translation of the PENTATEUCH), and eastern Aramaic (including the Aramaic in the BABYLONIAN TALMUD); and (3) New Aramaic, which is spoken by Nestorian Christians in SYRIA, Iraq, Turkey, Persia and Russia. Aramaic is closer to HEBREW than any other Semitic language. It was used as an international language, particularly for commerce from the period of the late Assyrian and Persian kingdoms in the sixth century BCE. In PALESTINE, Aramaic was the vernacular language for centuries, and the Bible was translated into Aramaic in SYNAGOGUES. It continued to be used in literary sources such as the ZOHAR and KABBALISTIC texts.

arba kosot

See FOUR CUPS.

Arbaah Turim

(Aramaic, 'Four Rows')

Code of Jewish law compiled by JACOB BEN ASHER in the 14th century. This work contains the decisions found in both versions of the TALMUD, and those of the geonim (*see* GAON), as well as those given in earlier commentaries and codes. The work is divided into four parts: (1) *Orah* *Hayyim,* which deals with daily conduct, including prayers, SABBATHS, and holidays; (2) *Yoreh Deah,* which lays down dietary laws: (3) *Even ha-Ezer,* which covers personal and family matters; and (4) *Hoshen Mishpat,* which describes civil law and administration.

Aristeas, Letter of

PSEUDEPIGRAPHIC work. It describes the glories of JERUSALEM and Judaism as well as the legendary origin of the SEPTUAGINT. Composed as a Greek letter, it was allegedly written by Aristeas, a Greek official of Ptolemy II of Egypt (285–246 BCE). In all likelihood it was actually written by an Egyptian Jew who was an admirer of Greek civilization. The work extols the Jewish people and their religious heritage, and seeks to illustrate the distinctiveness of Judaism in a HELLENISTIC environment.

ark

See HOLY ARK.

Ark of the Covenant

Chest in which the two Tablets of the Law (*see* TEN COMMANDMENTS) were placed as described in Exod. 25:10–22. It was made of acacia wood and inlaid and covered with gold. Measuring 2.5 cubits in length, 1.5 cubits in breadth, and 1.5 cubits in height, it was surrounded by a moulding of gold; four gold overlaid wooden staves were placed through four rings on its sides. A cover of gold was placed over it, and two golden CHERUBIM with outstretched wings screened the ark cover. According to Scripture, the golden cover and the cherubim symbolized the place where the SHEKHINAH (divine presence) dwelt. The ark which contained the Tablets of the Law symbolized the COVENANT between God and the Jewish nation. From the time of MOSES to the construction of SOLOMON'S TEMPLE, the ark was taken out from the HOLY OF HOLIES

The Ark of the Covenant from the Synagogue, Capernaum, Israel.

during times of national crisis. During the period of the First Temple, the ark was situated in the Holy of Holies and never removed.

Aron Kodesh

See HOLY ARK.

asceticism

Self-mortification. In the history of the faith, asceticism has been practised by individuals as well as various groups including the Essenes, THERAPEUTAE, ḤASIDEI ASHKENAZ, KABBALISTS and the ḤASIDIM. Nevertheless, Judaism generally opposes the practice, stressing instead the importance of enjoying God's gifts.

Asch, Sholem (1880–1957)

Polish YIDDISH author. He lived in the United States, France and Israel. In short stories, novels and plays, he portrayed life in Eastern Europe as well as the American Jewish experience. His later novels deal with the idea of messianic redemption. His works include *Motke the Thief*, *Kiddush ha-Shem*, *Three Cities*, *Salvation*, *East River*, *Moses, the Prophet*, *Mary*, *The Nazarene* and *The Apostle*.

Ashamnu

(Hebrew, 'We have trespassed')

First word of the alphabetic confession of sin which is recited on YOM KIPPUR.

Ashkenazim

One of the two main divisions of Jewry in the DIASPORA. Initially the term referred to the members of a biblical people (Gen. 10:3; Jer. 51:27). From the ninth century it was applied to Germans – hence German Jews were called Ashkenazim in contrast to the SEPHARDIM. After the period of the

Crusades, Ashkenazi Jews immigrated to Eastern European countries; subsequently they settled in Western Europe and America. The Hebrew pronunciation used by Ashkenazi Jews differs from that of the Sephardim; in addition, their ritual practices are of a distinctive type. The majority of Ashkenazi Jews spoke YIDDISH until the 20th century. After the HOLOCAUST, their numbers were greatly reduced.

Ashrei (Hebrew, 'Happy are those [who dwell in thy house]').

First word of Ps. 84:5. It is prefixed (with Ps. 144:15) to Ps. 145 and recited in the morning and afternoon SYNAGOGUE liturgy.

Asmodeus (Hebrew: *Ashmedai*)

Evil spirit frequently found in AGGADIC literature. According to most scholars, the name is derived from Aeshma Daeva, the Persian god of anger. Asmodeus is first referred to in the Book of TOBIT in the APOCRYPHA. In the TALMUD he is depicted as king of the demons. His name is invoked in spells and incantations in KABBALISTIC literature.

assimilation

Integration of Jews into another culture. It may refer to abandonment of external Jewish characteristics; abandonment of Jewish identity altogether; or conversion to another faith. In the HELLENISTIC period many Jews were influenced by Greek and Roman civilization. Under Islam, Jews were frequently attracted to various aspects of Islamic life and thought. During the middle ages anti-Jewish persecution coupled with Jewish cohesiveness deterred Jews from assimilation. However, since the 19th century assimilation in all its forms has become a dominant feature of Jewish life.

astrology

Belief that heavenly bodies influence terrestrial events. In biblical times it was criticized by the PROPHETS (Isa. 47:13; Jer. 10:2). Nonetheless, astrological speculation became a feature of Jewish life during the talmudic period and in later centuries. In the TALMUD there are various accounts of astrologers whose predictions came true. According to astrological theory, every living thing is born under a particular star, which determines its fate. Nonetheless the RABBIS emphasized that although the stars have a powerful effect upon the nations, Israel is above such stellar influence. During the middle ages, both rabbis and philosophers studied astrology, and some Jews served as court astrologers. Astrological theories are found in various philosophical tracts as well as in the ZOHAR and other KABBALISTIC sources.

atarah (Hebrew, 'crown')

Term applied since the middle ages to the symbol used as one of the TORAH ornaments.

atonement

Reconciliation with God following REPENTANCE for SIN. In Scripture it is connected with SACRIFICE (Lev. 5:14). The PROPHETS, however, declared that sacrifice alone is insufficient – moral action is also required. According to the RABBIS, PRAYER, repentance and CHARITY are of fundamental importance; in addition, they believed that SUFFERING, POVERTY, EXILE and DEATH bring about atonement. Among medieval KABBALISTS various ASCETIC practices were common ways of making atonement. According to the Jewish tradition, for sins committed against God, repentance is sufficient to earn atonement. However, if the sin involves injury to another person, restitution and FORGIVENESS are necessary. (*See also* FASTING; YOM KIPPUR.)

Auschwitz

Town in Poland, 30 miles west of Cracow. It was the site of the largest Nazi death camp, which, set up in 1940, had three large components: (1) Auschwitz I, the *Stammlager* (main camp); (2) Auschwitz II, Birkenau; (3) Auschwitz III, the *Aussenkommandos* (outside groups). With the installation of the gas chambers and the crematoria, thousands of people were killed every day. Nearly 1.6 million persons were murdered at Auschwitz by gassing, over-work, shooting and starvation.

Av 9

See NINTH OF AV.

Av 15

See FIFTEENTH OF AV.

av bet din

(Hebrew, 'Father of the Court')

Title conferred on the president of an ecclesiastical court. During the period of the Second TEMPLE the title was given to the vice-president of the Supreme Court in JERUSALEM. In all likelihood he was responsible for the procedure of the court. According to the TALMUD, the *av bet din* follows the NASI (president) and precedes the sage (*ḥakham*), who serves as the third member of the court. In gaonic times, the title designated the assistant to the GAON of the academies in BABYLONIA and Israel. From the 14th century a local RABBI, the head of a YESHIVAH, or the district rabbi of a large community used the title. In modern times the head of a rabbinical court is called *av bet din* or *rosh bet din*. (*See also* BET DIN.)

av ha-raḥamin

(Hebrew, 'Father of mercy')

Opening words of a medieval dirge in memory of MARTYRS. It is recited during SABBATH prayers among the ASHKENAZIM.

Avelei Zion

See MOURNERS FOR ZION.

Avinu Malkenu

(Hebrew, 'Our Father, Our King')

Poetic prayer recited on the TEN DAYS OF PENITENCE. It was composed during the time of the MISHNAH but subsequently underwent various changes. It has 25 verses in the SEPHARDI rite, and 44 in the ASHKENAZI.

Avodah   (Hebrew, 'Service', 'Prayer')

Term referring to the TEMPLE SACRIFI-CIAL service and to the DAY OF ATONEMENT ritual of the HIGH PRIEST. In addition, it refers to a section of the *musaf* (ADDITIONAL SERVICE) on the Day of Atonement depicting the Temple service on that day with its confession of SINS.

Avodah Zarah

(Hebrew, 'Idolatrous Worship')

Eighth TRACTATE of NEZIKIN in the MISHNAH. It deals with IDOLATRY.

Avot   (Hebrew, 'Fathers')

TRACTATE of the MISHNAH. It contains the teachings of sages from the third century BCE to the third century CE. Due to its importance, Avot (or Pirke Avot, 'Chapters of the Fathers') is incorporated in the liturgy – it is read in ASHKENAZI communities every SABBATH afternoon during the summer. Among SEPHARDIM, it is recited only at home on the Sabbaths between PASSOVER and SHAVUOT.

Avtalyon   (fl. first century BCE)

Palestinian scholar. He and SHEMAIAH constituted the fourth of the pairs of sages (ZUGOT) in PALESTINE. He served as AV BET DIN of the SANHEDRIN.

Azazel

Name designating the SCAPEGOAT or the demon to whom the scapegoat was sent out (Lev. 16). On the DAY OF ATONEMENT, two goats were designated as SIN OFFER- INGS for the nation. The HIGH PRIEST cast lots and declared one goat 'for the Lord'; the other was reserved for 'Azazel' and banished to the wilderness or cast over a cliff. In the APOCRYPHA and MIDRASHIC lit- erature, Azazel is portrayed as a fallen ANGEL or demon.

azei ḥayyim (Hebrew, 'trees of life') Staves which hold the TORAH SCROLLS.

B

Baal

Ancient CANAANITE agricultural god. Originally the term was applied to various local gods usually represented as bulls or human beings. They were generally worshipped as fertility gods. Once the Israelites entered the PROMISED LAND, they began to adopt the deities of the local inhabitants despite the rebuke of PROPHETS such as ELIJAH. This conflict is a central theme of the First Book of KINGS.

Baal Shem

(Hebrew, 'Master of the Divine Name')

Title applied to an individual who is able to perform MIRACLES by using divine names. Among the ḤASIDEI ASHKENAZ, it was given to liturgical poets. From the 13th century the title was used by Spanish KABBALISTS, and was also applied to writers of texts for AMULETS based on holy names. In the 17th and 18th centuries it referred to miracle workers who healed the sick.

Baal Shem Tov

See ISRAEL BEN ELIEZER.

baal teshuvah

One who has repented of his or her sins and is living an observant life. (*See also* REPENTANCE.)

Babylonia

Ancient country located in Western Asia between the Tigris and Euphrates rivers.

It was settled in the third millennium BCE by the Sumerians; Sargon I founded the Akkadian dynasty there in the 24th century BCE. Later, in the 19th century BCE, the Amorites ruled over northern BABYLONIA. Later rulers of the country were the Hittites and the Assyrians. After the conquest of the Assyrians by the Babylonians in the 6th century BCE, the Kingdom of JUDAH was devastated by a Babylonian onslaught and many Jews were led away into exile. In the centuries following the destruction of Jerusalem in 70 CE, Babylonian Jewry became increasingly important under the leadership of the EXILARCH. During this period the Babylonian ACADEMIES of NEHARDEA, SURA and PUMBEDITA served as centres of Jewish learning. In the 6th century CE the Babylonian TALMUD was compiled and served as the framework of Jewish learning in subsequent centuries.

Babylonian Talmud

See TALMUD.

badge, Jewish

Emblem which Jews were compelled to wear, normally made of cloth. From the seventh century Muslim rulers declared that Jews must wear special clothing. In 1215 the Fourth Lateran Council laid down a similar decree specifying that Jews should distinguish themselves from Christians. Usually the badge was yellow. In medieval England it depicted the two Tablets of the Law (*see* TEN COMMANDMENTS*)*; in France it was a circular patch; in Germany it was a large yellow circle. Under the Nazis it was a yellow STAR OF DAVID with the letter 'J' (or the word *Jude*) inside.

Baeck, Leo (1873–1956)

German RABBI and communal leader. He served as a rabbi in Oppeln (1897–1907), Düsseldorf (1907–12) and Berlin (from 1912), where he also lectured in MIDRASH and HOMILETICS at the Hochschule für die Wissenschaft des Judentums. Eventually he became the spiritual leader of German REFORM Jewry, and from 1922 served as chairman of the Rabbinerverband. Once the Nazis came to power, he was elected head of the Reichsvertretung der Juden in Deutschland. In 1943 he was sent to Theresienstadt concentration camp, surviving until its liberation in 1945, when he went to London. He became president of the World Union for Progressive Judaism, and served as visiting professor at the Hebrew Union College in Cincinnati, Ohio. His writings include *The Essence of Judaism*.

Bahir, Book of
(Hebrew: *Sefer Bahir*)

Kabbalistic text. According to tradition, it was written by Neḥunyah ben Ha-Kanah in the first century CE. However, most modern scholars believe it was composed in Provence in the 12th century. It deals with letter mysticism and alludes to the doctrine of the *sefirot*. Much of the terminology employed in this work became part of the vocabulary of the KABBALAH. In addition, it contains a reference to the belief in METEMPSYCHOSIS. (*See also* DIVINE EMANATIONS.)

Balaam (fl. 13th century BCE)

Aramean PROPHET. He was asked by Balak, King of Moab, to curse the Israelites when they camped in the steppes of Moab before entering the PROMISED LAND. Riding on a donkey, Balaam encountered an ANGEL wielding a sword, but was warned against proceeding by his donkey. Under divine inspiration he blessed Israel instead of cursing her (Num. 22–3).

Balfour Declaration

Statement issued on 2 November 1917 by the British Foreign Secretary Arthur James Balfour. It declared that the British government favoured the establishment in Palestine of a national home for the Jewish people. This declaration was the result of negotiations by Chaim WEIZMANN, Nahum Sokolow and others after the oubreak of the First World War. The document stated: 'His Majesty's government in Palestine view with favour the establishment in Palestine of a national home for the Jewish people, and will use their best endeavours to facilitate the achievement of this object, it being clearly understood that nothing shall be done which may prejudice the civil and religious rights of the existing non-Jewish communities in Palestine, or the rights and political status enjoyed by Jews in any other country.' (*See also* ZIONISM.)

ban (Hebrew: *herem*)

In biblical times, spoils taken in war were *herem;* they could not be used or enjoyed. Later, a *herem* was a ban placed on an individual. It was the ultimate sanction against an erring person, involving exclusion from the Jewish community for an indefinite period of time. It was employed against HERETICS.

baptism
See ANUSIM.

bar Kokhba, Simeon
(fl. second century CE)

Palestianian military leader in the war against Rome in 132–5. He proclaimed himself MESSIAH at the outbreak of the war. The name Bar Kokhba (Son of the Star) was applied to him because of this messianic role. Although his forces succeeded in capturing JERUSALEM, the Romans counter-attacked in 133 with an army of 35,000 under Hadrian and the commander Julius Severus. In 134–5 they besieged bar Kokhba's stronghold at Betar and he was killed in battle.

bar mitzvah

(Hebrew, 'son of the commandment')

Term applied to the attainment of legal and religious maturity; it also refers to the occasion on which this position is assumed. At the age of 13 a Jewish young man comes under the obligation to fulfil the commandments. In the SYNAGOGUE he is called up to read the TORAH and the HAFTARAH. A special service takes place when he reads for the first time, and the RABBI may deliver a sermon emphasizing his new responsibilities as a member of the community. After the service a festive KIDDUSH usually takes place. REFORM Judaism initially replaced the bar mitzvah with CONFIRMATION, but in recent years the bar mitzvah has come back into fashion and confirmation is now generally adopted as an additional ceremony.

baraita (Aramaic, 'external')

TANNAITIC sayings not contained in the MISHNAH. *Baraitot* are introduced by two formulae: (1) *teno rabbanan* (the rabbis taught); (2) *tanya, tena* (it was taught). The largest collection of HALAKHOT not contained in the Mishnah is the TOSEFTA; in addition, numerous *baraitot* are found in both TALMUDS.

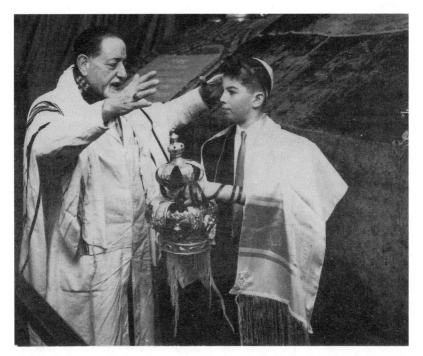

Bar mitzvah: The son of an American tourist comes to Israel for bar mitzvah, Mount Zion, Jerusalem.

Barcelona

Spanish city. From the ninth century Jews settled there; later it became one of the most important Jewish communities in Spain. It was the home of such scholars as Judah Al-Bargeloni, ABRAHAM BAR ḤIYYA, Abraham ben Ḥasdai, and Solomon ben ADRET. In 1263 the Disputation of Barcelona between NAḤMANIDES and Pablo Christiani took place there; after its conclusion, James I sought to convert the Jews to the Christian faith. In 1348 Jews in Barcelona were attacked, and in the massacres of 1391 the community was devastated.

Barekhu (Hebrew, 'Bless')

Opening word of the SYNAGOGUE formula of invitation to PRAYER. The phrase 'barekhu et Adonai ha-mevorakh' ('Bless ye the Lord who is [to be] blessed') is based on the biblical expression 'Bless ye the Lord'. It serves as the introduction to MORNING and EVENING SERVICE in the synagogue; in addition, it functions as the introduction to the reading of the TORAH. It was used for the Zimmun (invitation to Grace), but later replaced by the formula 'nevarekh' ('Let us bless'). When the reader recites 'BAREKHU', the congregation silently reads a prayer beginning 'yitbarakh'. On concluding the invitation to pray, the congregation responds: 'Blessed is the Lord who is [to be] blessed for ever and ever.'

Barukh, Apocalypse of

Apocalyptic work ascribed to JEREMIAH's scribe, Baruch. In the Syriac version, Baruch's visions on the eve of the destruction of JERUSALEM and its aftermath are depicted. The Greek version contains Baruch's journey through the HEAVENS, whereas the Ethiopic version contains stories about Baruch and Jeremiah during the period of the destruction of Jerusalem. (*See also* APOCALYPSE; EXILE; PSEUDEPIGRAPHA.)

Barukh ha-shem

(Hebrew, 'Blessed is the Name')

Expression of thanksgiving pronounced on hearing good tidings.

bat kol

(Hebrew, 'daughter of a voice')

Term used in rabbinic literature to depict the divine voice. It differs from the HOLY SPIRIT in that it can manifest itself to any person or group rather than to a select few. According to the sages, the *bat kol* is reputed occasionally to have given heavenly sanction to HALAKHIC DECISIONS, even though its judgement was not always accepted.

bat mitzvah (Hebrew, 'daughter of the commandment')

Ceremony for girls which corresponds to the boy's BAR MITZVAH. This takes place when a girl reaches the age of 12 years and one day. The ceremony which commemorates this occasion varies greatly: in some congregations girls read from the TORAH; in others they recite the HAFTARAH as well as certain PRAYERS.

Bathsheba

(fl. 11th–10th century BCE)

Wife of Uriah, then of King DAVID. When David, from his rooftop, spied her bathing, he had Uriah her husband killed in battle by putting him in the front lines. Bathsheba was the mother of King SOLOMON (2 Sam. 11–12; 1 Kgs. 1–2).

beard

According to Scripture, it is forbidden to cut the corners of the beard (Lev. 19:27). In the TALMUD the beard is regarded as the ornament of the face, and Jewish mystics ascribed esoteric significance to it. Among European Jews, the emphasis shifted from the obligation to wear a beard to the prohibition of shaving. However, it is permitted to clip the beard using scissors or an electric shaver with two cutting edges.

Begin, Menaḥem (1913–92)

Israeli statesman and prime minister. In 1942 he emigrated to PALESTINE and became the commander of the IRGUN TZEVAI LEUMI. From 1944 he led the Irgun's underground war against the British, and in 1948 founded the Herut party. In the general election of 1977 he led the Likud party to victory, becoming prime minister. His writings include *The Revolt* and *White Nights*.

Bel and the Dragon

Apocryphal book containing two stories about DANIEL's exposure to the falsity of pagan cults. In 'Bel' Daniel revealed the footprints of the priests who secretly removed the sacrifices placed before the idol Bel. In 'The Dragon' he caused the death of the dragon worshipped by the BABYLONIANS by feeding it a combination of pitch, fat and hair. (*See also* APOCRYPHA.)

Ben Sirah, Wisdom of

see ECCLESIASTICUS.

Bene Israel

(Hebrew, 'Sons of Israel')

Jewish community in India. According to tradition, its members originally left GALILEE because of persecution under ANTIOCHUS IV EPIPHANES in the second century BCE. They have retained many aspects of the Jewish faith. Although many have emigrated to Israel, a small community of Jews still survives in India.

benediction

The practice of making benedictions is found in the Hebrew Bible (1 Sam. 25:32). Benedictions follow a formulaic pattern. At the beginning of a PRAYER, it is customary to say '*barukh attah Adonai, Eloheinu, Melekh ha-Olam*' ('Blessed art thou O Lord, our God, King of the Universe'). Before fulfilling a commandment the following is added: '*asher kiddishanu b'mitzvotav vitzivanu*' ('who has sanctified us with your commandments and commanded us to . . . '). The AMIDAH, which is recited at all three daily services, consists of 19 benedictions. According to the TALMUD, every Jew should pronounce 100 benedictions each day.

Ben-Gurion, David (1886–1973)

Israeli statesman and prime minister. Born in Poland, he settled in PALESTINE in 1906. He was one of the labour leaders who founded the Ahdut ha-Avodah party in 1919, and later Mapai in 1930. From 1921 to 1935 he served as general secretary of the Histadrut (federation of Israeli trade unions). Subsequently he was chairman of the ZIONIST executive and the Jewish Agency. In April 1948 he became head of the provisional government, serving as prime minister and minister of defence. In 1956 he was responsible for the Sinai operation. His writings include speeches, articles and memoirs. (*See also* ZIONISM.)

David Ben-Gurion on his arrival at London airport on 2 June 1961 for a three-day visit.

Benjamin of Tudela
(fl. 12th century)

Spanish traveller. From Tudela in northern Spain he set out on his journeys in *c.*1165, returning *c.*1173. He visited about 300 places in France, Italy, Greece, SYRIA, PALESTINE, Iraq, the Persian Gulf, EGYPT and Sicily. His book of travels is a major source for understanding the history of the period.

bensh (Yiddish, 'bless')

Blessing. Term used for saying GRACE AFTER MEALS or blessing children. In addition, it is used in connection with the PRAYER for the new moon (*see* ROSH ḤODESH), the benediction recited by a person who has a perilous escape, and the kindling of lights on the SABBATH and FESTIVALS. (*See also* BENEDICTIONS.)

Ben-Yehudah, Eliezer
(1858–1922)

Hebrew writer and lexicographer of Lithuanian origin. In 1878 he went to Paris where he studied medicine; in 1879 he published articles encouraging settlement in PALESTINE. In 1881 he emigrated to JERUSALEM where he edited Hebrew journals. He was an advocate of HEBREW as a spoken language, and in 1890 he founded the Hebrew Language Council of which he was chairman. He wrote a comprehensive dictionary of ancient and modern Hebrew.

Berakhot (Hebrew, 'Blessings')

First TRACTATE of the MISHNAH order of ZERAIM (Seeds). It consists of nine chapters, with commentary in the Babylonian and Palestinian TALMUDS. It deals with BLESSINGS and PRAYERS.

Berdichevsky, Micah Joseph
(1865–1921)

Hebrew novelist. Also known as Micah Joseph Bin-Gorion, he was born in the Ukraine, and studied philosophy at Breslau and Berlin. Influenced by Nietzsche, he argued that Jewish universalism has led to EXILE. As a result, redemption from exile calls for a rejection of Judaism. In his writings he attacked the limited scope of Hebrew literature, the inadequacy of the HASKALAH, the ideology of AḤAD HA-AM and the ḤIBBAT ZION movement. His fiction depicts Jewish towns of Eastern Europe at the end of the 19th century and the life of East European Jewish students in Central and Western Europe.

Bereshit
See GENESIS.

berit
See CIRCUMCISION.

Berkovits, Eliezer (1900–1992)

American RABBI and theologian. Born in Transylvania, he served as a rabbi in Berlin, Leeds and Sydney. Subsequently he settled in the United States where he served as chairman of the department of Jewish philosophy at the Hebrew Theological College in Chicago. His writings include studies of FAITH after the HOLOCAUST.

Berlin

City in Germany. At the end of the 13th century Jews settled there, but the Jewish community was dispersed in 1510. Settlement recommenced at the end of the 17th century. The period of the ENLIGHTENMENT was ushered in there by Moses MENDELSSOHN in the 18th century. In the 19th century it became a major centre of REFORM JUDAISM. Under the Nazis the Jewish community of Berlin suffered the same fate as Jews elsewhere in Germany, but after the Second World War some Jews returned to the city.

bet din
(Hebrew, 'house of judgement')

Rabbinic court. During the TEMPLE period the SANHEDRIN, made up of 70 or

71 scholars, decided questions of religious law and appointed judges. Once the Temple was destroyed in 70 CE, the Sanhedrin became the focus of religious authority for the Jewish community. With the decline of Palestinian Jewry, the Sanhedrin was abolished and each Jewish community had a local court which exercised authority over communal matters. After Jewish emancipation in the 19th century the authority of the *bet din* was limited to voluntary arbitration and ritual matters.

bet ha-midrash
(Hebrew, 'house of study')

Rabbinic schools where Jews gather for study, discussion and PRAYER. During the Second TEMPLE period, the Great Bet Midrash stood in the Temple hall. In the TALMUD the term is used of an ACADEMY presided over by a legal scholar. Subsequently, most SYNAGOGUES had a *bet ha-midrash*.

Bet Hillel, Bet Shammai

Two schools of sages which existed in the first century CE. They differed in their decisions concerning more than 300 legal issues. Bet Shammai was generally more strict in interpretation. Rabbinic scholars subsequently adopted the majority of opinions of Bet Hillel. According to the TALMUD, a *bat kol* decreed that the law is in accord with Bet Hillel. Many of the debates between these two schools are recorded in the MISHNAH and BARAITA.

Bethel

Ancient Israelite city near JERUSALEM. ABRAHAM built an ALTAR near the site (Gen. 12:8), and it was the scene of JACOB's dream (Gen. 28). After the conquest of CANAAN, the TABERNACLE and ARK were placed there (Judg. 20:26–7). After SOLOMON built the TEMPLE in Jerusalem, its significance as a centre of pilgrimage declined. JEROBOAM set up a shrine there with the image of a calf which was condemned by the PROPHETS (1 Kgs. 12:25–33).

betrothal

Engagement to marry. According to Jewish LAW, betrothal creates no matrimonial relationship: either party may retract the promise of MARRIAGE. However, an aggrieved party can claim reimbursement for any loss suffered and demand compensation. It is customary to draw up the terms of betrothal in a document called the *tenaim*; this specifies the penalties payable by the defaulting party.

Bezazel (fl. ?13th century BCE)

Israelite craftsman. He constructed and decorated the ARK OF THE COVENANT (Exod. 36:2).

Bialik, Chaim Nachman
(1873–1934)

Russian Hebrew poet, essayist, storywriter and translator. Born in Zhitomir, he lived in Volozhin, Odessa, Korostyshev, Sosnowiec and Warsaw. In 1924 he settled in PALESTINE. His poetry, written in a lyrical style, is infused with Jewish hopes, memories and national aspirations. Throughout he uses HEBREW metrics and biblical parallelism. His essays discuss the course of Jewish culture, the state of Hebrew literature, and the development of language and style. With Yehoshua Hana Ravnitzky, he published *Sefer ha-Aggadah*, a collection of MIDRASHIC material classified by subject matter.

Bible

The HEBREW Bible is divided into three sections: TORAH (PENTATEUCH), Neviim (PROPHETS) and KETUVIM (Writings). The Torah is traditionally believed to have been given by God to MOSES on MOUNT SINAI, and contains the books of GENESIS, EXODUS, LEVITICUS, NUMBERS and DEUTERONOMY. The Neviim include JOSHUA, JUDGES, 1 and 2 SAMUEL, 1 and 2 KINGS (the former prophets), and ISAIAH, JEREMIAH, EZEKIEL, HOSEA, JOEL, AMOS, OBADIAH, JONAH, MICAH, NAHUM, HABAKKUK, ZEPHANIAH, HAGGAI, ZECHARIAH and MALACHI (the latter prophets). The Ketuvim consists of PSALMS, PROVERBS, JOB, the SONG OF SONGS, RUTH, LAMENTATIONS, ECCLESIASTES, ESTHER, DANIEL, EZRA, NEHEMIAH, and 1 and 2 CHRONICLES. The books which are included in the canon probably reached their present form between the ninth and second centuries BCE. With the exception of parts of Daniel, Ezra and Jeremiah, which are written in Aramaic, they are all written in Hebrew.

Bible, translations of

The earliest translation of the HEBREW Scriptures was the ARAMAIC TARGUM. This was followed in the second century by the Syriac translation, the PESHITTA, and in the third century by the Greek SEPTUAGINT. St Jerome produced the first Latin translation, the Vulgate, in the fourth century. In the 10th century SAADIAH GAON translated the Bible into Arabic. Spanish and YIDDISH editions were produced from the 15th century onwards.

Bible commentaries

There are two basic types of commentary: PESHAT (literal) and DERASH (homiletical). The interpretation of Scripture took place during three periods: (1) before the age of the *geonim* (until the sixth century); (2) from the GAONIC period to the HASKALAH (6th–18th century); and (3) from the Haskalah to modern times. In the earliest period the principles of exegesis were first formulated by HILLEL, and later expanded by ISHMAEL BEN ELISHA. Commentators of the second period include SAADIAH GAON, Abraham ibn Ezra, RASHI, David KIMHI and

NAHMANIDES. Prominent among commentators of the third period were Moses MENDELSSOHN, Samuel David LUZZATTO, and Abraham Kahana.

bikkur holim

See SICK, VISITING THE.

bimah (Hebrew, 'elevated place')

Platform in the SYNAGOGUE on which the reading desk stands. Traditionally it is located in the centre of the building. Among PROGRESSIVE Jews, however, it is usually situated in front of the ARK. The TORAH is read here. An alternative name is ALMEMAR. Among SEPHARDI Jews it is referred to as *tebah*.

binding (Hebrew: *akeda*)

Word used to depict ABRAHAM's binding and intended sacrifice of his son, ISAAC (Gen. 22:1–19). According to rabbinic sources, the AKEDA is a symbol of self-sacrifice in obedience to God. The passage from Genesis which describes this incident is read in the SYNAGOGUE on the first day of ROSH HA-SHANAH.

birkat ha-mazon

See GRACE AFTER MEALS.

birkat ha-minim

(Hebrew, 'blessing concerning sectarians')

The 12th BENEDICTION of the AMIDAH – actually a curse on sectarians. Instituted by GAMALIEL II, it was composed or copied from earlier sources by Samuel ha-Katan. It has been used against SADDUCEES, collaborators, persecutors, heretics and Judeo-Christian sects. Jews have in the past been accused of working against Christianity in their prayers, but the original intention was against Jewish heretics. (*See also* APIKOROS.)

birkat ha-torah

(Hebrew, 'blessing of the Law')

The benediction which is said before reading the TORAH.

birth control

According to MIDRASHIC sources, this practice goes back to the wicked generation before the FLOOD. In GENESIS, birth control is referred to in connection with ONAN, who spilled his seed on the ground (Gen. 38:9–10). The TALMUD and RESPONSA deal with the subject in detail. Birth control procedures can only be used by the wife; the main preference is for oral contraceptives. (*See also* ABORTION.)

bitter herbs (Hebrew: *maror*)

A Pesach (PASSOVER) food. According to Exodus 12:8, on Passover Jews are commanded to eat *matzah* (UNLEAVENED BREAD) with bitter herbs. It symbolizes the bitterness of Egyptian slavery.

black Jews

African Americans who have established Jewish congregations. They are generally centred on individual charismatic figures. Their services are influenced by KABBALISTIC and rabbinic sources as well as the Christian Pentecostal tradition. They have little contact with mainstream Jewry, and are not recognized as Jews by the Israeli government under the LAW OF RETURN. (*See also* FALASHAS.)

blasphemy

Insult directed against God or sacred things. It is forbidden in Scripture and punishable by death (Lev. 24:10–23). Subsequently this punishment was replaced by EXCOMMUNICATION. According to the MISHNAH, blasphemy is restricted to cases where God's name is pronounced. During trials for blasphemy, witnesses were not permitted to quote the offending words until the closing stages when the public was excluded from the court. One of the witnesses repeated the blasphemy and the judges rent their garments. (*See also* CAPITAL PUNISHMENT.)

blessing

See BENEDICTION.

blood

In the Hebrew Bible, blood is referred to as life itself (Lev. 17:11, 14; Deut. 12:23). The prohibition against consuming blood is one of the seven laws given to NOAH (Gen. 9:4). According to Jewish law, blood must be drained from a slaughtered animal before it is eaten. During TEMPLE times, blood was sprinkled on the ALTAR during the sacrifice as a symbol of ATONEMENT. (*See also* SACRIFICE; SHEHITA.)

blood libel

Accusation that Jews murder non-Jews to obtain blood for PASSOVER or other rituals. In Christian countries Jews were accused of killing children at Easter to use their blood to make UNLEAVENED BREAD or in the SEDER rites. This led to trials and massacres of Jews in the middle ages and in the early modern period.

Bnai Brith

(Hebrew, 'Sons of the Covenant')

International Jewish organization. Founded in NEW YORK in 1843, its aims are social, moral, educational and philanthropic. From 1880 to 1920 it helped in the settlement of immigrants to the USA. A number of subsidiary sections have been formed: women's chapters were created in 1897, the Anti-Defamation League in 1913, the Hillel Foundation in 1913, youth organizations in 1924, the Vocational Service Bureau in 1938 and the Department of Adult Education in 1948. It has lodges and chapters in 45 countries. (*See also* CHARITY.)

Boethusians

Jewish religious and political sect, active in the first century BCE. It was named after Boethus, a disciple of Antigonus of Sokho (or possibly after the High Priest

Simeon ben Boethus). Its adherents denied belief in the RESURRECTION of the body and the AFTERLIFE.

Book of Creation
(Hebrew: *Sefer Yetsirah*)

Early BABYLONIAN or PALESTINIAN mystical work from the third to sixth centuries. According to this work, the cosmos is derived from the HEBREW alphabet and the ten sefirot (DIVINE EMANATIONS). Knowledge of these mysteries, including letter combinations, allegedly confers magical powers on the initiated. Hence the GOLEM (an artificially created human being) was created by means of formulae from this book. The *Sefer Yetsirah* influenced later KABBALISTS. From the GAONIC period various commentaries were written on it.

Book of Life

Book kept in HEAVEN. It lists the names of the righteous. The belief in the existence of a heavenly ledger is alluded to several times in the Hebrew Bible. In the MISHNAH, AKIVA describes the heavenly book in which all human actions will be inscribed until the DAY OF JUDGEMENT. The same belief is expressed in the liturgy of the HIGH HOLY DAYS.

Book of the Covenant

Laws set out in Exod. 20:23–23:33. These laws in all likelihood date from before the days of the monarchy. They cover cultic legislation, laws of slavery, capital offences, theft, idolatry, charity and social organization, and the religious calendar.

Borochov, Dov Ber (1881–1917)

Ukrainian socialist ZIONIST leader and writer. He was one of the the the founders of POALE ZION, and served as secretary of the World Confederation of Poale Zion. After leaving Russia in 1914, he became a spokesman for the American Poale Zion and the World and American Jewish Congress movements. Subsequently he returned to the USSR. He analysed the economic and social position of the Jewish nation along Marxist lines, arguing for settlement in PALESTINE.

Bratslav Hasidim

Followers of NAḤMAN OF BRATSLAV. One of the largest ḤASIDIC groups. Bratslav Hasidim emphasize simple FAITH and PRAYER centred on the ZADDIK.

breastplate

Sacred object worn by the HIGH PRIEST (Exod. 28:15ff). It consisted of a square gold frame in which were set 12 gems of different colours which represented the tribes of Israel. It also held the URIM AND THUMMIM. The term is now applied to the silver ornament placed in front of the cover of the TORAH SCROLL in ASHKENAZI congregations.

bridegroom of the law

Reader called up to recite the last portion of the PENTATEUCH on the festival of SIMḤAT TORAH. The person who comes after and begins again at Genesis is referred to as 'the bridegroom of the beginning'. In many communities it is usual for the 'bridegrooms' to host a party after the service.

Buber, Martin (1878–1965)

Philosopher. Born in Vienna, he lived in Lvov and studied at German universities. In 1898 he joined the ZIONIST movement, becoming editor of *Die Welt* in 1901. From 1903 he engaged in literary activity, and in 1906 founded the German monthly *Der Jude*. Together with Franz ROSENZWEIG, he published a German translation of the BIBLE. From 1924 to 1933 he served as professor of Jewish religion and ethics at Frankfurt on the Main. In 1938 he settled in JERUSALEM, and was appointed professor of the sociology of religion at the

Hebrew University. His writings include *I and Thou*.

burial

According to the Jewish faith, burial of the dead is a central duty. Traditionally the corpse was put in a grave or rock-cut cave. In ancient times the body was first buried in the ground; subsequently the bones were placed in stone ossuaries in the family's burial cave. During the Second TEMPLE period, tombs and rock-cut graves with architectural façades became common. If possible, burial took place on the day of death. Initially many of the dead were dressed in costly garments; however, it eventually became the norm to use simple linen clothing. When coffins are used, they should be made of simple wood. A *ḥevra kaddisha* (BURIAL SOCIETY) provides for all the details of burial: its role is to help read the CONFESSION

(*viddui*), wash and dress the corpse, conduct the service and the burial, and provide a meal for the mourners after the funeral. (*See also* FUNERAL.)

burial society
(Aramaic: *ḥevra kaddisha*)

The term refers to associations devoted to visiting the sick, burying the dead and comforting the bereaved. Because the dead cannot be buried for material gain, the duty of burial devolves on the community as a whole. Membership of the *ḥevra kaddisha* is a communal duty and viewed as a great honour. Among the SEPHARDIM such a society is generally called Ḥesed ve-Emet ('kindness and truth'). (*See also* FUNERAL.)

burnt offering
See SACRIFICE.

A burial society making a shroud in which a dead person is buried, Prague, c. 1780.

C

Cain

Eldest son of ADAM and EVE. When God rejected his offering consisting of the fruit of the earth while accepting his brother Abel's animal sacrifice, Cain murdered Abel. As a punishment he was condemned to wander through the land of Nod. He built a town called Enoch and became the progenitor of several peoples (Gen. 4).

calendar (Hebrew: *luaḥ*)

The Jewish calendar consists of 12 months based on the lunar cycle: Nisan, Iyyar, Sivan, Tammuz, Av, Elul, Tishri, Marḥeshvan, Kislev, Tevet, Shevat and Adar. In a leap year there are two months of Adar. According to tradition, the numbering of years is calculated from creation, which coincides with 3760 BCE. The year 5000 began on 1 September 1239. To calculate the Jewish date since 1240, 1,240 should be deducted from the year of the Common Era and 5,000 added. For dates in September–December, another year is added.

calf, golden

Idol made by AARON. The ancient Israelites became impatient when MOSES remained on MOUNT SINAI for a long period of time, and demanded that Aaron make a golden calf to worship. When Moses descended from the top of the mountain, he burned the golden calf and ground its gold to dust. At Moses' pleading, God forgave the Israelites for their iniquity (Exod. 32). (*See also* IDOLATRY.)

Canaan

Name of Syria in the 15th–13th century BCE. In a narrower sense the term was applied to the coast of PALESTINE in biblical times. Before the Hebrew conquest, the country was divided into small city-states. The Israelites referred to the land as Eretz Israel ('the Land of Israel'); the northern part was called Aram. (*See also* CANAANITES; ISRAEL, LAND OF; PROMISED LAND).

Canaanites

Inhabitants of the land of CANAAN. Traditionally they were descended from Canaan, the son of Ham. Divided into 11 peoples, they occupied the area between the Nile and Euphrates rivers. The name first appears in inscriptions from the 15th century BCE. From the 14th century BCE, the inhabitants of this region applied the name to themselves. Originally this people appears to have been a mixture of Horites, Hittites and Hebrews dating back to the 17th century BCE. They were nearly all destroyed or absorbed by the invading Hebrew tribes (*c.*13th century BCE), the Philistines along the coast (12th century BCE) and Arameans (11th century BCE).

Those who remained were eventually absorbed by DAVID and SOLOMON.

candelabrum

See MENORAH.

candles

In the Jewish faith the lighting of candles symbolizes joyful as well as sorrowful occasions. As a symbol of joy, it is a feature of the SABBATH as well as feast days. This was instituted by the PHARISEES during the period of the Second TEMPLE. The lighting of candles on such occasions, accompanied by the appropriate blessing, is the prerogative of the principal woman of the household. Candles are also placed at the head of a dead person, and are used during the week of MOURNING for the dead, on the anniversary of a death, and on the eve of the DAY OF ATONEMENT.

canon of Scripture

See BIBLE.

cantillation

Chanting of Scripture or liturgical texts in the SYNAGOGUE. A system of accent marks is used to aid cantillation: these indicate both punctuation and stress and show the rise and fall of the chant. The chanting is led by the CANTOR (*ḥazzan*).

cantor (Hebrew: *ḥazzan*)

SYNAGOGUE offical who leads the congregation in prayer and is in charge of the music. In the TEMPLE the liturgy was intoned by the PRIESTS and LEVITES. During synagogue services a prominent member of the community conducts the prayers. During the middle ages more complex music – known as cantorial music (*ḥazzanut*) – came into fashion and the office of the cantor was created. Further musical developments took place in the 18th century and had an impact on cantors, who studied musical composition and instrumental playing.

In the 19th and 20th centuries outstanding cantors included Joseph Rosenblatt, Zavel Kwartin, Mordecai Hershman, David Roitman, Aryeh Leib Rutman, Mosheh Kusevitsky and Leib Glanz.

capital punishment

According to Scripture, the death penalty was decreed for murder, sexual crimes (including adultery and incest), BLASPHEMY, IDOLATRY, desecration of the SABBATH, witchcraft, kidnapping, and dishonouring parents. According to the TALMUD, it may not be carried out unless two eye witnesses testify to the crime. In addition, the perpetrator must have previously been warned about the crime and its punishment. The Hebrew BIBLE specifies three types of capital punishment: stoning, burning and hanging. The RABBIS also specified slaying by the sword and strangulation. Capital punishment was rarely imposed under Jewish LAW, and many rabbis advocated its abolition. In the DIASPORA, Jews were subject to the laws of the lands in which they lived, and particular forms of execution were inflicted on them because of their religious affiliation. In the middle ages they were frequently executed by being hung by their heels; it was also common to exacerbate the punishment by stringing up dogs on either side of the condemned person.

Cardozo, Abraham (1626–1706)

Spanish MARRANO physician and mystic. Born in Rio Seco, he became a follower of SHABBETAI ZEVI, supporting him even after he converted to Islam. He expounded Shabbetean doctrines in a number of works. His theology was based on GNOSTIC dualism. He disparaged the value of the hidden First Cause and placed supreme importance on the God of Israel.

Caro, Joseph (1488–1575)

Spanish TALMUDIC codifier. Born in TOLEDO, he settled in Turkey after the expulsion of the Jews from Spain. In

1536 he set out for SAFED, where he became the head of a large YESHIVAH. His *Bet Yosef* (*House of Joseph*) is a commentary on the ARBAAH TURIM by JACOB BEN ASHER. He also compiled an abbreviation of this work, the SHULḤAN ARUKH (*The Prepared Table*). His codes were criticized by ASHKENAZI scholars who argued that they ignored French and German traditions. Nonetheless, the Shulḥan Arukh (printed with Moses ISSERLES strictures) became the authoritative code of Jewish LAW for ORTHODOX Judaism.

celibacy

See ASCETICISM.

ceremonial objects

Used in the SYNAGOGUE as well as in the home on the SABBATH and FESTIVALS and during ceremonies marking life-cycle events. These objects include: TORAH SCROLLS, Torah cases and covers, Torah crowns, Torah BREASTPLATES, pointers, ARKS, curtains for the ark, lamps, SPICE BOXES, Sabbath candlesticks, KIDDUSH cups, Sabbath tablecloths, ḤANUKKAH MENORAHS, ESTHER scroll cases, SEDER plates, ETROG containers, CHAIRS OF ELIJAH, wedding rings, wedding canopies and MEZUZAHS.

Chagall, Marc (1887–1985)

French artist of Russian origin. Born in Vitebsk, he studied in St Petersburg and Paris. In May 1914 he had a one-man show in Berlin; three years later he was appointed commissar for fine arts in Vitebsk and director of the Free Academy of Art. Subsequently he became designer for the Chamber State Jewish Theatre. He settled in France in 1923, but emigrated to New York in 1941. Later he returned to France. His paintings are dominated by themes from East European Jewish life.

chair of Elijah

Symbolic chair reserved for the PROPHET ELIJAH at the CIRCUMCISION ceremony. It is positioned to the right of the SANDAK, and the child is placed for a moment in the chair before being moved to the SANDAK's lap for the circumcision to be performed.

Chanukah

See ḤANUKKAH.

Chariot mysticism

Also known as Maaseh Merkavah ('Work of the Chariot') or Merkavah mysticism, this mystical doctrine is based on the vision of the divine chariot in Ezek. 1. It depicts the mystic's ascent to HEAVEN, his visions of the divine palaces, and personal experience of the divine presence. It formed the basis of a complex of speculations, homilies and visions connected with the throne of glory and the divine chariot. (*See also* HEKHALOT, BOOKS OF.)

charity (Hebrew: *zedakah*)

Giving money or material goods to help the poor or needy. In Scripture it is regarded as an obligation to give succour to the widow, the orphan, the stranger and the aged. According to the MISHNAH, charity assumes a well-defined system of organized relief. The RABBIS argued that the highest form of charity is that in which the donor and recipient are unknown to one another. MAIMONIDES maintained that the best kind of charity involves helping a needy person to support himself in some occupation. By the middle ages philanthropic institutions were established in the Jewish community. In the 19th and 20th centuries Jews have undertaken an active role in a wide range of Jewish charitable work, although in recent times the development of the welfare state has significantly altered the nature of Jewish philanthropy as the state has taken over some of the traditional functions of charity, such as the care of the aged and destitute.

chastity

Abstinence from sexual contact. The scriptural emphasis on sexual purity is linked to the condemnation of IDOLATRY. Of the 12 curses in Deut. 27, four are directed against those guilty of sexual sin. The rabbis listed ADULTERY along with IDOLATRY and MURDER as the cardinal offences which must not be committed on pain of death. Sexual relations outside MARRIAGE are forbidden by Jewish LAW. Early marriage was perceived as the best safeguard against sexual impurity. (*See also* SEXUAL MORALITY.)

cherub

Supernatural being depicted variously in Scripture as a winged figure with human, animal or bird's head and body. According to the Book of GENESIS, cherubim guarded the gates to the GARDEN OF EDEN (Gen. 3:24). In the TABERNACLE images of cherubim were placed on either side of the ARK, forming the THRONE OF GOD (Exod. 25:18–20, 37:7–9). Subsequently such images were placed in the HOLY OF HOLIES in the TEMPLE. The PROPHET EZEKIEL describes four cherubim carrying the divine throne (Ezek. 1). In post-biblical literature cherubim are identified with the ANGELS.

chief rabbi

Principal rabbinic authority of a national or provincial Jewish community. In the middle ages, chief rabbis were appointed in various countries. In the modern period Napoleon desired to set up consistories presided over by a grand rabbi. In Germany before unification the chief rabbinate existed in various provinces. In England the chief rabbi represents British Jewry. In ISRAEL there are two chief rabbis, one each from the ASHKENAZI and the SEPHARDI populations. However, not all countries have a chief rabbi.

Chief Rabbis of Israel: Sephardi Chief Rabbi Nissim (1896–1981) and Ashkenazi Chief Rabbi Unterman (1886–1976).

Chmielnicki massacres

Attacks on the Jewish community in the 17th century, led by the Ukrainian Cossack leader Bogdan Chmielnicki. These events shocked the Jewish world and gave rise to a wave of messianic longing, culminating in the widely held belief that SHABBETAI ZEVI was the MESSIAH.

chosen people

The belief that God chose the Jews is based on the COVENANT between God and ABRAHAM (Gen. 15). The covenant was renewed on MOUNT SINAI; however, the nation's election was made conditional on their observance of the TORAH (Deut. 7:6). ISRAEL is described in Exodus as a kingdom of priests and a holy nation (Exod. 19:6). According to the PROPHETS, the election of the people is based on righteousness. In the MISHNAH and TALMUD, the role of Israel as a teacher of all peoples is stressed. The Jewish idea of chosenness does not imply superiority, but rather the obligation to fulfil religious and moral duties.

Chronicles, Books of

Name of two biblical books in the HAGIOGRAPHA containing genealogical lists of the Israelite tribes from ADAM to the time of DAVID (1 Chr. 1–9), an account of David's rule (1 Chr. 10–29), a description of SOLOMON's reign (2 Chr. 1–9) and a history of the Kingdom of JUDAH up to its destruction by the BABYLONIANS (2 Chr. 10–36).

circumcision

Removal of the foreskin of the penis. In Jewish practice it is carried out by an official called the *mohel* at a ceremony which also includes the naming of the child and is held when he is eight days old. It is a sign of the COVENANT and is performed according to instructions given to Abraham (Gen. 7:11–12).

cities of refuge

MOSES decreed that six cities should serve as places of refuge for those who accidentally committed manslaughter (Num. 35:13; Deut. 19:9). In such cities a person was free from persecution by an avenger. (*See also* SANCTUARY.)

codes of Jewish law

The earliest codes of LAW date from the GAONIC period: *Halakhot Pesukot* and *Halakhot Godolot*. In these works the order of law is based on the TALMUDIC sequence. The later code of Isaac ALFASI, *Sefer ha-Halakhot* (11th–12th century), gives a synopsis of talmudic law, omitting legislation which was not applicable in post-TEMPLE times. The MISHNEH TORAH of MAIMONIDES includes all talmudic law. The code of Asher ben Jehiel, *Piske ha-Rosh* (13th–14th century), follows Alfasi's code with the addition of the opinions of later authorities. His son, JACOB BEN ASHER, compiled the ARBAAH TURIM, which formed the basis for the SHULḤAN ARUKH of Joseph CARO. Moses ISSERLES added supplementary notes (MAPPAH) to this code, incorporating ASHKENAZI practices. Every generation produced POSEKIM (halakhic scholars) who interpreted the law in practice and thereby contributed to its codification.

cohen

See PRIEST.

Cohen, Hermann (1842–1918)

German philosopher. Born in Coswig, he served as professor of philosophy at the University of Marburg until 1912; subsequently he taught at the Hochschule für Wissenschaft des Judentums. In 1880 he resumed his lapsed links with Judaism and defended the Jewish people and tradition. His writings include *Religion of Reason out of the Sources of Judaism*.

commandments

See HALAKHAH; MITZVAH; TEN COMMANDMENTS.

compassion

According to rabbinic Judaism, compassion is one of the three distinguishing characteristics of the Jewish people. It is among the highest virtues, and should be extended to animals as well as human beings.

confession

Scripture mentions the efficacy of the public and individual confession of SIN. Sin offerings accompanied by PRAYER played a major role in the TEMPLE SACRIFICAL service. In the SYNAGOGUE the confession of sin is part of the daily prayer service as well as the liturgy for the DAY OF ATONEMENT. At death a special confession (VIDDUI) is recited.

confession of faith

Declaration that the Lord God is One is the major confession of the Jewish FAITH. It is said on rising in the morning, on going to bed at night, and ideally at the moment of death. (*See also* SHEMA.)

confirmation

Ceremony for young adults to affirm their commitment to Judaism. Prevalent primarily in non-Orthodox communities, it was originally designed to replace the BAR MITZVAH. Today, however, it usually supplements this ceremony. One of its main objectives is to ensure the continuation of Jewish education past the age of BAR MITZVAH and BAT MITZVAH. It is normally held on the festival of SHAVUOT.

Conservative Judaism

Religious movement which emerged in the middle of the 19th century in Europe and the USA. Reacting against ORTHODOXY as well as REFORM JUDAISM, its founders argued that the traditional forms and precepts of Judaism are valid; however, they permitted some modifications of the HALAKHIC system. In the USA it has its own rabbinical school (Jewish Theological Seminary of America), rabbinic association (Rabbinical Assembly of America) and congregational organization (United Synagogue of America). Elsewhere, too, it has become a major force in Jewish life.

consistory

Official organization of Jewish congregations in France. The consistory was introduced by Napoleon in 1808. Each local consistory represented the Jews in a particular area and sent delegates to Paris to the Central Consistory: this body was responsible for the maintenance of the chief rabbinate as well as the RABBINICAL SEMINARY. The consistory has remained the official French Jewish representative organization.

contraception

See BIRTH CONTROL.

conversion from Judaism

See ANUSIM; APOSTASY; MARRANO.

conversion to Judaism

See PROSELYTE.

Copper Scroll

One of the DEAD SEA SCROLLS. Made of copper, it was discovered in 1952. It includes an inventory of the QUMRAN community's treasures as well as the places where they were hidden when its headquarters were abandoned in the first century CE.

Córdoba

City in Andalusia, southern Spain. When it became the capital of the western Caliphate in the 10th century, it was a major centre of Jewish culture. This was largely the result of the activity of Ḥasdai ibn Shaprut, who served as a physician and diplomat in the service of the caliph. Under his influence, the city attracted Jewish philosophers, poets and scholars to the city. MAIMONIDES was born there.

Cordovero, Moses (1522–70)

Palestinian KABBALIST of Spanish origin. Known as Ramak, he was the most important kabbalist in SAFED before Isaac LURIA. His first systematic work, *Pardes Rimmonim*, covers a wide range of mystical topics. He also composed a second tract, *Elimah Rabbati*, as well as a commentary on the ZOHAR.

corporal punishment

Physical chastisement is one of the forms of PUNISHMENT specified in Scripture. According to the Bible, 40 lashes were the maximum that could be inflicted for a single offence. Three JUDGES were to be present at the time of punishment: one ordered it, another counted the lashes, and a third read the relevant passage from DEUTERONOMY (28:58–9). The RABBIS decreed that corporal punishment should take place only in PALESTINE, except for the offence of disobedience. MAIMONIDES listed 207 cases for which corporal punishment was prescribed.

cosmogeny

See CREATION.

Costa, Isaac de (1798–1860)

Dutch writer and poet. Born into a distinguished SEPHARDI family in AMSTERDAM, he converted to Christianity in 1822. He published studies of Jews in Spain, Portugal and the Netherlands. His *Israel and the Gentiles* is an account of the Jewish people written from a Christian perspective. Many of his poems are based on Scripture.

courses, priestly

Rota of PRIESTS who participated in the TEMPLE ritual. They were divided into 27 groups; each group conducted the SACRIFICIAL liturgy for two weeks every year. (*See also* LEVITE.)

court Jews

Individuals who served as financial or other agents of European rulers. They functioned in absolutist states, especially in Central Europe, from the end of the 16th century. Court Jews enjoyed special privileges, were exempt from wearing the Jewish BADGE, and were permitted to live where they wished. Many were extremely wealthy. Due to their position in society, they were often influential in obtaining rights for their co-religionists.

courts

See BET DIN; SANHEDRIN.

covenant

Binding agreement between persons, nations or parties. In Scripture a covenant was established by a ceremony such as passing between two halves of a SACRIFICED animal (Gen. 15:9–11). The covenant between God and individuals or nations was accompanied by an external sign. Thus the covenant made with NOAH was symbolized by a rainbow (Gen. 9:13); the covenant with ABRAHAM by the act of CIRCUMCISION (Gen. 17:10); and the covenant with the children of Israel by the SABBATH (Exod. 31:13). God made a covenant with the house of AARON to ensure them the PRIESTHOOD (Num. 25:12–13). He also made a covenant with DAVID to establish that the monarchy would continue through his offspring (2 Sam. 23:5).

creation

According to the Bible, God created the cosmos. The biblical description of creation resembles the myths found in the BABYLONIAN religion. The RABBIS of the TALMUD accepted GNOSTIC ideas of creation, while various rabbinic scholars believed in *creatio ex nihilo*. Speculations about the nature of the visible universe, MAASEH BERESHIT ('Work of Creation') and the transcendental world, MAASEH MERKAVAH ('Work of the Chariot') are found in KABBALISTIC sources. Medieval Jewish philosophy was influenced by the Ptolemaic conception of the universe. The ZOHAR expounds various theories about the nature of creation, which were subsequently modified by Isaac LURIA.

creed

Authoritative statement of belief. Judaism does not contain a credal formulation. However, a number of Jewish scholars have drawn up the basic PRINCIPLES of the Jewish faith. PHILO set out five essential beliefs, and MAIMONIDES listed 13 principles of the Jewish faith which have been generally accepted. Other scholars such as Ḥasdai CRESCAS and Joseph ALBO produced different formulations. Some scholars believed it impossible to identify the essential beliefs of Judaism.

cremation

Disposal of a corpse by burning. Although cremation was known in the ancient world, Judaism prescribes BURIAL either in the ground or in a mausoleum. In modern times REFORM JUDAISM has permitted cremation, thereby incurring the wrath of ORTHODOX RABBIS.

Crescas, Ḥasdai (*c.*1340–*c.*1412)

Spanish RABBI and theologian. Born in BARCELONA, he was active as a merchant and communal leader there. In 1367 he was imprisoned on a charge of DESECRATING THE HOST, but later released. With the accession of John I in 1387 he was associated with the royal household of the Court of Aragon. Subsequently he settled in SARAGOSSA, where he functioned as a rabbi. In 1391 his son was killed in an anti-Jewish riot in Barcelona, which he described in a Hebrew account. His *Light of the Lord* is a refutation of MAIMONIDES.

cruelty

The Jewish faith condemns cruelty in either words or deeds.

crypto-Jews

Jews who outwardly practised another religion, which they were compelled to accept, while remaining faithful to Judaism. The phenomenon arose after the FORCED CONVERSIONS under the Visigoths in Spain in the seventh century, and under the Alhomades in north Africa and Spain in the 12th century. Other groups of crypto-Jews were the Neofiti in southern Italy from the end of the 13th century to the 16th century, and the *conversos* (or MARRANOS) in Spain after the persecutions of 1391 and the expulsion of 1492, and in Portugal after 1497. In Majorca such Jews were known as *chuetas*. In Persia in the 19th century forcible conversion to Islam gave rise to a group known as Jedid Al-Islam.

cup of Elijah

Cup of wine placed on the table at the PASSOVER SEDER; it is prepared to welcome ELIJAH the PROPHET, who is believed to visit every Jewish home on Passover night.

curse

Appeal to a supernatural power to bring harm on a person or group; as a profane expresion of anger. The BIBLE prohibits cursing God, one's parents, authorities or the deaf. The TALMUD expresses belief in the power of curses. Uttering a curse is permitted in some instances if it is done for religious reasons. Any curse which involves God's name is prohibited.

custom (Hebrew: *minhag*)

Many Jewish regulations are not based on written or oral LAW, but are binding because they are observed by custom. Different customs developed among Jews living in different parts of the DIASPORA, giving rise to variations in practice. These differences were noted by codifers of Jewish law. Joseph CARO, for example, cited the customs of Spanish Jews in his SHULḤAN ARUKH, while Moses ISSERLES in his glosses to this work refers to the customs among the ASHKENAZIM.

Cyrus the Great
(fl. 6th century BCE)

King of Persia 559–529 BCE. According to Scripture, God instructed him to rebuild JERUSALEM. In 538 BCE he granted permission to the Jews to return to the HOLY LAND and rebuild the TEMPLE (Ezra 1:1–44; 2 Chr. 36:22–3).

D

daily prayer

During the period when the JERUSALEM TEMPLE was functioning, SACRIFICES were offered daily. After the Temple was destroyed by the Romans in 70 CE, sacrifice ceased. In their place MORNING (*shaharit*), AFTERNOON (*minhah*) and EVENING (*maariv*) SERVICES took place in the synagogue; this pattern was established by the sages to correspond to the morning and afternoon sacrifices and the nightly burning of fats in the Temple. Ideally a MINYAN (quorum of ten men) should be present for each of these services since, without it, certain parts of the liturgy cannot be recited. On weekday mornings, a TALLIT (fringed prayer shawl) is worn, and TEFILLIN (phylacteries) are put on.

Damascus affair

In 1840 a superior of the Franciscan convent in Damascus disappeared. Prominent Jews were tortured and a confession of murder was obtained. This resulted in a campaign against the Jewish community. Through the intervention of Sir Moses MONTEFIORE and Isaac-Adolphe Crémieux, the murder charge was dismissed and the surviving imprisoned Jews were released.

dance

In biblical times dancing was associated with religious celebration. However, in the SYNAGOGUE, dancing plays no role except for the custom of dancing with the SCROLLS on SIMHAT TORAH. Mixed dancing was traditionally frowned on by the RABBIS, although it was permitted for men to dance with one another at weddings. Among HASIDIC Jews the dance is perceived as a form of worship.

danger to life

The TALMUD prescribes various prohibitions in order to prevent danger to life. The duty of preserving life (as well as health) takes precedence over keeping any of the commandments with the exception of IDOLATRY, sexual immorality and MURDER. The concern for avoiding danger is derived from the biblical injunction: 'Take good heed to your souls'. (Deut. 4:9).

Daniel, Book of

Biblical book among the HAGIOGRAPHA. It contains the story of Daniel, who was exiled to BABYLON. His upbringing, miraculous escapes from persecution, and visions of the rise and fall of empires are depicted. The book is unusual in that much of it was composed in ARAMAIC, and it should probably be dated in the fourth century BCE. Daniel is also the hero of the APOCRYPHAL books of SUSANNA AND THE ELDERS and BEL AND THE DRAGON.

darshan (Hebrew, 'expounder')

Preacher. Originally the person given this title expounded the biblical text.

During the middle ages the term was applied to a professional preacher. In some East European countries a person was appointed to be the official *darshan* of the community. An alternative title, MAGGID, was given to both the official and the itinerant preacher.

daven

ASHKENAZI term meaning 'to pray'.

David   (fl. 11th–10th century BCE)

King of JUDAH and ISRAEL. His adventures are described in the biblical books of SAMUEL and CHRONICLES. While King SAUL was alive, David emerged as a great military hero, having been anointed by the PROPHET Samuel. He was successful in uniting the 12 tribes after Saul's death and became king of both Israelite kingdoms. He dominated the surrounding nations, made his capital in JERUSALEM, and attained riches and power. After various crises within his family circle, he was successful in passing on the crown of the united kingdom to his son, SOLOMON. In later centuries, David's reign was viewed as a golden age, and it was believed that the future MESSIAH would come from the Davidic line. David was also credited with composing many of the PSALMS.

David, City of

See JERUSALEM.

David, Star of
(Hebrew: *Magen David*)

Name given in Judaism to the symbol consisting of two superimposed triangles forming a star. It was used in the SYNAGOGUE at Capernaum as early as the third century CE, but was not adopted as a Jewish symbol until much later. From the 13th century the name figures in practical KABBALAH, and the symbol – believed to have magical properties – is found in association with the pentagram (Star of SOLOMON). The *Magen David*

occurs in a Jewish context in PRAGUE in the 17th century. In the 19th century it was adopted by the First ZIONIST Congress as its symbol, and appeared on the flags of the Zionist Organization as well as the State of ISRAEL. The Nazis employed a yellow six-pointed star as a Jewish BADGE.

Star of David.

Day of Atonement
(Hebrew: *Yom Kippur*)

Fast observed on 10 Tishri (Lev. 23:32). According to Scripture, it is obligatory to refrain from work during the Day of Atonement and cleanse oneself from sin (Lev. 16:30). Yom Kippur ends the TEN DAYS OF PENITENCE. In biblical times on the Day of Atonement, the HIGH PRIEST entered the HOLY OF HOLIES dressed in white linen. The SYNAGOGUE liturgy contains numerous prayers for FORGIVENESS. (*See also* SIN.)

Day of Judgement

Occasion of the last judgement by God at the end of the world when the final fate of every person will be determined. According to Scripture, there will be an eschatological Day of Judgement. The MISHNAH asserts that the judgement of the world is continuing and takes place at four different periods during the year. In the Jewish LITURGY, the NEW YEAR (Rosh Ha-Shanah), which occurs on 1 Tishri, is viewed as an annual day of judgement for all peoples. Decrees are then subsequently sealed on the DAY OF ATONEMENT. (*See also* BOOK OF LIFE.)

Day of the Lord

Period when divine punishment will be meted out to the wicked and justice will be triumphant. The term is found in various PROPHETIC passages, the prevailing feature of which is a dramatic sense of doom. The usual message is that the Day of the Lord is near.

Dayan, Moshe (1915–81)

Israeli military commander and politician. The son of Shemuel Dayan, he was born in Degan-Alef. In 1948, during the WAR OF INDEPENDENCE, he commanded the defence of Jewish settlements in the Jordan valley. He was subsequently appointed chief of operations at GHQ and later became commander-in-chief. In 1959 he was elected to the KNESSET as a member of the Mapai party. Later he was elected to the Sixth Knesset representing Rafi. He conducted the SIX DAY WAR in 1967, and the Yom Kippur War in 1973 as minister of defence.

Days of Awe

(Hebrew: *Yamim Noraim*)

Term applied to the NEW YEAR (Rosh Ha-Shanah) and DAY OF ATONEMENT (Yom Kippur), as well as the period between them: the TEN DAYS OF PENITENCE. According to the Jewish tradition, all individuals stand before the divine throne of judgement at the New Year, and judgement is decreed on the Day of Atonement.

dayyan

See JUDGE.

dayyenu

(Hebrew, 'It would have satisfied us')

Refrain of a song of thanksgiving recited at the PASSOVER SEDER. The song enumerates the 15 stages of redemption of the Jews from Egyptian bondage.

dead, prayers for the

See KADDISH.

Dead Sea Scrolls

Ancient manuscripts found between 1947 and 1956 in caves in areas west of the Dead Sea. They are written in HEBREW and ARAMAIC and date mainly from *c.*150 BCE to 68 CE, when the monastic community at QUMRAN which owned them was destroyed by the Romans. The Dead Sea Scrolls contain fragments of nearly every book of the BIBLE, as well as copies of the Book of ISAIAH. Fragments have also been discovered of the APOCRYPHA and PSEUDEPIGRAPHA. In addition, they contain the plan of a struggle between the Sons of Light and the Sons of Darkness, religious hymns, the rule by which the community was governed, details of a hidden treasure and descriptions of the TEMPLE. Many scholars believe they were written by the ESSENES. They are now housed in the Shrine of the Book in Israel. (*See also* COPPER SCROLL; MANUAL OF DISCIPLINE; WAR SCROLL.)

death

Belief in the RESURRECTION of the dead was not a feature of Judaism during the biblical period. Rather, the dead were believed to dwell in a shadowy place beneath the earth known as SHEOL. In the period of the Second TEMPLE, the concepts of the resurrection of the body, the DAY OF JUDGEMENT, and reward and punishment in the world to come became centrally important in the teaching of the PHARISEES. The SADDUCEES, however, rejected these doctrines on the grounds that they were not contained in Scripture. Belief in the resurrection of the dead was one of MAIMONIDES' PRINCIPLES OF THE FAITH and is still maintained by ORTHODOX Jews. (*See also* FUNERAL.)

death anniversary

See YAHRZEIT.

death penalty

See CAPITAL PUNISHMENT.

Deborah (fl. 12th century BCE)

Israelite JUDGE and prophetess. Her exploits are described in the Book of JUDGES. She encouraged the war of liberation from the oppression of Jabin, King of Cannan (Judg. 4). In addition, she was the author of the Song of Deborah (Judg. 5), which depicts the battle and subsequent victory. The song is believed to be one of the oldest passages in Scripture.

Decalogue

See TEN COMMANDMENTS.

decree (Hebrew: *gezerah*)

In Jewish law, a technical term for a rabbinic prohibition. It is distinct from a positive enactment (TAKKANAH). In a non-legal context the term came to denote an evil or anti-Jewish decree. By extension, it referred to anti-Jewish persecutions and POGROMS.

demonology

Study of demons or demonic beliefs. Scripture as well as rabbinic sources refer to various demonic beings. In KABBALISTIC literature there is a dichotomy between the demonic and the divine realms. Demons also play a role in Jewish folklore and legend. AMULETS and MAGIC formulae were used to protect Jews from their evil influence.

derekh eretz

(Hebrew, 'way of the land')

Desirable behaviour, in conformity with accepted social and moral principles. It includes rules of etiquette and polite behaviour. In rabbinic literature it refers to normal human behaviour, worldly occupation and correct conduct.

desecration of the host

Defilement of the consecrated bread or wafer used in the Christian sacrament of the Eucharist. In 1215 the Lateran Council recognized the doctrine of transubstantiation (according to which the bread becomes the body of Christ). Subsequently the accusation that Jews defiled or tortured the host became common in Europe. It was the pretext for a number of Jewish massacres, the first of which took place in Belitz in 1243. Other outbreaks occurred in Paris in 1290, in Brussels in 1370 and in Segovia in 1410. (*See also* ANTI-SEMITISM; BLOOD LIBEL.)

Deutero-Isaiah

See ISAIAH.

Deuteronomic historian

Editor and redactor of the Books of SAMUEL and KINGS. The Deuteronomic historian is so named because he was influenced by the ideas in the Book of DEUTERONOMY, including the conviction that the one true SANCTUARY is in JERUSALEM and that the kings of ISRAEL and JUDAH were judged on the basis of their dedication to the COVENANT. The books recount the history of the Israelites from the end of the period of the JUDGES to the destruction of the TEMPLE in 586 BCE. In all likelihood the editor was writing in the late sixth century in an attempt to understand the events of his country's history.

Deuteronomy, Book of

Fifth book of the PENTATEUCH. It contains MOSES' description of the events after the TORAH had been given on MOUNT SINAI. This is followed by an ethical exhortation and a summary of Jewish LAW. Moses then makes his final speeches to the Israelites, including his blessing. An account of his death concludes the book. A version of Deuteronomy was found in the TEMPLE during the reign of King JOSIAH in the seventh century BCE. This prompted a reform of the cult and a centralization of worship in JERUSALEM. Although traditionally believed to be of Mosaic authorship, the book probably dates from the seventh century.

devekut (Hebrew, 'cleaving to God')

Spiritual state of communion with God. It is achieved during PRAYER and MEDITATION. The term is derived from the phrase 'Love the Lord your God and cleave unto him' (Deut. 11:22). Usually *devekut* is described as the highest stage on the spiritual ladder.

devil (Hebrew: *Satan*)

In Scripture the term 'Satan' means an adversary; in later books, Satan came to refer to a supernatural being who accused men in the heavenly assembly, as in the Book of JOB. In the APOCRYPHA and later Jewish literature, Satan is depicted as a more powerful figure who acts independently in tempting humanity to defy God. In the TESTAMENT OF THE TWELVE PATRIARCHS he is known as Behal, and in the DEAD SEA SCROLLS as the Angel of Darkness. Nevertheless Judaism is not a dualistic system: it is understood that God is all-powerful. Yet before the days of the MESSIAH, the devil is a powerful figure. In modern times Jews prefer to speak of the forces of evil rather than a personal Satan. (*See also* DEMONOLOGY.)

devotion (Hebrew: *kavvanah*)

The BIBLE and rabbinic sources stress that observances and PRAYERS should be conducted with inner devotion and steadfast intent. The concept of devotion is of special importance in KABBALISTIC literature, since prayer can influence the upper realms. Kabbalists maintain that devotion in prayer can be attained by the mystical action of combining the letters of God's name. (*See also* DIVINE EMANATIONS; GOD, NAMES OF.)

dialogue

In medieval times, DISPUTATIONS took place between Jews and Christians with the aim of converting the Jewish community to the Christian faith. In modern times there has been an increasing awareness of the need for Jews and Christians to engage in positive encounter and dialogue.

diaspora

Dispersion and settlement of Jews outside PALESTINE after the Babylonian captivity. When the TEMPLE was destroyed in the sixth century BCE, large numbers of Jews settled in BABYLONIA. From the hellenistic period onwards Jews lived in many lands, including Islamic and Christian countries. In the middle ages Jews in Northern and Western Europe were persecuted and often expelled from the countries in which they resided. Eventually they gravitated to Eastern Europe, then to the USA; many also sought to return to Palestine. The establishment of the State of ISRAEL and the emigration there of millions of Jews have profoundly influenced Jewish life in the diaspora. (*See also* EXILE.)

dibbuk

Evil spirit which takes possession of an individual. Dibbuks were believed to cause madness, speak through the mouth and cleave to the human soul. They can be exorcised by pronouncing and conjuring the name of God (*see* GOD, NAMES OF). Such EXORCISM was practised in the circle of Isaac LURIA, and by ḤASIDIC ZADDIKIM. Among 20th-century Jews, such beliefs have largely disappeared. (*See also* DEMONOLOGY.)

dietary laws (Hebrew: *kashrut*)

Biblical and rabbinic legislation permits certain foods for consumption. These are referred to as KOSHER ('fit'). Other foods, however, are prohibited. These include meat from birds and animals which are unclean or not ritually slaughtered; certain parts of animals (such as the sinew of the hip); meat and milk products eaten together; and any kind of fish that does not have both fins and scales. Jewish sources also deal with the preparation of food: for example, since Jews may not consume blood in any form, all meat must be soaked and salted before it is eaten. Although no reason is given in Scripture or rabbinic literature for these regulations, various explanations have been given, among them that dietary restrictions in themselves regulate holiness in everyday life, encourage self-discipline, keep Jews separate from gentiles, and protect the community from disease.

din Torah

See JUDGEMENT OF THE LAW.

dina de-malkuta dina (Aramaic, 'The law of the country is the law')

The halakhic rule that the law of the country is binding. In certain cases the law of the country is to be preferred to Jewish law. The principle was laid down in the third century by sage Samuel, who imbued BABYLONIAN Jews with the consciousness that they must be reconciled with the government of the Sassanid kingdom.

Discipline, Manual of

One of the DEAD SEA SCROLLS. It depicts the organization and some of the beliefs of the sect that originally owned the scrolls.

dispersion

See DIASPORA.

disputations

See BARCELONA, DISPUTATION OF; TORTOSA, DISPUTATION OF.

divine emanations
(Hebrew: *sefirot*)

In KABBALISTIC literature the *sefirot* are depicted as emanations or manifestations of God. The concept, coloured by Neoplatonism and GNOSTIC thought, was used to explain how a transcendent, inaccessible Godhead (EN SOF) can relate to the world. Among kabbalists the nature of the *sefirot* was a matter of controversy. In the *kabbalah* a distinction is often made between the first three *sefirot* (regarded as the highest), and the remaining (lower) *sefirot*. The ten *sefirot* are: (1) The Supreme Crown; (2) Wisdom; (3) Intelligence; (4) Love; (5) Power; (6) Beauty; (7) Endurance; (8) Majesty; (9) Foundation; (10) Kingdom.

divorce

The dissolution of a MARRIAGE. It is effected in Jewish LAW by a bill of divorce termed *sefer keritut* in Scripture (Deut. 24:3) or *get* in the TALMUD. This bill is written by the husband and handed to his wife in the presence of witnesses. Biblical law stipulates that divorce is permitted if the husband finds an 'unseemly thing' in his wife (Deut. 24:1). This phrase was variously interpreted by rabbinic scholars. Although the power of divorce is vested in the husband, Jewish divorce law has developed in the direction of establishing greater equality between husband and wife.

documentary hypothesis

The belief that the PENTATEUCH was composed from different documentary sources. Traditionally Jews maintained that the Five Books of Moses were composed in their entirety by MOSES, and this has remained a central tenet of the faith. However, the 19th-century

German biblical scholar Wellhausen argued that different strands within the text can be discerned. He identified them as J (because God is called YHWH), E (God is Elohim), D (the writer of Deuteronomy), and P (the Priestly source). Most non-ORTHODOX Jews have accepted the documentary hypothesis in at least a modified form.

dogma

Despite the formulations of the central PRINCIPLES OF THE FAITH by MAIMONIDES and other philosophers during the middle ages, thinkers of the ENLIGHTENMENT such as Moses MENDELSSOHN argued that Judaism does not prescribe a set of fundamental beliefs. This view – that Judaism is a religion without dogma – was later propounded by Solomon SCHECHTER and others.

Dome of the Rock

Mosque in the TEMPLE area in JERUSALEM. It was built on the site of Mount Moriah over the rock on which ABRAHAM was prepared to sacrifice ISAAC, on which King SOLOMON built his Temple, and from which the Muslim prophet Mohammed ascended to heaven. ORTHODOX Jews today do not walk over the TEMPLE MOUNT for religious reasons and pray instead by the outer western wall. (See WAILING WALL.)

Donmeh

Judeo-Muslim sect, formed in the 17th century. As followers of SHABBETAI ZEVI, its members converted to Islam, but continued to observe many Jewish customs.

doorpost

See MEZUZAH.

Dov Baer of Liubavitch
(1773–1828)

ḤASIDIC leader. He was the son and successor of SHNEOUR ZALMAN of Lyady.

Dov Baer of Mezhirech
(c.1710–72)

ḤASIDIC leader. Known as the Maggid of Mezhirech, he was originally a folk preacher. Eventually he came under the influence of the Baal Shem Tov (ISRAEL BEN ELIEZER), becoming his most influential disciple. After the death of the Baal Shem Tov, Dov Baer emerged as the leader of Ḥasidic Jewry, and the centre of the movement was transferred from Medzibozh to Mezhirech. He was responsible for the growth of Ḥasidism in the Ukraine, Lithuania and Galicia. Although Dov Baer wrote no books, his teachings were collected and published by his disciple, Solomon of Lutsk. The central role of the ZADDIK in Ḥasidic Judaism is largely due to Dov Baer's teaching.

dowry

Property which a wife brings to her husband at marriage. Scripture mentions gifts brought by the husband to the bride as well as by the wife to the husband. In the TALMUDIC period, the practice of giving a dowry was well established. The dowry is recorded in the MARRIAGE contract; it reverts to the wife upon DIVORCE or the death of the husband.

dream

In Scripture, dreams are frequently perceived as divine communications. JOSEPH and DANIEL were noted for their ability to interpret dreams. In the TALMUD various views are presented concerning the significance of dreams. Interest in dreams continued into the middle ages and through the modern period, especially among KABBALISTS and the HASIDIM.

dreidel (Yiddish, 'spinning top')

The word is applied to a traditional Jewish toy which bears the initial letters of the Hebrew words: 'A great miracle happened there.' It is used in a game played at ḤANUKKAH.

dress

During biblical times the dress of Jews was similar to that of other peoples. During the HASMONEAN period Greek and Roman costumes became fashionable among the Jewish upper classes. Later the wearing of fringes (ZITZIT) on four corners of a garment distinguished Jews from gentiles. From the middle ages Jews were frequently compelled to wear a Jewish BADGE or other distinctive forms of clothing. In North Africa the prohibition of bright colours in Jewish dress resulted in the evolution of the black robe and skullcap (YARMULKE). In Eastern Europe the wearing of a fur-trimmed hat (*streimel*) and a long kaftan reflected current customs. In certain Mediterranean areas, Jews wore Spanish fashions introduced by SEPHARDI exiles in 1492.

Dreyfus, Alfred (1859–1935)

French soldier. Born in Alsace, he became a captain on the general staff of the French army in 1892. Two years later he was accused of treason, found guilty and sentenced to life imprisonment. After protesting his innocence, he was eventually exonerated. The case plunged France into a state of virulent ANTI-SEMITISM for a decade. The Dreyfus affair deeply troubled Theodor HERZL, convincing him of the need for a Jewish state. Dreyfus' *The Letters of Captain Dreyfus to his Wife* and *Five Years of my Life* describe his ordeal.

drink offering

Offering of wine added to all SACRIFICES in the JERUSALEM TEMPLE. The quantities of wine varied from a fourth part of a *hin* for a lamb, a third part of a *hin* for a ram, and half a *hin* for a bullock (Num. 15:5–9).

dualism

Religious or philosophical system. The term is applied to two different beliefs. (1) The belief in a cosmic struggle between the powers of good and evil. This doctrine was taught in the ancient Persian religion and later by GNOSTICS. The RABBIS condemned those who acknowledged the existence of two powers. Despite such criticism, dualistic theories affected some Jewish theologians, and this belief became a central feature of Jewish mystical thought. (2) The belief in a radical opposition of matter and spirit. Derived from Greek thought, such ideas influenced PHILO as well as medieval Jewish philosophers.

dukhan

See TEMPLE PLATFORM.

Duran, Simeon ben Zemah (1361–1444)

North African rabbinic scholar, philosopher and scientist. Known as Rashbatz, he was born in Majorca and served as a physician and surgeon in Palma. After the massacre there in 1391, he settled in Algiers where he became chief rabbi. His works include an encyclopedic philosophical study, *Magen Avot*. His RESPONSA deal with religious and legal issues as well as grammar, philology, exegesis, literary history, philosophy, KABBALAH, mathematics and astronomy.

duty

Action that an individual is obligated to perform for God or another person. Jewish LAW stipulates different types of duty: *hovah* (an obligation) is distinct from MITZVAH, which can signify both a duty and a commendable act (*reshut*). In the view of Baḥya ibn PAKUDA, a distinction should be made between the duties of the limbs (involving ceremonial and practical duties) and those of the heart (involving the spiritual life).

E

earlocks (Hebrew: *pais*)

Ringlets of hair worn in front of the ears by strict ORTHODOX Jews. *Pais* are not cut, in fulfilment of the commandment in Lev. 19:27.

early rising (Hebrew: *hashkamah*)

Early MORNING SERVICE held before the official morning prayers.

Eban, Abba (b. 1915)

Israeli statesman and diplomat. Born in Cape Town, he lectured in Arabic at Cambridge University from 1938 to 1940. After the Second World War, he moved to PALESTINE. He was a member of the Jewish Agency delegation to the UN in 1947–8, and then represented the new State of ISRAEL at the UN in 1948–9, before serving as Israel's ambassador to the USA from 1950 to 1959. He served as president of the Weizmann Institute from 1958 to 1966. After being elected to the KNESSET as a Mapai delegate, he was successively minister of education and culture (1960–3), deputy prime minster (1963–6) and foreign minister (1966–74).

Ebionites

Judeo-Christian sect which was active in PALESTINE in the second to fourth centuries. The Ebionites observed the Mosaic law, believed that Jesus was the MESSIAH, viewed poverty as a central principle, and held property in common.

Ecclesiastes, Book of

Biblical book, one of the five scrolls in the HAGIOGRAPHA. The name 'Ecclesiastes' is Greek, meaning 'convoker', and is a rendering of the HEBREW word *kohelet* by which the author is referred to. The book discusses the meaning of life – a central theme is that all is futile, but the end of the book is pious and optimistic. Ecclesiastes is read in the *synagogue* during SUKKOT.

Ecclesiasticus

APOCRYPHAL book. Known also as the Wisdom of Ben Sira, it was composed by Ben Sira and translated into Greek by his grandson in 132 BCE. It contains moral teaching, as well as liturgical poems and psalms.

ecstasy

Spiritual exaltation. It is closely associated with DEVEKUT ('cleaving to God'), an ideal emphasized in ḤASIDIC sources. The only comprehensive study of ecstasy is found in the *Tract on Ecstasy* by DOV BAER OF LIUBAVITCH.

education

Scripture decrees that God's precepts should be taught to the people, especially children. The religious revival introduced by EZRA in the fifth century BCE centred on the regular reading of the TORAH (Ezra 7:1–10:44). During the rabbinic period there was a comprehensive educational system for Jewish boys. SYNAGOGUES had a *bet sefer* for elementary study and a BET HA-MIDRASH for advanced learning. In the BABYLONIAN ACADEMIES Jewish scholarship reached great heights; subsequently YESHIVOT (rabbinical academies) were created throughout the Jewish world which carried on the traditions of Jewish study. In modern times traditional Jewish educational institutions have been established, as well as neo-ORTHODOX religious schools and day schools. All such institutions are in different ways committed to perpetuating Jewish learning. (*See also* ḤEDER; TALMUD TORAH.)

Egypt

Country in north-east Africa. From its beginnings, the history of the Jewish people has been linked with Egypt. According to the Book of GENESIS, the PATRIARCHS visited the country, and early Jewish history is connected with the bondage of the Jews there and the EXODUS. Throughout the period of the monarchy, there were frequent Judeo-Egyptian contacts. After the conquest of Egypt by Alexander the Great, a significant number of Jewish immigrants settled there. In later centuries there was a continual presence in Egypt.

eḥad mi yodea
(Hebrew, 'Who knows one?')

Opening words of a medieval HEBREW riddle of numbers. It is apppended to the PASSOVER HAGGADAH in certain rites.

Eibeschütz, Jonathan
(*c.*1690–1794)

Bohemian TALMUDIST and KABBALIST. He served as the head of a YESHIVAH in PRAGUE, becoming rabbi at Metz in 1741. From 1750 he served in turn at Altona, Hamburg and Wandsbeck. He was accused of being a follower of SHABBETAI ZEVI, but denied the charge.

Eighteen Benedictions
See AMIDAH.

El
See GOD, NAMES OF.

el male raḥamim
(Hebrew, 'O God, full of compassion')

Opening words of the PRAYER for the dead. It is recited at a FUNERAL service, on the anniversary of a death, on visiting the grave of a relative or after being called up for the reading of the law. Among the ASHKENAZIM, it is frequently included in the memorial service on FESTIVALS and the DAY OF ATONEMENT. The prayer originated in Jewish communities of Western and Eastern Europe, where it was recited for the MARTYRS of the crusades as well as the CHMIELNICKI MASSACRES.

elder

One of the members of the governing body of the nation or community. During the biblical period the elders helped rule the Israelites; MOSES appointed 70 elders to aid him in this task (Num. 11:16ff). The elders served as judges and representatives of the people until the Second TEMPLE period. During the middle ages the title *zaken* was attributed to communal councillors in some areas.

Elders of Zion, Protocols of the

Forged tract, purporting to demonstrate the existence of international Jewish aspirations to gain world power. It was widely used to evoke anti-Jewish sentiment. It was first published in Russia at the beginning of the 20th century. After the Russian civil war, the work was introduced into Western Europe by Russian émigrés. It depicts a plan supposed to have been made by a conference of leaders of world Jewry to attain global domination and the overthrow of Christian society. The *Protocols* circulated in many countries, played a part in Nazi propaganda, and continues to be reprinted, particularly in the Arab world.

Eleazar ben Judah of Worms
(*c.*1165–*c.*1230)

German TALMUDIST, KABBALIST and liturgical poet. Known as Eleazar Rokeaḥ, he was born in Mainz and spent most of his life in Worms. He witnessed the murder of his wife and children by the crusaders. He published works on HALAKHAH, liturgical poetry, theology, ethics and exegesis. His *Sefer ha-Rokeaḥ* was intended to educate the common reader in Jewish LAW. He was the last major scholar of the ḤASIDEI ASHKENAZ movement.

election

See CHOSEN PEOPLE.

Elephantine

Ancient fortress town on the western bank of the Nile, opposite Aswan, on the border between Ethiopia and EGYPT. From the end of the Egyptian royal period (*c.*590 BCE) to the end of the Persian period (333 BCE), a military garrison of Jewish soldiers was stationed there. The temple used by the Jews in the town was devastated by an Egyptian mob, but was subsequently rebuilt. The episode is depicted in Elephantine papyri.

Elijah (fl. 9th century BCE)

Israelite PROPHET. He was active during the reigns of AHAB and AHAZIAH (1). He sought to restore the purity of Israelite worship when Ahab's wife, JEZEBEL, introduced the cult of BAAL into the country. In a contest with the prophets of Baal, he was victorious (1 Kgs. 18). According to 2 Kgs. 2:1–11, Elijah did not die; instead, he was carried to HEAVEN in a chariot of horses and fire. In rabbinic sources he is portrayed as the harbinger of the MESSIAH. At the PASSOVER SEDER a glass of wine is poured out for him.

Elijah, Apocalypse of

APOCRYPHAL work. It portrays the archangel MICHAEL's account to ELIJAH of the end of Rome, the destruction of the wicked, the last judgement and the heavenly Jerusalem.

Elijah ben Solomon Zalman
(1720–97)

Lithuanian talmudist. Known as the Vilna Gaon, he travelled throughout Poland and Germany, eventually settling in Vilna. He encouraged the translation of works on natural science; nonetheless, he was opposed to philosophy and the Haskalah (Jewish ENLIGHTENMENT). He was also critical of the HASIDIC movement and was viewed as the spiritual leader of the MITNAGDIM. He wrote commentaries on the Bible, annotations on the TALMUD, MIDRASH and ZOHAR, and works on mathematics, the geography of PALESTINE, and HEBREW grammar. In his studies of Jewish law he sought to establish critical texts of rabbinic sources. He avoided PILPUL and based his rulings on the plain meaining of the text.

Elimelech of Lyzanhsk
(1717–87)

Galician RABBI. He was one of the founders of the ḤASIDIM in Galicia. A follower of DOV BAER OF MEZHIRECH, he is viewed as the theoretician and creator of practical ZADDIKISM. His *Noam Elimelekh* depicts the role of the *zaddik* in the Ḥasidic movement, stressing the holiness and perfection of the *zaddik* and his influence in the earthly and spiritual realms.

Elisha (fl. 9th century BCE)

Israelite PROPHET, active during and after the reign of Jehoram. He was the disciple and successor of ELIJAH. He foretold Hazael's accession to the Syrian throne, and anointed JEHU king over Israel.

Elisha ben Avuyah
(fl. 2nd century)

PALESTINIAN sage. Born in JERUSALEM, he came to doubt the unity of God, divine providence, and reward and punishment. Eventually he renounced Judaism. Although he was a friend of Meir, the sages disassociated themselves from him and referred to him as Aher (the other).

Elohim
See GOD, NAMES OF.

emanation
Philosophical and theological theory which explains the origin of the universe as flowing from a primary source. It was adopted from Neoplatonism by Arab philosophers, and eventually passed into medieval Jewish philosophy and KAB-BALAH. In mystical sources, it is an essential part of the concept of the *sefirot* (*see* DIVINE EMANATIONS).

emancipation
In Jewish usage the term is applied to the removal, particularly in the Western world in the 18th–20th centuries, of restrictions imposed on Jews. From the fourth century the Holy Roman Empire imposed various discriminatory restrictions on Jews, which were intensified in medieval Europe. Jewish emancipation derived from utopian political and social ideas in the 18th century. In the 19th and 20th centuries Jews have been granted full civil equality in nearly all countries where they reside. (*See also* ENLIGHTENMENT.)

Emden, Jacob (1697–1776)
Danish HALAKHIC authority. Born in Altona, he was a RABBI in Emden from 1728–1733. He then returned to Altona, where he established a printing press. He viewed SHABBETAIANISM as a danger to Judaism and engaged in a dispute about the movement with Jonathan EIBESCHÜTZ. He composed works dealing with halakhic topics as well as polemical pamphlets.

emissary (Hebrew: *meshullah*)
Meshullahim travelled from place to place in the GAONIC period carrying the decisions of the ACADEMIES. They served as an important link in the Jewish world, and provided informative accounts of their travels.

En Sof (Hebrew, 'infinite')
Name given to the divine infinite in KAB-BALISTIC thought. Early kabbalists conceived of the En Sof as the absolute perfection in which there is no distinction or plurality. It does not reveal itself and transcends human thought. In kabbalistic literature creation is bound up with the manifestation of the hidden God as En Sof. (*See also* ZOHAR.)

engagement
See SHIDDUKH.

Enlightenment
(Hebrew: *Haskalah*)

Hebrew social, spiritual and literary movement. It developed in the last quarter of the 18th century and continued until 1880. The Jewish Enlightenment began in Germany and spread to Austria, Poland and Russia. Its advocates (MASK-ILIM) argued that Jews should reform their schools, learn the language of the countries in which they resided, increase their knowledge of secular subjects, and adopt the manners of their gentile neighbours. The movement was challenged by ORTHODOX leaders, who viewed such innovations as a threat to the traditional Jewish way of life. (*See also* MENDELSSOHN, MOSES; MITNAGDIM; PROGRESSIVE JUDAISM; REFORM JUDAISM.)

Enoch, Book of
APOCRYPHAL work. It was translated in the 10th or 11th century from Greek into Slavonic. It depicts Enoch's ascent,

his journey through the seven heavens, his return to earth, his address to his son and his second ascent.

entertaining travellers
(Hebrew: *hakhnasat orehim*)

The obligation to care for travellers and strangers is a central feature of the Jewish faith. Such hospitality is mentioned in various biblical narratives, and in rabbinic literature it is frequently extolled. During the middle ages and later it became common to provide special lodging for the vagrant poor in a guest house. (*See also* CHARITY.)

ephod

Upper garment worn during sacred rites in ancient Israel. In Scripture the term is usually used to refer to the ornamented vestment which the HIGH PRIEST wore over his blue robe. To this he bound the BREASTPLATE with the URIM AND THUMMIM. Although soothsaying and divinations were forbidden, the *ephod* and the *Urim* and *Thummim* were used as a means of seeking God's counsel. By the beginning of the Second TEMPLE period, consulation of the *ephod* no longer occurred.

Ephraim   (fl. ?16th century BCE)

Israelite, younger son of JOSEPH. Eventually his name became attached to one of the tribes of Israel and of the more northern of the two Israelite kingdoms. During the period of the JUDGES, the tribe of Ephraim claimed priority. After SOLOMON's death, the northern tribes seceded, and the first king of the NORTHERN KINGDOM of Israel (JEROBOAM) belonged to this tribe. The prophets later referred to the House of JUDAH and the House of Ephraim.

epicoros

See APIKOROS.

epitropos
(Greek, 'trustee', 'guardian')

TALMUDIC term which refers to one who cares for the property of minors, the deaf or someone of unsound mind.

Eretz Israel
See ISRAEL, LAND OF.

eruv

Term which applies to various symbolic acts which facilitate the accomplishment of otherwise forbidden actions on the SABBATH and FESTIVALS. These include carrying burdens on the Sabbath (permitted through *eruv hatzerot* – amalgamating individual holdings), walking further than the permitted 2,000 cubits beyond the inhabited area of the town (through *eruv tehumim* – amalgamating boundaries), and cooking for the Sabbath on a festival day falling on Friday (through *eruv tavshilin* – amalgamating meals).

Esau   (fl. ?16th century BCE)

Israelite, father of ISAAC and REBEKAH, and twin brother of JACOB. After Jacob obtained Esau's birthright and the blessing given to the first-born son, Esau became Jacob's enemy and Jacob fled to Haran. When he returned 20 years later, his brother greeted him affectionately (Gen. 35ff).

eschatology

Theology, biblical exegesis or doctrine concerning the end of days. All eschatological theology supposes an alteration of the present world through divine intervention. Originally Jewish eschatology was an expression of faith in a glorious future for Israel after a period of suffering. Subsequently it was introduced by the PROPHETS into their teaching: they added moral content and threatened catastrophe in the absence of repentance. Such expectations were later transformed into APOCALYPTIC beliefs, which viewed the end as a sign of the coming of the MESSIAH who would bring about the ingathering of the EXILES, the Kingdom of God, and the DAY OF JUDGEMENT when the righteous would receive eternal reward and the wicked would be punished. (*See also* RESURRECTION; HEAVEN; HELL.)

Esdras

Two books of the APOCRYPHA. They are known as 3 and 4 Esdras since EZRA and NEHEMIAH are also known as 1 and 2 Esdras. Supposedly written by Ezra the Scribe, 3 Esdras covers the history of Israel from the days of King JOSIAH to the reading of the law to the exiles by Ezra; 4 Esdras, also known as the Apocalypse of Ezra, examines the problem of suffering, the future of the Jewish nation and the coming of the MESSIAH. Both books date from early during the Second TEMPLE period (*See also* APOCALYPSE.)

eshet ḥayil

see WOMAN OF VALOUR.

Essenes

Monastic Jewish sect in Palestine at the end of the Second TEMPLE period. They are described by Pliny and JOSEPHUS. Located on the north-western shore of the Dead Sea, their religious outlook was closer to the PHARISEES than that of the SADDUCEES; nonetheless, they formulated their own specific beliefs and observances. They withdrew from everyday life to their own communities, where they placed emphasis on meticulous ritual purity. The DEAD SEA SCROLLS provide a detailed account of their beliefs and practices. Among the Scrolls, the MANUAL OF DISCIPLINE depicts the customs of the sect and other scrolls reveal their particular APOCALYPTIC beliefs. The sect appears to have been completely destroyed in the Jewish War of 66–70 CE.

Esther, Book of

Biblical book from the HAGIOGRAPHA. The Book of Esther relates how a Jewish woman, Esther, became the wife of King Ahasuerus of Persia. Encourged by her uncle, Mordecai, she foiled the plans of the grand vizier, HAMAN, who sought to destroy the Jewish community. An addition to the book is found in the APOCRYPHA. Composed in *c*.350 BCE, the Book of Esther reflects the conditions of the Jews in the Persian empire. It is read in entirety in the SYNAGOGUE on the FESTIVAL of PURIM.

Esther, Fast of

Fast on 13 Adar before the FESTIVAL of PURIM. If the fast falls on a SABBATH, it is observed the preceding Thursday.

Esther, Feast of

See PURIM.

eternal light   (Hebrew: *ner tamid*)

Name given to the light which is kept burning in the SYNAGOGUE. It is a symbol of the golden seven-branched candelabrum (MENORAH) which burned continuously in the TEMPLE. Originally this was placed in a niche in the western wall, but subsequently was suspended in front of the ARK. The *ner tamid* has been interpreted alternatively as the symbol of God's presence and as the spiritual light emanating from the Temple. In ancient times it was created by a wick burning in olive oil; however, in the modern period an electric light is normally used.

ethical literature

See MUSAR.

Ethiopian Jews

See FALASHAS.

etrog

Citrus fruit which is eaten on SUKKOT. It was a popular Jewish symbol on coins as well as graves, and was used in the decoration of SYNAGOGUES during the Second TEMPLE period. Silver boxes for the *etrog* have been a common subject of Jewish ritual art.

etz ḥayyim

See TREE OF LIFE.

eulogy

FUNERAL or memorial oration. From ancient times it was customary to praise and lament the dead. In later times a eulogy was recited at the funeral. Among the SEPHARDIM the eulogy consists of a TALMUDIC discourse after the expiration of the 30 days' mourning period. (*See also* SHELOSHIM.)

euthanasia

Mercy killing. The Jewish faith teaches that life is a blessing from God; hence, hastening death is equivalent to bloodshed. The SHULḤAN ARUKH specifies that a dying person has the same rights as a person who is alive, and 'it is forbidden to cause him to die quickly'. Nonetheless, with the advent of modern technology, some scholars permit the cessation of artificial means of prolonging life when there is no possibility of recovery. Among PROGRESSIVE Jews, there is some discussion of voluntary euthanasia, but in general there is an acceptance of the traditional view.

Eve

First woman. According to GENESIS 1:27, both male and female were created in the image of God. In Gen. 2:22, EVE was formed from the rib of ADAM. In the GARDEN OF EDEN she was seduced by the serpent to disobey God and persuaded Adam to follow her example. As a result, both Adam and Eve were expelled from the Garden, and Eve was condemned to labour in childbirth and to be subservient to her husband. Her name means the mother of all living things. (*See also* LILITH.)

evening service (Hebrew: *maariv*)

Service of evening prayer. According to tradition, it was ordained by JACOB. The

TALMUD relates a dispute about whether it was obligatory or optional. In time it became a requirement. The service includes the SHEMA, its blessings, and the AMIDAH. During the medieval period, poems called MAARAVOT were composed for it.

Eve, from Michelangelo's depiction on the ceiling of the Sistine Chapel: Eve is shown being created from a rib taken from Adam's side (Gen. 2: 21–2.).

evil eye (Hebrew: *en ha-ra*)

Glance which has evil consequences. Belief in the evil eye is found in rabbinic sources and KABBALISTIC texts. Various remedies are recommended, such as the wearing of AMULETS, reading Scripture and reciting spells. These folk beliefs are now rare in the Jewish community. (*See also* DIBBUK; MAGIC.)

evil inclination
(Hebrew: *yetzer ha-ra*)

According to rabbinic psychology, each person is driven by both a GOOD INCLINATION (*yetzer ha-tov*) and an evil inclination (*yetzer ha-ra*).

excommunication
(Hebrew: *ḥerem*)

Term used in various senses to do with prohibitions and bans. In the biblical period it applied to the prohibition against making use of spoils taken during war, which were to be destroyed. In the rabbinic period, it came to mean the most serious form of BAN, or excommunication, used as a punishment for individuals who committed offences harmful to the Jewish people. (*See also* HERESY.)

execution

See CAPITAL PUNISHMENT.

exegesis

See MIDRASH.

exilarch (Aramaic: *resh galuta*)

Head of the BABYLONIAN Jewish community during the 1st–13th centuries. The office was hereditary, and its holder was traditionally a member of the House of DAVID. He was recognized by the royal court, served as chief tax collector among Jewry, appointed judges and exercised criminal jurisdiction in the Jewish community. There was a close relationship – and also frequent conflicts – between the exilarch and the heads (GAONIM) of the Babylonian ACADEMIES.

exile (Hebrew: *galut*)

State of exclusion from the PROMISED LAND. The term *galut* implies degradation and alienation; it is an expression at the despair of the Jews in the face of persecution and expulsion in the DIASPORA. Only by returning to ZION will the Israelite people be restored. By extension, the KABBALISTS explained the evil in the world as a consequence of the '*galut* of the Divine Presence'.

exile, Babylonian

Exile of the Jews in BABYLONIA in the sixth century. The period of exile commenced with the destruction around 586 BCE of the Kingdom of JUDAH by NEBUCHADNEZZAR and ended with the return of the Jews from captivity in *c*.538 BCE. Encouraged by the prophecies of JEREMIAH and EZEKIEL, the Jewish exiles maintained their identity, worshipped in the SYNAGOGUE, and prospered under foreign rule.

exiles, ingathering of

During the period of the BABYLONIAN EXILE, EZEKIEL prophesied the return of the exiles to their ancestral homeland. He addressed himself first to Judean exiles; subsequently he extended his prophecy to include the exiles of the NORTHERN KINGDOM. The conviction that the exiles would be restored became a central feature of rabbinic belief, and was incorporated into the liturgy. In modern times the concept of the ingathering of the exiles (*kibbutz galuyyot*) is frequently used to designate the immigration of Jews in the DIASPORA to the State of ISRAEL.

Exodus, Book of

Biblical book. It consists of 40 chapters. Chapters 1–17 describe the oppression of the Israelites by the Egyptians, the rise of MOSES, the TEN PLAGUES, and the exodus from Egypt. Chapters 18–24 depict the divine revelation on MOUNT SINAI, and the legislation and COVENANT between God and Israel. The episode of the GOLDEN CALF and subsequent events are contained in chapters 25–40.

exorcism

Driving out of an evil spirit. The practice is discussed in the APOCRYPHA, the New Testament and the TALMUD. Magical formulae were employed to expell evil spirits, and AMULETS were used to ward off their influence. Exorcism was frequently performed by KABBALISTS and ḤASIDIM, who were anxious to rid individuals of the souls of the dead who possessed them. (*See also* METEMPSYCHOSIS.)

expulsion

Throughout history, Jews have been expelled from the countries where they resided. They were driven out of Rome in 139 BCE; from England in 1290; from France in 1306, 1322 and 1394; from Germany in 1348; from Andalusia in 1484; from Spain in 1492; from Portugal in 1497; from Navarre in 1498; from Provence in 1412; from Naples in 1541; and from the Papal States in 1569. The Russian community was expelled from Little Russia in 1727, 1739 and 1742, and in the 19th century Jews were restricted to the Pale of Settlement. Initially the Nazis were anxious to encourage Jews to emigrate; only after the borders were closed did the Final Solution take place. (*See also* HOLOCAUST.)

Ezekiel, Book of

Biblical book of a sixth-century PROPHET. Ezekiel prophesied among the BABYLONIAN EXILES from 592 to 570 BCE and consoled those in captivity after the destruction of JERUSALEM. The first chapter describes the divine CHARIOT (*merkavah*), which served as the basis of later mystical speculation. Chapters 1–24 contain prophecies of destruction before the fall of Jerusalem. Chapters 25–32 prophesy disasters that will befall the gentiles. Chapters 33–9 contain works of compassion for Israel. Finally, chapters 40–8 record visions of the restored TEMPLE and kingdom.

Ezra, Apocalypse of

See ESDRAS.

Ezra, Book of

Biblical book, part of the HAGIOGRAPHA. It depicts the story of the Jews return from EXILE in BABYLONIA from the return of ZERUBABBEL to JUDAH in the sixth century BCE until the return of Ezra, an Israelite PROPHET who was originally a scribe in the Persian government. Subequently Ezra received permission from Artaxerxes I to lead the Jewish exiles back to JERUSALEM. Together with NEHEMIAH, he persuaded the people to return to the TORAH, observe the SABBATH and the SABBATICAL YEAR, pay TEMPLE dues, and refrain from INTERMARRIAGE.

ezrat nashim

(Hebrew, 'court of women')

Court in the TEMPLE at Jerusalem beyond which women were not allowed to go. Subsequently, *ezrat nashim* came to refer to the section of the synagogue in which women sit.

fable (Hebrew: *mashal*)

Short moral tale in which characters are often animals. Fables are found in MIDRASHIC LITERATURE and the TALMUD. In the middle ages popular collections of fables were written by Jewish authors, who based their writings on Arab sources. Some modern Jewish writers have also produced fables.

Fackenheim, Emil (b. 1916)

Canadian theologian. Born in Halle, Germany, in 1940 he emigrated to Canada, where he was professor of philosophy at the University of Toronto. His major work concerns the religious response to the HOLOCAUST. His writings include *God's Presence in History*, *The Jewish Return into History* and *To Mend the World*.

faith

Judaism distinguishes between faith meaning 'believing in' (*emunah*) and faith meaning 'trusting in' (*bittaḥon*). The Hebrew Bible takes it for granted that God exists; the term *emunah* was used for believing in the fulfilment of his promises. During the middle ages, it was used for believing in such statements as MAIMONIDES' THIRTEEN PRINCIPLES. At the same time, it was accepted that the Jewish religion is based not on belief, but on a unique personal relationship which involves trust and obedience.

faith, confession of

See CONFESSION OF FAITH; SHEMA.

Faith, Thirteen Principles of

See MAIMONIDES; THIRTEEN PRINCIPLES OF FAITH.

Falashas

The ancient Jewish community of Ethiopia. The Falashas claim to be descended from notables of JERUSALEM who accompanied Menelik, the son of King SOLOMON and the Queen of Sheba, back to his own land. Their form of Judaism derives from the Bible including the APOCRYPHA, as well as other post-biblical books. The Falashas are not familiar with the views of the sages in the TALMUD. Rumours of a black Jewish community were current among world Jewry for many centuries, and the Falashas were subsequently recognized as members of the House of Israel. In the mid-1980s many Falashas were airlifted to ISRAEL. (*See also* BLACK JEWS.)

Fall

ADAM and EVE's disobedience to God, described in the Book of GENESIS. As a result of the Fall, the first human beings were expelled from the GARDEN OF EDEN – Adam was condemned to earn his own livelihood, and Eve to suffer pain in childbirth and be subservient to her husband. The sages taught that death was the result of the Fall, but, unlike Christianity, Judaism does not teach a doctrine of original sin.

false witness

According to the TEN COMMANDMENTS, bearing of false witness is condemned (Exod. 20). This prohibition includes perjury, slander, defamation and lying. In Jewish LAW courts (BET DIN), the accused can be convicted only on the testimony of two witnesses – a single hostile report is insufficient.

family

The Jewish faith attaches great importance to family life. Each person in the family has a particular role, and individual rights are safeguarded by the tradition.

fasting

Abstention from food. Individuals are permitted to fast as a sign of REPENTANCE or MOURNING. Through fasting, ATONEMENT can be made. The entire Jewish community observes fast days. The two major fasts, the NINTH OF AV and YOM KIPPUR, last from sunset to sunset. They involve abstaining from food, drink, sexual intercourse and wearing leather. Other fasts last from sunrise to sunset and involve abstaining only from food and drink.

fasts

See FASTING; ESTHER, FAST OF; FIRST-BORN, FAST OF; NINTH OF AV; YOM KIPPUR.

fathers, merits of

Doctrine that through the deeds of one's ancestors, blessings may be secured. In particular, the merits of the PATRIARCHS, ABRAHAM, ISAAC and JACOB, are believed to obtain benefits for the Jewish people.

Fathers, Sayings of
(Hebrew: *Avot*)

Section of the MISHNAH. *Avot*, or PIRKE AVOT (Sayings of the Fathers), is a collection of the sayings of the sages going back in an unbroken chain from the TANNAIM to MOSES. It is the best-known of all rabbinic compositions, and is frequently studied in the SYNAGOGUE on the SABBATH. The full text is often printed in the traditional PRAYER BOOK. In the Mishnah, it is located at the end of NEZIKIN.

fear of God

Traditonally the fear of God has been viewed as the start of religious consciousness. According to the Book of PROVERBS, 'the fear of the Lord is the beginning of wisdom' (10:10).

feminism

A number of prominent 20th-century feminists have been of Jewish origin, and the feminist movement has brought about marked changes in Jewish life. Traditionally there is a rigid distinction between the role of men and women in the Jewish faith. However, since the 1970s in the PROGRESSIVE movement, women have served congregations as RABBIS, CANTORS and educationalists as well as SYNAGOGUE officers. Such changes have been resisted by the ORTHODOX as contrary to the HALAKAH. (*See also* ABORTION; BIRTH CONTROL; KETUBBAH; MARRIAGE.)

fence around the law

Rabbinic legislation designed to safeguard traditional observances. According to the MISHNAH, one of the central aims of the men of the GREAT SYNAGOGUE was to make a fence around the law. Hence they formulated regulations that were more stringent than the original commandments to ensure that they would be followed.

festivals

Days of rejoicing in the Jewish calendar. On biblical festivals (which include the first and last days of festal seasons), all work is forbidden. In the DIASPORA, the ORTHODOX celebrate most festivals on two consecutive days, whereas they are

kept for only one day by most
PROGRESSIVE Jews. The later post-bibli-
cal festivals do not involve absention
from work. (*See also* HANUKKAH; HIGH
HOLY DAYS; LAG BA-OMER; PASSOVER;
PILGRIM FESTIVALS; PURIM; ROSH HA-
SHANAH; SABBATH; SHAVUOT; SUKKOT;
FIFTEENTH OF AV; FIFTEENTH OF SHEVAT;
YOM ATZMAUT; YOM TOV.)

Fez

City in north central Morocco. Its Jewish
community dates from the ninth century
and has produced a number of rabbinic
scholars. Persecutions there were instigated against the Jews by the Almohades
in the 12th century and the Marabout
movement during the 13th century. As a
consequence, Jews were allotted a special
quarter of the city (the Mellah). Spanish
refugees fled there in 1391 and after 1492.

Fifteenth of Av (Hebrew: *Tu B'Av*)

FESTIVAL marking the beginning of the
wine harvest. At the time of the Second
TEMPLE, *Tu B'Av* was celebrated on Av
15. Dancing took place in the vineyards
and offerings of wood were brought to
the Temple.

Fifteenth of Shevat
(Hebrew: *Tu Bi-Shevat*)

Date on which the new year begins for the
purposes of tithing fruit. It is celebrated as
the 'New Year for Trees', and special fruits
are consumed. In modern ISRAEL the day
is celebrated by tree-planting.

Final Solution

Genocide against the Jews planned by the
Nazis in the 1930s and 1940s. Formulated
at a secret meeting by the Nazi leaders, it
resulted in the setting up of the death
camps. (*See also* HOLOCAUST.)

fine

In Scripture, fines are imposed for rav-
ishing a virgin (50 shekels), seducing a
virgin (50 shekels), falsely accusing one's

wife of not being a virgin at marriage
(100 shekels), and one's ox killing a
slave (30 shekels). Later fines were
imposed by rabbinic courts (BET DIN) for
a variety of violations. From early times,
CAPITAL PUNISHMENT for many offences
was transmuted into a fine.

first-born

During the biblical period special privileges and a double share of the father's
inheritance belonged to the first-born son.
(*See also* REDEMPTION OF THE FIRST-BORN.)

First-born, Fast of the

Fast day which is celebrated by the first-
born on the day before PASSOVER (Nisan
14). The fast day is designed to express
gratitude to God for sparing the first-
born of the Israelites in the tenth plague
of Egypt (Exod. 12). This custom has
largely disappeared.

First-born, Redemption of

See REDEMPTION OF THE FIRST-BORN.

first fruits

Portion of the harvest dedicated to God.
Deut. 26:1–11 specifies that every
Israelite must offer the first fruits of his
crop to the PRIESTS of the TEMPLE.
Traditionally on the second day of
PASSOVER (Nisan 16) a sheaf of barley
was given. SHAVUOT was also known as
the festival of the first fruits (HAG HA-
BIKKURIM); this PILGRIM FESTIVAL was a
time for making the offering. Although
this practice ended with the destruction
of the Temple, first-fruit celebrations
still take place in the State of ISRAEL.

fish

According to Jewish law, the only fish
which may be consumed are those that
have both fins and scales. Because creeping
things are forbidden, no shellfish of any
sort is allowed. (*See also* DIETARY LAWS.)

Five Scrolls
See SCROLLS, FIVE.

Flood

Gen. 6–9 describes the Flood. Because human beings were so evil, God decided to destroy them in a great deluge. Only NOAH, his family, and a male and female of each non-human species were permitted to survive. After the waters abated, God sent a rainbow as a sign of his promise that such an event would never take place again. Great flood legends are found in other cultures, and the biblical version is similar to that in the Babylonian Epic of Gilgamesh.

forced conversion

See ANUSIM.

forgiveness

The ancient Israelites believed that by making SACRIFICE, God's forgiveness could be obtained. However, the PROPHETS continually stressed that it is necessary to make restitution for wrongdoing. There must be full REPENTANCE accompanied by a complete change of heart. Nonetheless, the Israelites could feel confident of God's forgiveness because God is loving and longs to have a fatherly relationship with his CHOSEN PEOPLE. After the destruction of the TEMPLE in 70 CE, there were no more sacrifices. Instead, God's forgiveness could be obtained through PRAYER and FASTING. Yet it was still necessary to receive forgiveness from an injured party as well as from God. This is why it is customary to ask for forgiveness from those who have been wronged before the DAY OF ATONEMENT.

former prophets

The books of the former PROPHETS are JOSHUA, JUDGES, I and II SAMUEL and I and II KINGS.

Formstecher, Solomon

(1808–89)

German philosopher and RABBI. He was born in Offenbach and served as a rabbi there from 1842. He was active in the REFORM movement and edited Der *Freitagabend* and *Die Israelitische Wochenschrift*. His *Die Religion des Geistes* presents a basis for the aims of the EMANCIPATION and REFORM JUDAISM.

Fostat

Old Cairo. Jews lived in Fostat from the period of the Arab invasions. The city was the centre of Egyptian Jewry, serving as the seat of the local EXILARCHS in the 11th–12th centuries, and later of the NAGID. In 1896 the Cairo GENIZAH was discovered there in the Ben-Ezra SYNAGOGUE.

four captives

Medieval legend. Four RABBIS were captured by Muslim pirates and ransomed by various Jewish communities. The legend originated in Spain and possibly has some basis in fact.

four cups (Hebrew: *Arba Kosot*)

The four cups of wine which are drunk at the PASSOVER SEDER service. According to the sages, even the poorest person should obey this custom, which is based on the four ways God was said to have delivered the Israelites from Egyptian bondage. (*See also* HAGGADAH.)

four questions

Questions asked during the PASSOVER SEDER. During the course of the meal, the youngest competent person asks why the FESTIVAL night is different from every other night. This provides an opening for the person officiating to explain the nature of the PASSOVER.

four spices

Term used to refer to the four types of plants used during SUKKOT, as stipulated in Lev. 23:40: 'And you shall take on the first day [of Sukkot] the fruit of goodly trees, branches of palm trees, and boughs of thick trees, and willows of the brook.' The four species are the ETROG, palm, myrtle and willow. They are held or waved during the festival.

Frank, Jacob (1726–91)

Polish founder of the Frankist movement. Born in Podolia, he was viewed as the successor to SHABBETAI ZEVI. His mystical festivities were alleged to be accompanied by sexual orgies. He and his disciples were EXCOMMUNICATED in 1756. Subsequently the Frankists renounced the TALMUD. Debates were held between Frankists and the RABBIS – this episode concluded with the baptism of members of the Frankist sect. When the Polish authorities discovered that the Frankists viewed Jacob Frank as their lord, he was tried and held in a monastery. Later he was released by the Russians and settled in Offenbach, which became the centre of the movement.

Frankel, Zecharias (1801–75)

German RABBI and scholar. Born in PRAGUE, he served as a rabbi in Litomerice and Teplice, becoming CHIEF RABBI of Dresden in 1836. In 1854 he became director of the Breslau Rabbinical Seminary. He was the founder of the positivist-historical school which later influenced CONSERVATIVE JUDAISM in the USA. At the second REFORM rabbinical conference at Frankfurt am Main in 1845, he objected to the gradual abolition of HEBREW in the liturgy, and withdrew from the conference. He published studies of HALAKHIC topics, the history of the ORAL LAW, and the methodology of the MISHNAH and TALMUD. He also founded and edited the *Monatsschrift für Geschichte und Wissenschaft des Judentums*.

free will

The ability to make choices which are not predetermined. According to Scripture, each person is able to choose between good and evil. The concept of punishment and reward is based on this assumption. The TALMUD specifies that God is omniscient: nonetheless, human beings have capacity to choose their own lifestyle. Although rabbinic scources do not discuss the seeming contradiction between free will and divine omniscience, this subject was discussed at length by medieval Jewish philosophers.

Freud, Sigmund (1856–1939)

Austrian psychologist, founder of psychoanalysis. Born in Freiberg, he worked as a neuropathologist and clinical neurologist in Vienna. He formulated a new approach to understanding human motivation. In addition to writing numerous psychoanalytic studies, he published *Moses and Monotheism*. He was a member of the Jewish community in Vienna and belonged to the local BNAI BRITH.

Sigmund Freud (1856–1939).

fringes

See ZITZIT.

fromm (Yiddish)

Strictly observant.

funeral

See BURIAL.

G

gabbai

Officer of the community. Originally, the *gabbai* collected dues or charitable contributions. The term has come to mean any official of the community.

Gabirol, Solomon ibn
(*c.*1021–*c.*1056)

Spanish poet and philosopher. Born in Saragossa, he wrote secular and religious poetry and philosophical studies. His poem *Keter Malkut* ('Crown of Divine Kingship') is incorporated into the liturgy. His philosophical writings are based on Neoplatonic theories.

Gabriel

Archangel. Together with MICHAEL, he is the only ANGEL mentioned by name in the Hebrew Bible (Dan. 8–10). In rabbinic sources he is referred to as a leader of the angelic host, and is one of the highest angels in the celestial hierarchy.

Fisherman on the sea of Galilee at sunrise.

Galilee

Northernmost region of ISRAEL. During the reign of Tiglath-Pileser III of Assyria in the eighth century BCE, it was separated from Israel. In 104 BCE it was reunited with JUDEA by Aristobulus I. Subsequently it became the main centre of Judaism in PALESTINE. It became the seat of the patriarchate, and TALMUDIC ACADEMIES were established in its cities of TIBERIAS and SEPPHORIS. From the 16th and 17th centuries SAFED in Galilee was an important centre of KABBALISTIC Judaism.

galut

See EXILE.

Gamaliel (fl. 1st century CE)

Palestinian elder, grandson of HILLEL. He served as president of the SANHEDRIN. According to the Acts of the Apostles, Paul was one of his pupils. He maintained close contacts with Jews in PALESTINE as well as in the DIASPORA. He was responsible for various TAKKANOT (rabbinical rulings).

gambling

According to Jewish LAW, gambling is forbidden. A distinction is made between those who gamble for pleasure and professional gamblers. So untrustworthy are the latter that they are not permitted to act as witnesses for a BET DIN.

Gaon

Head of the BABYLONIAN academies of SURA and PUMBEDITA between the 6th–11th centuries. During this period the *geonim* were viewed as the most important religious authorities in the Jewish world. They were selected by the hereditary EXILARCHS, and their responsibilites including interpreting TALMUDIC law, responding to HALAKHIC questions from Jews living in the DIASPORA, and presiding over the BET DIN. They were supported by voluntary contributions as well as local taxes, and were expected to maintain a large establishment. After the ninth century their influenced waned. In the 10th century the title was used by the head of the ACADEMY in Israel, and also in EGYPT, Damascus and Baghdad in the 12th and 13th centuries. Famous *geonim* include Yehudai Gaon, SAADIAH GAON, Sherira Gaon and Samuel ben Hophni. (*See also* YESHIVAH.)

Garden of Eden

Abode of ADAM and EVE (Gen. 2–3). They were expelled from the garden because they disobeyed God and ate the forbidden fruit. In rabbinic sources the Garden of Eden is portrayed as the place where the righteous dwell after death.

gartel (Yiddish, 'girdle')

Girdle made of either black silk or wool. It is worn by HASIDIC men at prayer, in fulfilment of the decree that one should make a division between the upper and lower halves of the body while praying. It is symbolic of the injunction to gird one's loins in the service of God.

Gedaliah, Fast of

Fast which is observed on 3 Tishri (after ROSH HA-SHANAH) to commemorate the assassination of Gedaliah who served as the BABYLONIAN governor of JUDAH. He was appointed after the destruction of the TEMPLE in 586 BCE and dwelt at Mizpah. He was killed by Ishmael ben Nethaniah who aspired to overthrow Babylonian rule. Gedaliah's followers fled to EGYPT, taking the PROPHET JEREMIAH with them (2 Kgs. 25:25–6; Jer. 41.1ff).

Gehenna

See HELL.

Geiger, Abraham (1810–74)

German REFORM leader and scholar. After becoming a RABBI in Wiesbaden in

1832, he reformed the SYNAGOGUE service and published the *Wissenschaftliche Zeitschrift für judische Theologie*. In 1837 he convened the first synod of Reform rabbis. Later he served as rabbi in Breslau, where he founded a school for religious studies and led a group that worked on HEBREW philology. He was a participant in subsequent Reform synods; from 1863 he served as rabbi in Frankfurt am Main. In 1870 he became rabbi of the Berlin congregation, and he helped establish the Hochschule für Wissenschaft des Judentums in the city. His works include studies of the Bible, the SADDUCEES and PHARISEES, Jewish history, MISHNAIC Hebrew and MAIMONIDES.

gemara (Aramaic, 'completion')

Commentary on the MISHNAH. Together the Mishnah and the Gemara make up the TALMUD.

gematria (Greek, 'geometry')

Science of interpreting a sacred text according to the numerical value of the letters of the words. There are various different systems of *gematria*. It was much used in the middle ages, and later by the KABBALISTS and the followers of SHABBETAI ZEVI. It derives from the second century CE, when Rabbi Judah argued that Jer. 9:10 ('No one pases through ... and the beasts are fled') implies that JUDAH was deserted for 52 years. This is because the numerical value of the Hebrew word for beasts is 52.

gemilut ḥasadim

See GIVING OF KINDNESS.

Genesis, Book of

First book in the BIBLE. It recounts the CREATION of the universe, the story of ADAM and EVE, the history of the FLOOD, the exploits of ABRAHAM, ISAAC and JACOB, and the story of JOSEPH. It concludes with the Israelites settling in the land of EGYPT. It is traditionally believed to have been written by MOSES, although modern scholars contend it is a composite source. The main theme of the book is the development of the COVENANTAL relationship with God, first on the part of humanity in general as represented by Adam and NOAH, and later on the part of the Jews in particular. God's saving plan in history is unfolded in the book, and the chronology is highly schematized. (*See also* PENTATEUCH; TORAH).

genizah

A place for storing old sacred books. It is forbidden in Jewish LAW to destroy anything which contains the name of GOD. Consequently it was the practice to store damaged or obsolete books in small rooms attached to the synagogue.

gentile

See GOYIM.

geonim

See GAON.

ger

See PROSELYTE.

ger toshav

See RIGHTEOUS STRANGER.

gerousia

Council of ELDERS. According to JOSEPHUS, the *gerousia* dates from biblical times, and during the HELLENISTIC period it served as a legislative and judicial body. It was in all likelihood the forerunner of the Great SANHEDRIN in JERUSALEM.

Gersonides

See LEVI BEN GERSHON.

get

Bill of divorce. It is known as a *sefer keritut* in the Book of DEUTERONOMY (24:3), and consists of a document written by the husband and delivered to the wife in the presence of witnesses. This document is required if the woman wishes to remarry. Jewish scholars disagreed as to the reasonable grounds for divorce. Today the practice is that a religious divorce is not granted until the secular legal formalities are completed. In the State of ISRAEL a *get* is the only form of divorce. Because it is the husband who gives the wife a divorce, serious hardship can arise if the husband refuses to comply. There have been some attempts in modern times to remedy this difficulty. Most PROGRESSIVE movements do not issue *gittin*, and do not require them for REMARRIAGE. (*See also* DIVORCE.)

geullah (Hebrew, 'redemption')

Title given to several PRAYERS. The section between the SHEMA and AMIDAH in the MORNING SERVICE is known as *geullah*, as is the seventh benediction of the AMIDAH and the benedictions recited after the Great HALLEL in the PASSOVER SEDER.

gezerah

See DECREE.

ghetto

Jewish residential area. The first enclosed ghetto was established in VENICE in 1516. Subsequently several other cities in Christian Europe restricted the living quarters of their Jewish population. Nonetheless, because of SABBATH regulations Jews have voluntarily chosen to live in specific areas. By extension the term 'ghetto' came to apply to any area predominantly occupied by ethnic minorities. Compulsory Jewish ghettos were instituted under the Nazis. (*See also* HOLOCAUST.)

Gideon (fl. 12th century BCE)

JUDGE of the tribe of MANASSEH. He was defeated by the Midianites near En

Harod. When he was offered the kingship of ISRAEL, he refused. In his view, God is the King of Israel and no human should usurp this role (Judg. 6–8). In Judges 6:32 he is referred to by the name 'Jerubaal'.

gilgul

See METEMPSYCHOSIS.

giving of kindness
(Hebrew: *gemilut ḥasadim*)

Acts of CHARITY. This encompasses various obligations of sympathetic consideration towards others. The sages taught that the whole religion rests on three pillars: TORAH, TEMPLE service, and *gemilut ḥasadim*.

giving of the law
(Hebrew: *mattan torah*)

Giving of the LAW by God to MOSES on MOUNT SINAI.

gleanings (Hebrew: *leket*)

Remnants of the crop left in the field after harvesting. During the biblical period gleanings were left for the poor (Lev. 19:9–10; 23:22; Deut. 24:19–21) in the corners of the field. The laws regarding gleaning are found in the tractate PEAH in the TALMUD.

glory (Hebrew: *kavod*)

Glory of God. According to the PROPHETS, there will come a time when the whole world is full of glory.

gnosticism

Religious movement characterized by the belief that through intuitive knowledge the spiritual element of man can be released from its earthly bondage. It flourished during the HELLENISTIC period and in later centuries. Gnostics believe that the material world has resulted from a primeval fall, and was created by an intermediary fallen from the divine realm. Gnosticism contains oriental mythological elements combined with Greek philosohical ideas. Gnostic DUAL-ISM was viewed by rabbinic scholars as HERESY and the condemnation of such heretics (*minim*) is found in rabbinic literature. Gnosticism subsequently influenced Jewish mysticism (*See* KABBALAH.)

God

Divine creator and ruler of the universe. The belief in God is the foundation of the Jewish religion and the basis of the legal system. The BIBLE portrays CREATION and God's activity in the history of ancient Israel. Medieval Jewish philosophers sought to demonstrate the existence of God, and investigated the nature of the divine attributes. KABBALISTS explored the hidden depths of the Godhead, and God's activity in the world.

God, attributes of

Scripture ascribes various traits to God, such as mercy, justice and benevolence. In addition, God is described as possessing human characteristics. Medieval Jewish philosophers debated whether such anthropomorphic descriptions should be understood literally or figuratively. Such thinkers as Moses MAIMONIDES argued that only negative attributes are permissible. Others, such as Hasdai CRESCAS, maintained that positive attributes were also acceptable. In rabbinic sources God is described as omnipotent, omniscient, incorporeal and all-good. (*See also* THIRTEEN ATTRIBUTES OF MERCY.)

God, names of

Because it is forbidden to pronounce the TETRAGRAMMATON (YHWH), substitutions and circumlocutions were used to refer to God. Various HEBREW terms are employed in the BIBLE. Other names arose as a result of rabbinic, philosophical and KABBALISTIC usage. Such names include El (God); El Elyon (most high);

El Olam (eternal God); El Shaddai (God almighty); El Brit (God of the covenant); Elohim (God); Adonai (Lord); Yahweh Zeva'ot (Lord of hosts); Ha-Shem (the name); Shem ha-Mephorash (the ineffable name); Kedosh Yisrael (the holy one of Israel); Ha-Makom (the place); SHEKHINAH (divine presence); Ha-Kadosh Barukh Hu (the holy one, blessed be he); Ha-Gevurah (the strength); Ha-Rahaman (the merciful); Attik Yomin (ancient of days).

Gog and Magog

APOCALYPTIC figures mentioned in EZEKIEL 38–9 in the vision of the end of days. Ezekiel depicts the war of God against Gog of the land of Magog. In rabbinic literature the wars of Gog and Magog will occur before the coming of the MESSIAH.

going up (1) (Hebrew: *aliyah*)

Calling up of a member of the congregation to read from the TORAH in the SYNAGOGUE service. Originally each individual who was called up read a section of the weekly Torah portion. Later a special reader was appointed who performed this function; those who were called up read blessings instead.

going up (2) (Hebrew: *aliyah*)

Term used specifically for the immigration of Jews to ISRAEL. There have been three major waves of immigration: the first from 1882 to 1903; the second from 1904 to 1914; and the third from 1918 to 1923. Subsequently Jews immigrated to the HOLY LAND from many countries both before and after the Second World War. All Jews are allowed to settle in Israel in accordance with the LAW OF RETURN.

golem

Artifically created being, usually human. It is brought to life through a MAGICAL act or the use of holy names. The concept is connected with the magical interpretation of the SEFER YETZIRAH and the idea of the creative power of HEBREW letters. Various accounts of the creation of a *golem* are recorded in the TALMUD as well as in Jewish literature from the 12th century. The ḤASIDEI ASHKENAZ viewed the creation of a *golem* as a symbolic ecstatic experience following a solemn ceremony. From the 15th century a *golem* was regarded as a real creature.

good inclination
(Hebrew: *yetzer ha-tov*)
Tendency to do good rather than evil. According to rabbinic sages, each person has both a good and an EVIL INCLINATION (*yetzer ha-ra*).

Gordon, Aaron David
(1856–1922)
Palestinian Hebrew writer. Born in Troyanov, Russia, he held a post in the financial management of the estate of Baron Horace Ginzburg. In 1904 he settled in PALESTINE, where he worked as an agricultural labourer. In his writings he stressed the importance of such activity; in his view, self-realization can only be attained through working the land.

government, prayer for the
(Hebrew: *ha-noten teshuah*)
This prayer is recited during the SABBATH and festival MORNING SERVICE. It begins with the phrase: '*ha-noten teshuah*' (He who gives salvation).

gown (Hebrew: *kittel*)
White, shroud-like garment worn by the officiant and many members of the congregation during the prayer service on the HIGH HOLY DAYS, and by the CANTOR at the additional service on SHEMINI ATZERET and the first day of PASSOVER. In addition, it is worn by the person conducting the Passover SEDER, and by the groom during the MARRIAGE ceremony.

goyim (Yiddish, 'gentiles')
Non-Jews. The original meaning of the word means 'nations'. Through the centuries Jewish attitudes towards non-Jews have varied. Sometimes friendship and at other times hostility has been shown. Gentiles are not expected to keep the 613 commandments found in Scripture nor the rabbinic expansion of this legislation. It is sufficient for them to observe the seen laws given to NOAH. A distinction is made between IDOLATORS and those who believe in one God such as Christians and Muslims. Intercourse with non-Jews was always problematic because of the DIETARY LAWS, and since the time of EZRA, INTERMARRIAGE has been forbidden. (*See also* NOACHIDE LAWS.)

grace after meals
(Hebrew: *birkat ha-mazon*)
PRAYER consisting of four BENEDICTIONS. It is recited after a meal where bread has been eaten. If bread has not been consumed, a shorter form of grace is recited. The benedictions praise God for providing for food, express gratitude for his blessings, ask him for mercy and support, and thank him for his goodness.

grace before meals
Prayer consisting of one or more BENEDICTIONS which are recited before a meal or before the separate courses of a meal. Rabbinic sages instituted separate blessings for various types of food. The blessing for bread ('Who brings forth bread from the earth') is based on Psalm 104:14. When said at the beginning of the meal, it exempts one from the obligation to recite blessings for other courses.

Graetz, Heinrich (1817–91)
German historian and biblical scholar. Born in Xions in the district of Posen, he lectured in Jewish history and the Bible at the Jewish Theological Seminary in

Breslau. In 1869 he became an honorary professor at the university there. His multi-volume *History of the Jews* influenced generations of Jewish scholars.

Great Assembly

Supreme religious body of Jewry during the Second TEMPLE period. Traditionally the Great Assembly was composed of 120 ELDERS known as 'the men of the Great Assembly'. Much of the liturgy goes back to the dicussions and formulations of this body (see Neh. 8–9).

Great Hallel

See HALLEL HA-GADOL.

Great Sanhedrin

See SANHEDRIN, GREAT.

Great Synagogue

See SYNAGOGUE, GREAT.

greetings

Common HEBREW greetings include: '*Shalom*' ('Peace') or '*Shalom aleikhem*' ('Peace be with you'). On the SABBATH it is customary to say '*Shabbat shalom*' ('Sabbath peace'), or the YIDDISH expression '*Gut shabbos*' ('Good Sabbath'). On FESTIVALS, one should say '*Ḥag sameaḥ*' ('Good festival'), or the Yiddish '*Gut yomtov*' ('Good festival'). On the New Year, Jews wish each other '*Le shanah tovah tikkatevu*' ('May you be inscribed for a good year').

gregger

Rattle noisemaker. The *gregger* is sounded on the FESTIVAL of PURIM when the name HAMAN is mentioned in the reading of the Book of ESTHER. This is so that the name of Haman is blotted out while the Book of Esther is read.

Guide for the Perplexed

(Hebrew: *Moreh Nevukhim*)

Philosophical work by Moses MAIMONIDES, composed in the 12th century. In this study Maimonides attempted to reconcile the truths of Scripture with Aristotelianism. The work was accused by some of excessive rationalism which might lead to HERESY, while others supported Maimonides' views.

guilt offerings

See SACRIFICE.

H

Ḥabad

ḤASIDIC movement. The name is derived from the intitials of the words *Ḥokhmah* (wisdom), *Binah* (understanding) and *Daat* (knowledge). Ḥabad was founded in the 18th century by SHNOEUR ZALMAN of Lyady. He was opposed by Ḥasidic leaders living in Volhynia, as well as the MITNAGDIM led by the Vilna Gaon (ELIJAH BEN SOLOMON ZALMAN). His teaching is contained in the TANYA, where he developed a theosophical doctrine based on the KABBALISTIC doctrines of Isaac LURIA. Originally Ḥabad was centred in Belorussia, but after the First World War it spread to other lands.

Habakkuk, Book of

Biblical book, one of the 12 MINOR PROPHETS. It recounts the prophecies of Habakkuk, who was active during the seventh century BCE. It consists of three chapters which contain a protest against injustice, a complaint about the victory of the Chaldeans, God's reply, a prayer, and a description of the DAY OF THE LORD.

Habiru

Ancient people living in the Fertile Crescent (Mesopotamia) during the second millennium BCE. The name is recorded on the TEL EL AMARNA tablets and other documents. According to some scholars, the term refers to the ancient Hebrews.

Hadassah

Alternative name for ESTHER (Esther 2.7). It also refers to the Women's ZIONIST Organization of America, founded in 1912 by Henrietta SZOLD to raise the standard of health in PALESTINE, encourage Jewish life in the USA and foster the Jewish ideal. In ISRAEL, Hadassah sponsors medical training, research, care and special education. Its members in the USA are involved in fund-raising and educational activities.

Hafetz Ḥayyim (1838–1933)

TALMUDIC scholar. His real name was Israel Meir Kagan; although he did not occupy an official position, he was universally recognized as a an ethical and religious teacher, particularly among Lithuanian Jews. He wrote both scholarly and popular works.

haftarah (Hebrew, 'conclusion')

Second reading in the SYNAGOGUE on SABBATHS and FESTIVALS. The Haftarah reading is from the PROPHETS and is selected for its connection with the TORAH reading of the day. One BENEDICTION is recited before it is read, and four afterwards. The Haftarah is chanted according to particular rules of CANTILLATION.

Haganah

Underground military organization in PALESTINE. It succeeded Ha-Shomer in

1920 and operated until 1948 when its members transferred to the Israeli army. In 1931 the movement split and a minority formed the IRGUN TZEVAI LEUMI. The organization carried out undergound training within individual settlements, supervised illegal immigration and manufactured equipment. After the Second World War, its operations were directed against the British in order to secure the rejection of the anti-ZIONIST White Paper of 1939. From 1947 it focused its activity against Arab attack.

hagbahah (Hebrew, 'lifting')

Term used in a liturgical context to refer to the raising of the TORAH SCROLL in the SYNAGOGUE. This is done before or after the reading so that the congregation can see the writing.

Haggadah

Ritual service which is performed in the home on the first PASSOVER evening, or on the first two evenings in traditional Jewish households. Originally a narrative recounting the EXODUS from EGYPT, it consists of BENEDICTIONS, PRAYERS, MIDRASHIC commentary and PSALMS, recited during the FESTIVAL meal. The order of the Passover Haggadah became an established custom and is recorded in the MISHNAH. Subsequently it took on a more elaborate form which is contained in the prayer books of Amram Gaon (eighth century) and SAADIAH GAON (10th century). It is the subject of various commentaries as well as manuscript illuminations.

Haggai, Book of

Biblical book, one of the books of the 12 MINOR PROPHETS. It recounts the prophecies of Haggai, which date from the second year of the reign of Darius I, King of Persia (*c*.520 BCE). They deal with the building of the TEMPLE, the restoration of the nation and the grandeur of ZERUBBABEL.

Hagiographa
(Greek, 'Holy Writings')

Third section of the BIBLE. It is known in Hebrew as KETUVIM and includes the books of PSALMS, PROVERBS, JOB, the SONG OF SONGS, RUTH, LAMENTATIONS, ECCLESIASTES, ESTHER, DANIEL, EZRA, NEHEMIAH, and 1 and 2 CHRONICLES.

Hai Gaon (939–1038)

Babylonian GAON. Initially he assisted his father, Sherira Gaon, in administering and teaching in the ACADEMY of PUMBEDITA. He became *gaon* in 998. Under his leadership the academy became a centre of Jewish learning. He issued thousands of RESPONSA dealing with various areas of Jewish LAW. In addition, he composed a commentary on several TRACTATES of the TALMUD, poetry and a treatise on commerce.

hair

See PAIS.

ḥakham (Hebrew, 'wise')

Rabbinic title. Originally Jewish scholars who had not formally received *semikhah* (rabbinic ordination) were known as *ḥakhamim*. The title was also used for the third in status after the NASI and AV BET DIN. Among the SEPHARDIM, the title is used for the local RABBI.

hakhel (Hebrew, 'assembly')

Assembly of the seventh year. According to Deut. 31:10, the Israelites were to assemble every seventh year to 'hear and learn to fear the Lord your God'. Although this practice is mentioned in the MISHNAH, it ceased after the destruction of the TEMPLE.

hakhnasat kallah
(Hebrew, 'bringing in the bride')

The practice of providing a DOWRY for poor brides. During the middle ages, societies were set up to raise dowries, known as *hakhnasat kallah* societies.

hakhnasat orehim

See ENTERTAINING TRAVELLERS.

halakhah (Hebrew, 'way of going')

Jewish LAW. ORTHODOX JUDAISM teaches that the entire legal system goes back to MOSES, who received the TORAH from God on MOUNT SINAI. The *halakhah* is made up of the WRITTEN LAW, as recorded in the PENTATEUCH, and the ORAL LAW, which includes later RESPONSA as well as established customs. During the period of the TEMPLE the SADDUCEES denied the authority of the oral law; this view was also adopted later by the KARAITES. However, the oral law was collected by JUDAH HA-NASI in the MISHNAH, and the discussions of the AMORAIM are recorded in the TALMUD. Subsequently Jewish law was codified in such works as the MISHNEH TORAH by MAIMONIDES and the SHULHAN ARUKH compiled by Joseph CARO. While ORTHODOXY accepts the *halakhah* as binding, PROGRESSIVE JUDAISM has adapted it to contemporary life. This process has been condemned by Orthodox Jews. (*See also* CODES OF JEWISH LAW.)

halitzah

See LEVIRATE MARRIAGE.

hallah (Hebrew, 'dough offering')

In Scripture the word refers to a portion of dough given to the PRIEST (Num. 15:17–21). It is now applied to a special SABBATH loaf. The term also denotes the ninth TRACTATE in the MISHNAH order of ZERAIM, which deals with the setting aside of the *hallah*.

hallel

Psalms 113–18. The *hallel* is chanted on the FESTIVALS of PASSOVER, SUKKOT and HANUKKAH. It is mentioned in the TALMUD as being incorporated into the synagogue liturgy from an early period.

hallel ha-gadol (Hebrew, 'great Hallel')

Name given to Ps. 136. It is recited on the SABBATH and at FESTIVAL MORNING SERVICES as well as on the last day of PASSOVER.

hallelujah (Hebrew, 'praise ye the Lord')

Word used as a refrain at the beginning and end of certain PSALMS.

halutz

See PIONEER.

Haman

Persian official in the court of King Ahasuerus. He sought to kill all Jews, but his plans were defeated by ESTHER. He was subsequently hanged on a gallows which he had made for Mordecai. He became the object of hatred among Jews, and a symbol of villainy. These events are recorded in the Book of Esther, and in memory of them the Jews celebrate the FESTIVAL of PURIM.

hamesh megillot

See SCROLLS.

hametz

See LEAVEN.

hands, laying on of (Hebrew: *semikhah*)

Rabbinic ordination. During the period of the sages, religious leaders were ordained as RABBIS by laying on of hands. Membership of the SANHEDRIN was restricted to those who were ordained; nonetheless, any teacher could ordain his students by using the formula 'Yoreh, yoreh. Yadin, yadin.' (May he decide? He may decide. May he judge? He may judge.) In the early days, rabbinical ordination did not take place outside Israel and BABYLONIAN teachers were called rav rather than rabbi. However, from the fifth century, licence to judge was frequently given in a written document. From the 12th century this document came to be called *semikhah*. Today all RABBINICAL SEM-INARIES and some YESHIVOT grant *semikhah* using the ancient formula.

hands, washing of

According to Jewish LAW, hands must be ceremonially washed after rising from sleep, touching a corpse, urinating or defecating, and before eating or praying. (*See also* ABLUTION.)

ha-noten teshvah

See PRAYER FOR THE GOVERNMENT.

Ḥanukkah (Hebrew, 'Dedication')

Winter FESTIVAL of lights. It lasts for eight days, beginning on Kislev 25.

Ḥanukkah: A family lighting candles.

Ḥanukkah commemorates the victory of the MACCABEES over the HELLENISTS and the miraculous lasting of holy oil for eight days rather than one. In fact, the festival has an older history: in the days of the TEMPLE, torches and lamps were kindled in the Temple courts and water poured out so it was reflected by the lights. In modern times it has become a major festival as a substitute for the Christian Christmas, which occurs at much the same time. All observant households have a MENORAH for eight candles; one is lit on the first day, two on the second and so on. Card playing and spinning the DREIDEL are associated with the festival. It is forbidden to FAST, and the HALLEL is chanted in the SYNAGOGUE. It is a particularly important holiday in ISRAEL since it symbolizes the survival of Jews against enormous odds.

ḥaroset

Paste composed of fruit, spices, wine and *matzah* meal. It is eaten at the PASSOVER SEDER. The BITTER HERB is dipped into *ḥaroset* to make it less strong. Ḥaroset symbolizes the mortar which was made by the Israelites during their period of slavery in EGYPT.

Ha-shem (Hebrew, 'The Name')

Term referring to God. It is used to avoid mentioning his name. It is found in such phrases as '*Barukh ha-Shem*' (Blessed be God), '*Be ezrat ha-Shem*' (With the help of God) and '*Im yirtze ha-Shem*' (God willing).

hashkamah

See EARLY RISING.

hashkavah

Memorial PRAYER. *See* KADDISH; YAHRZEIT; YIZKOR.

hashkivenu (Hebrew 'cause us to lie down [in peace]')

Opening word of the second BENEDIC-TION which follows the evening SHEMA.

It is a PRAYER for protection and peace during the night.

Ḥasidei Ashkenaz
(Hebrew, 'Pious ones of Germany')

12th- and 13th-century German Jewish movement, influenced by Merkavah mysticism (CHARIOT MYSTICISM). Its leaders included Samuel ben Kolonymus, and the works of Abraham ibn Ezra and SAADIAH GAON were much studied. Disciples of the movement displayed intense religious fervour. The ultimate sign of love for God was MARTYRDOM (*kiddush ha-Shem*), and adherents of the Ḥasidei Ashkenaz demonstrated great courage. The movement was similar in certain respects to Christian pietism. The movement had a significant impact on communities in Spain, Poland and Lithuania.

ḥasidei ummot ha-olam
(Hebrew, 'the pious ones of the world's nations')

Righteous gentiles. The *ḥasidei ummot ha-olam* are those individuals who observe the seven commandments of NOAH. As such, they are viewed as worthy to enter into the world to come. Since the Second World War, the term has increasingly been used to refer to those gentiles who helped individuals escape from the Nazi HOLOCAUST. (*See also* NOACHIDE LAWS.)

Ḥasidim (Hebrew, 'the Pious')

Those who lead pious lives. During the TALMUDIC perod, the *ḥasidim ha-rishonim* (just and pious men) were famous for their ritual purity and scrupulousness in keeping the MITZVOT. The *ḥasidim ve-anshei maaseh* (pious who were also men of action) were notable for their good works and miracles. Although the Ḥasidim were always admired, the sages emphasized that intelligence as well as piety are necessary to gain God's favour.

Ḥasidim, Sefer
(Hebrew, 'Book of the Pious')

Medieval moral guide. It dates from the 13th century. It was the major ethical tract of the Ḥasidei Ashkenaz, and is attributed to Rabbi Judah he-Ḥasid.

Ḥasidism

Religious and social movement founded by the Baal Shem Tov (ISRAEL BEN ELIEZER) in Volhynia and Podolia in the 18th century. He taught that all human beings are created equal before God, purity of the heart is superior to study, and devotion to prayer and God's commandments is of fundamental importance. He was succeeded by DOV BAER OF MEZHIRECH, who systematized Ḥasidic

A Ḥasidic Jew in Jerusalem wearing traditional Hasidic clothing.

teaching. Although the Ḥasidim were opposed by TALMUDISTS (MITNAGDIM), the movement spread throughout Eastern Europe and beyond. The major centres of Ḥasidism were destroyed during the Second World War, but several dynasties emigrated to the USA, such as the Lubavitcher and the SATMAR. These groups established their own training colleges and schools, and through them the movement continues to exert an important influence on world Jewry.

Haskalah

See ENLIGHTENMENT.

haskamah (Hebrew, 'agreement')

Formal rabbinic approval of a printed book. From the 16th century, some communities insisted that books should be published only if they carried a *haskamah*.

Hasmoneans

Term used in the TALMUD to refer to the MACCABEES. The Hasmoneans led the rebellion under the Seleucid kings in the second century BCE. Under the leadership of Matthias and his sons JUDAH, Simon and Jonathan, an independent Jewish kingdom was created which lasted until the time of the Roman conquest in 67 BCE.

ha-tikvah (Hebrew, 'hope')

National anthem of the State of ISRAEL. The verse was written by Naphtali Herz Imber in 1878, and the tune is based on a SEPHARDI melody and Smetana's *Vltava*.

havdalah (Hebrew, 'distinction')

Ceremony which ends the SABBATH. BENEDICTIONS are recited over wine, a candle and spices, and a final blessing thanks God for the distinction between the sacred and the profane. Different customs prevail in various communities; a lighted candle is usually extinguished in the wine. The ceremony reputedly stems from the days of the GREAT SYNAGOGUE.

haver (Hebrew, 'member')

Member of a group which observed certain TITHING laws in MISHNAIC and talmudic times. The regulations outlined in the TALMUD for becoming a *haver* are similar to the rules in the QUMRAN MANUAL OF DISCIPLINE. In the time of the *geonim*, a *haver* was simply a scholar.

havurah

Mutual benefit society. Originally a *havurah* was established for a specific aim such as VISITING THE SICK or burying the dead. In the 20th century, the term has come to refer to a small informal worship group. The *havurah* movement has been responsible for various innovative liturgies in recent years.

hazzan

See CANTOR.

head, covering of

See SHEITEL; YARMULKE.

Hear, O Israel

See SHEMA.

heave offering
(Hebrew, 'sacrifice')

Offering made to the SANCTUARY or to the PRIESTS. It refers to the TITHES, to the HALLAH (dough offering) given to the priests, and to the half-shekel that had to be contributed to the sanctuary.

heaven

Abode of God. In Scripture, heaven is located in the upper part of the universe. The sages taught that there were several heavens in which the ANGELS dwell. REWARD AND PUNISHMENT are fundamental concepts in Jewish theology, and it is held that the righteous will ascend to heaven after death. The term 'heaven' is also often used as an alternative to God, as in 'the fear of heaven' and 'for the sake of heaven'. (*See also* GARDEN OF EDEN.)

Hebrew

Hebrew belongs to the CANAANITE branch of Semitic languages. It was used by the ancient Israelites until about 500 years after the Babylonian EXILE. MISHNAIC Hebrew is an altered form of biblical Hebrew, used by the TANNAIM from the second century BCE to the second century CE. In time it was superseded by ARAMAIC and Greek. In about 500 CE a literary revival of Hebrew commenced, which lasted through the middle ages. From 900–1400 Jews in North-western Europe wrote in Hebrew, while in Muslim countries Arabic was used. In Eastern Europe Jews spoke and wrote in YIDDISH. Though Hebrew continued as a religious language, Jews used the vernacular. The Haskalah (*see* ENLIGHTENMENT) revived interest in Hebrew, and it was subsequently adopted as the language of the State of ISRAEL.

Hebrews

Name given to various groups of Jews. In Scripture it refers to the descendants of Eber, grandson of Shem (Gen. 10:24), and the people who originated from beyond the River Euphrates. ABRAHAM is referred to as 'the Hebrew' (Exod. 9:1). Some scholars identify the people known as the HABIRU with the Hebrews. The word 'Hebrew' was frequently employed in place of 'Jew' in the 19th century, but in Europe 'Israelite' was more common.

Hebron

Ancient city of JUDAH. In Scripture, ABRAHAM purchased a plot of land in Hebron (the cave of MACHPELAH) in which to bury SARAH (Gen. 13:18).

Hebron was assigned by JOSHUA to Caleb; subsequently it became a LEVITICAL city and one of the CITIES OF REFUGE (Josh. 20:7). DAVID reigned there before transferring the capital to JERUSALEM (2 Sam. 2:11).

ḥeder (Hebrew, 'school')

A school dedicated to teaching children about Judaism. Many SYNAGOGUES have a *ḥeder* attached to them.

hefker

See OWNERLESS PROPERTY.

heifer, red

See RED HEIFER.

hekdesh

Property sacred to God. Property consecrated to the TEMPLE came into this category, and the LAWS relating to *hekdesh* are complex in character. The practice fell into disuse after the destruction of the TEMPLE in 70 CE. Nonetheless, it was still possible to give away property to a CHARITY or the SYNAGOGUE. Because of its charitable connection, the term *hekdesh* came to refer to a shelter for the poor, sick or old.

Hekhalot, Books of

Collections of MIDRASHIC material concerning the Heavenly Halls. They contain descriptions of the ascent to HEAVEN to behold the divine CHARIOT (*merkavah*), heavenly places (*hekhalot*) and the throne of glory. Embracing ecstatic experiences and hymns in praise of God, some of this material has been incorporated into the ASHKENAZI HIGH HOLY DAY liturgy. The books are attributed to ISHMAEL BEN ELISHA (second century CE), but were written at a later period.

hell (Hebrew: Gehenna)

Originally the name Gehenna referred to a valley to the south-west of JERUSALEM. During the period of the monarchy it was the site of a cult that invoved the burning of children (2 Kgs. 23:10; Jer. 7:31; 32:35). In rabbinic literature the name is used to refer to the place of torment for the wicked after death.

Hellenism

Principles, ideals and way of life associated with classical Greek civilization. Hellenism spread over the Mediterranean and the Middle East from the fourth century BCE. During this period PALESTINE was under Greek rule and JUDEA was surrounded by numerous Hellenized cities. In addition, the Jewish DIASPORA was expanding into EGYPT, Cyrenaica, Syria, and Asia Minor, which were all under Hellenistic influence. By the MISHNAIC period, Jewish life in Palestine and the diaspora was largely dominated by Hellenistic influences.

heresy

Opinion or doctrine contrary to the orthodox tenets of the faith. Because Judaism does not have an official creed, it has no clear definition of heresy. Nonetheless, rabbinic Judaism views as heretics those who renounce the teaching of TORAH. They are refered to by such terms as *min* (sectarian), *apikoros* (epicurean), *kopher* (freethinker) and *mumar* (one who has changed). The punishment of heretics was justified as a means of preventing them from leading others to false belief. During the middle ages, heresy was punished by EXCOMMUNICATION (*ḥerem*).

heretic

See APIKOROS.

hermeneutics

Method of interpreting Scripture. It proceeds according to TALMUDIC principles. Various collections of rules (*middot*) governing the methodology of exegesis existed during the rabbinic period, including the seven rules of HILLEL; the 13 rules of ISHMAEL BEN ELISHA; and the 32 rules of Eliezer ben Yose ha-Galili. In addition, Nahum of Gimzo formulated a system of interpretation based on the assumption that the marking on every letter has a specific meaning; this was subsequently developed by AKIVA.

Herod (fl. 1st century BCE)

King of JUDEA (37–4 BCE), son of Antipater II. Appointed Governor of GALILEE by his father in 47 BCE, he successfully crushed a Galilean revolt. In response, he was censured by the SANHEDRIN. Later he became tetrarch of Judea and eventually king. He constructed a Greek theatre and amphitheatre in JERUSALEM, transformed SAMARIA into a Greco-Samaritan city, built the port of Caesarea, and rebuilt the TEMPLE in Jerusalem. During his reign he dealt harshly with anyone he viewed as a threat to his power. He put a number of people to death, including his wife Mariamne and her sons.

Herzl, Theodor (1869–1904)

Austrian writer and journalist, founder of political ZIONISM. Born in Budapest, he served as Paris correspondent for the Vienna *Neue Freie Presse* from 1891 to 1895. In his play *Das neue Ghetto* he criticized Jewish assimilation. After the DREYFUS case he wrote *The Jewish State* in which he encouraged the creation of a Jewish homeland. He convened the First Zionist Congress in Basle in 1897, at which the World Zionist Organization was established. By acclamation he became its president. He later began negotiations with world leaders to create a Jewish state. After the founding of the State of ISRAEL, his remains were transported to JERUSALEM.

Heschel, Abraham Joshua (1907–72)

American Jewish theologian. Educated in Berlin, he was deported by the Nazis to Poland in 1938. He subsequently emigrated to England. From 1940 he taught philosophy and rabbinics at the Hebrew Union College in Cincinnati; in 1945 he was appointed professor of Jewish ethics and mysticism at the Jewish Theological Seminary in New York. He wrote studies of medieval Jewish philosophy, the BIBLE, KABBALAH, HASIDISM and the philosophy of religion.

Hess, Moses (1812–1875)

German socialist. Born in Bonn, he helped found the socialist daily *Rheinische Zeitung*, of which Karl MARX became editor. Later he lived in Belgium, Switzerland and Paris. In 1862 he published *Rome and Jerusalem*, in which he argued for the creation of a Jewish homeland. Subsequently he engaged in the work of the Alliance Isráelite Universelle. His other writings include *The Holy History of Humanity* and *The European Triarchy*.

hessah daat
(Hebrew, 'removal of the mind')

Lack of attention when performing religious duties, causing the action to become invalid.

hevra kaddisha

See BURIAL SOCIETY.

Hexateuch

First six books of the BIBLE comprising GENESIS, EXODUS, LEVITICUS, NUMBERS, DEUTERONOMY and JOSHUA.

Hezekiah
(fl. eighth to seventh century BCE)

King of JUDAH from 715 to 687 BCE. Unlike his father, Ahaz, he sought to free Judah from Assyrian influence. He removed pagan images and altars from the TEMPLE and renewed religious life. Such reforms were supported by the prophet ISAIAH. During his reign the Assyrian king Sennacherib invaded Judah; as a consequence, Hezekiah was compelled to pay tribute to the Assyrians.

Hibbat Zion
(Hebrew, 'Love of Zion')

International ZIONIST movement. It originated in the 1860s and served as a focus for early Zionist aspirations. It had widespread appeal among the Jewish minorities in Russia and Romania.

High Holy Days

The festivals of Rosh Ha-Shanah (NEW YEAR) and Yom Kippur (DAY OF ATONEMENT). The ten days between the two are frequently described as the High Holy Day period.

high places

Shrines built on a hill in the HOLY LAND. When the TEMPLE in JERUSALEM had been built, it was condemned as idolatrous to worship at a high place. However, once the NORTHERN KINGDOM had separated from the SOUTHERN KINGDOM, the northern kings encouraged worship at the high places so that the people would not go down to Jerusalem.

High Priest

Chief PRIEST of the Jewish people from ancient times until the destruction of the TEMPLE in 70 CE. The term is first found in reference to AARON and his descendants who were anointed with holy oil (Lev. 21:10; Num. 35:25,28; Josh. 20:6). Subsequently, the title was applied to the chief priest of the First and second Temple. In addition to the priestly garments (breeches, tunic, girdle and mitre), the High Priest wore a robe, EPHOD, BREASTPLATE and frontlet. Attached to the breastplate were the URIM AND THUMMIM. On the DAY OF ATONEMENT he wore white linen. The High Priest was the principal officiant in the Temple. He was entitled to be present at all SACRIFICES, and among his responsibilities was the administration of the treasury. In addition, he administered the divine oracle and the Urim and Thummim. He was the sole celebrant on the Day of Atonement when he entered the HOLY OF HOLIES to offer INCENSE. The office of High Priest ceased after the destruction of the Temple.

Hillel (fl. first century BCE)

Palestinian rabbinic scholar. Born in BABYLONIA, he settled in PALESTINE where he studied with SHEMAIAH and AVTALYON. Subsequently he was appointed president of the SANHEDRIN. Together with SHAMMAI, he was the last of the pairs (ZUGOT) of scholars. He formulated seven rules of scriptural interpretation. He was also the originator of the golden rule: 'Do not do unto others that which you would not have them do unto you.' He was the founder of the school known as BET HILLEL. (*See also* HERMENEUTICS.)

ḥillul ha-Shem
(Hebrew, 'profanation of the name')

Expression used to designate any action that desecrates God's name. Such an action should be avoided not only because it is a sin (as forbidden by the TEN COMMANDMENTS), but also because it sets a bad example to others. The phrase has come to designate any action that is likely to bring disgrace on Judaism or the Jewish nation.

Hinnom, Valley of
See GEHENNA.

Hirsch, Samson Raphael
(1808–88)

German RABBI and writer. Born in Hamburg, he served as rabbi in Oldenburg and Emden, and later as chief rabbi of Moravia. From 1851 he was rabbi in Frankfurt am Main. He was the founder of NEO-ORTHODOXY, which attempted to combine European culture with loyalty to traditional Judaism. His works include *Nineteen Letters on Judaism* and *Horeb: Essays on Israel's Duties in the Diaspora.* He became the leader and foremost exponent of ORTHODOXY in Germany in the 19th century.

ḥol ha-moed
(Hebrew, 'weekday of the festival')

Name given to each of the days between the first and last days of the PASSOVER and SUKKOT FESTIVALS. The first and last days are holy days; however, on the intermediate days essential work may be undertaken. Nonetheless, no MARRIAGES may occur and MOURNING is forbidden.

Holdheim, Samuel (1806–60)

German REFORM RABBI. Born in Kempno near Posen, he served as rabbi in Frankfurt an der Oder, Mecklenburg-Schwerin and Berlin. He advocated radical reform at rabbinical conferences in Braunschweig (1844), Frankfurt am Main (1845) and Breslau (1846).

ḥolent

SABBATH dish among ASHKENAZIM. It is prepared the day before the Sabbath and cooked in an oven overnight to avoid breaking the Sabbath law against kindling a light on the Sabbath. It is usually made of beans. The SEPHARDI equivalent is known as *hamin.*

holiness (Hebrew: *kedushah*)

The Hebrew word for holiness denotes separation, particularly separation for holy purposes. As a dimension of the moral life, holiness is stressed in Lev. 19: 'You shall be holy for I, the Lord your God, am holy.' In ceremonial practice, it is associated with the DIETARY LAWS, laws of ritual PURITY and spirituality. Special holiness is ascribed to the TEMPLE, PRIESTS and LEVITES. Holiness is required of the entire nation, who are referred to as a 'holy people'. The land of ISRAEL is known as the 'HOLY LAND'.

holiness code

Laws in Lev. 17–26. They deal with SAC-RIFICE, sexual conduct, the priesthood, the HOLY DAYS, SABBATICAL YEARS, and various BENEDICTIONS and warnings. The holiness code is traditionally thought to have been written by MOSES, although most scholars now date it to the First TEMPLE period. It parallels the codes in Deut. 12–28 and Exod. 20–23.

Holocaust (Hebrew: *Shoah*)

Destruction of the European Jewish community during the Second World War (see map on p. 96). The Nazi government was committed to ANTI-SEMITIC policies. Until the declaration of war in 1939, Jews were systematically excluded from public office as well as intellectual and cultural life in Germany. After 1939 emigration was no longer possible. Jews were then herded into GHETTOS and transported east where they were slaughtered in concentration camps. Six million Jews are estimated to have died during the Holocaust. Nisan 27 is kept as the Holocaust Memorial Day, and YAHRZEIT is observed for the unknown dead on Tevat 10. The Holocaust destroyed the SHTETLS and YESHIVOT of East European Jewry, and persuaded the world community that the ZIONIST demand for a Jewish homeland should be met. The State of ISRAEL was created in 1948.

Holy Ark (Hebrew: *Aron Kodesh*)

Alcove in the SYNAGOGUE where the TORAH scrolls are kept. It is built in the wall facing JERUSALEM and is the focal point of the synagogue. The congregation usually stands when the Ark doors are opened, and an ETERNAL LIGHT (*ner tamid*) is kept burning before it. Among the SEPHARDIM, the *Aron Kodesh* is called the *Heikhal*.

holy days

In Scripture the following holy days are mentioned: the three PILGRIM FESTIVALS –

PASSOVER, SHAVUOT and SUKKOT – which in biblical times were harvest festivals as well as commemorations of historical events; and the days of solemnity, which are NEW YEAR and the DAY OF ATONEMENT. On all holy days work is forbidden. (The first and last days of Passover and Sukkot are holy days when work is not allowed; however, some work is permitted on the intermediate days [HOL HA-MOED]). Traditional Jews observe the holy days (except the DAY OF ATONEMENT) for two days. REFORM JUDAISM limits observance to one day. Work may take place on the post-biblical festivals of HANUKKAH and PURIM, which are the best-known and most frequently observed of the many minor festivals.

Holy Land

The land of ISRAEL was promised by God to ABRAHAM and his descendants. The area is indicated in Scripture in the PATRI-ARCHAL COVENANT (Gen. 15:18–19). Other boundaries are described in Num. 34:2–12 and other biblical books, as well as in talmudic sources. It is viewed as an inalienable gift to the Jewish people. Love of the land is expressed in the BIBLE, the TALMUD, the liturgy, religious thought and Jewish LAW.

Holy of Holies

Inner shrine of the TEMPLE in JERUSALEM. The Holy of Holies was entered by the HIGH PRIEST once a year on Yom Kippur (DAY OF ATONEMENT). It had no windows and a raised floor so that it was the highest spot in the Temple. Here the ARK OF THE COVENANT was kept. It was regarded as the most holy place in the Jewish world.

holy places

In modern Jewish life the principal holy places are the western wall (*see* WAILING WALL – a relic of the TEMPLE of HEROD) and the graves of biblical figures or famous scholars from the MISHNAIC

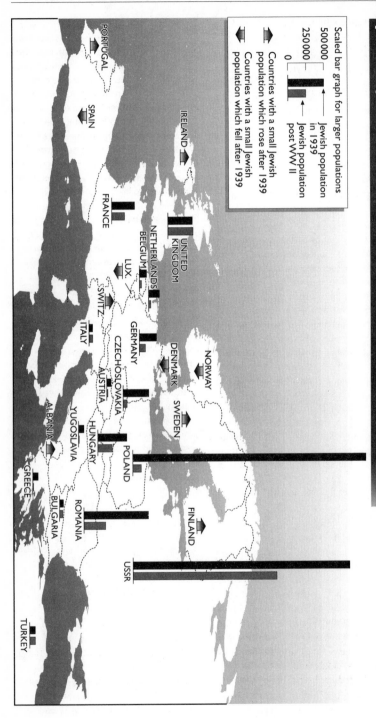

Jewish Population of Europe before and after the Second World War

Scaled bar graph for larger populations

500000 — Jewish population in 1939
250000 — Jewish population post WW II
0

Countries with a small Jewish population which rose after 1939

Countries with a small Jewish population which fell after 1939

PORTUGAL
SPAIN
IRELAND
FRANCE
NETHERLANDS
BELGIUM
UNITED KINGDOM
LUX
SWITZ
ITALY
GERMANY
CZECHOSLOVAKIA
AUSTRIA
DENMARK
NORWAY
SWEDEN
ALBANIA
YUGOSLAVIA
HUNGARY
POLAND
FINLAND
GREECE
BULGARIA
ROMANIA
USSR
TURKEY

period to the present day. Increasingly, since the destruction of European Jewry during the HOLOCAUST, the death camps such as AUSCHWITZ and the remains of Jewish quarters in towns which had important Jewish communities have also become holy places. Among the ḤASIDIM, the court of the ZADDIK is a place of PILGRIMAGE.

Holy Spirit
(Hebrew: *Ruaḥ ha-Kodesh*)

In Scripture the Hebrew term means literally 'divine spirit' (Isa. 63:10–11; Ps. 51:13). In rabbinic sources it refers to 'divine inspiration'. The criterion for determining the biblical CANON was whether each book had been inspired by the Holy Spirit. According to rabbinic tradition, the communication to an individual of the Holy Spirit takes place only after long religious discipline resulting in spiritual ascent.

home

In Judaism the home is a central focus of Jewish life. The MEZUZAH, fixed to the doorposts, is a reminder of the sacred nature of the home. The SABBATH CANDLES are reminiscent of the TEMPLE, and the dining table on which KIDDUSH and HAVDALAH are celebrated recalls the Temple ALTAR. In an ORTHODOX home, GRACE is said before and after meals, the Sabbath is kept, the laws of SHATNES and KASHRUT are observed, and sexual relationships are regulated according to the laws of NIDDAH. Both PASSOVER and SUKKOT are largely home FESTIVALS, with the SEDER meal and the construction of the SUKKAH. ḤANUKKAH candles are lit at home, and PURIM is a time of home merrymaking. Life-cycle ceremonies such as CIRCUMCISION, the REDEMPTION OF THE FIRST-BORN and MOURNING are all conducted at home. The home is also the fundamental place of education of children into the faith.

homiletics

Art of preaching. Traditionally sermons begin with a biblical verse which is illustrated in turn by another biblical verse, and so on. Eventually the preacher returns to his original text and expounds on the ethical or ritual implications of the law. The preliminary biblical verses are selected from sections of the PENTATEUCH, PROPHETS and HAGIOGRAPHA associated with the week. The use of a scriptural verse at the beginning of the sermon has continued into the present era.

homosexuality

Sexual relationships between individuals of the same gender. This practice was condemned unequivocally in the Bible (Lev. 18:22), and this stand was continued by the sages. Homosexuality is viewed as debasing human life, as being contrary to the biblical command to be fruitful and multiply, as 'spilling the seed in vain' and as being threatening to the Jewish home. PROGRESSIVE JUDAISM has taken a more tolerant position, and there are even a few 'gay congregations' in the USA.

Hosea, Book of

Biblical book, one of the 12 books of the MINOR PROPHETS. Living in the eighth century BCE, Hosea exhorted the Israelite nation to concentrate on religious and moral reform rather than dabble in international affairs. He adopted a compassionate stance, using his own matrimonial difficulties as a symbol of God's love for his wayward people.

Hoshanah Rabbah

Seventh day of SUKKOT. According to rabbinic teaching, God's decrees are sealed on this day. It became a widespread practice to spend the night before Sukkot in prayer. In biblical times on this day seven circuits were made around the TEMPLE ALTAR. Now seven circuits are made around the BIMAH in the SYNAGOGUE. The TORAH SCROLLS and the branches of the *lulav*, myrtle and willow, as well as the ETROG, are carried in the procession. When the seventh circuit is completed the willow branches are beaten.

hoshanot

PRAYERS recited during the circuits (*hakkaphot*) of the SUKKOT FESTIVAL. They consist of brief lines, each of which opens and concludes with the response 'Hoshanah [O deliver]', spoken by the congregation. They address God by different epithets and ask for his deliverance. Originally these were prayers for rain recited on Sukkot. Some of the *hoshanot* were written by liturgical poets such as Eleazar KALLIR.

hospitality

Rabbinic sages gave advice on how to entertain guests, and in the middle ages *hakhnasat orehim* (hospitality) societies were established to look after Jewish travellers. (*See also* ENTERTAINING TRAVELLERS.)

host, desecration of

See DESECRATION OF THE HOST.

house of worship

See BET HA-MIDRASH; HIGH PLACES; SANCTUARY; SYNAGOGUE.

Hovevei Zion

See LOVERS OF ZION.

hukkat ha-goy
(Hebrew, 'custom of the gentile')

A custom forbidden because of its IDOLATROUS or heathen connotations. According to Lev. 20:23, Jews may not 'walk in the custom of the nation'. As a consequence, wearing particular kinds of clothing is forbidden as leading to lewdness, and the ORTHODOX have condemned the REFORM movement for its use of organs and mixed choirs on this basis.

Humanistic Judaism

Movement founded by Sherwin Wine in the 1960s in Detroit, Michigan, USA. Humanistic Judaism rejects the belief in a supernatural deity, and regards humanistic values in the Jewish tradition as of fundamental significance. The movement now consists of approximately 30,000 members, comprising organizations in the USA, Canada, Britain, France, Belgium, Israel, Australia, Argentina and Uruguay.

hummash

See PENTATEUCH.

huppah

See MARRIAGE CANOPY.

ibn Daud, Abraham (c.1110–80)

Spanish historian, philosopher, physician and astronomer. Born in CORDOVA, he settled in TOLEDO. His *Emunah Ramah* (*Sublime Faith*) is a philosophical study based on Aristotelian principles. In this work he discusses central problems related to GOD, the SOUL, PROPHECY, CREATION, and FREE WILL. His *Sefer ha-Kabbalah* (*Book of Tradition*) relates the history of TALMUDIC scholarship until his own day.

ibn Ezra, Abraham (1089–1164)

Spanish poet, grammarian, biblical commentator, philosopher, astronomer and physician. Born in TOLEDO, he settled in Spain and later journeyed to Italy, France, England and PALESTINE. He composed poetry, biblical commentaries, grammatical studies, philosophy and astrological texts.

ibn Shaprut, Ḥasdai (c.915–c.970)

Spanish statesman and physician. He served at the courts of the caliphs Abder Raḥman III and Ḥakam II at CORDOVA. He was employed on various missions. In addition to his political activity, he supported Jewish scholars and scholarship and defended Jewish communities. He composed a well-known letter to the king of the KHAZARS expressing his joy at their independent Jewish kingdom. His scholarly work included collaboration in translating the work of Dioscorides into Arabic.

ibn Tibbon, Jacob (c.1230–1312)

French astronomer, physician, writer and translator. Known as Don Profiat, he was born in Marseilles. He lived at Montpellier, where he taught medicine at the university. He translated Euclid, Averroes and Al Ghazzali from Arabic into HEBREW. In addition, he produced astronomical tables, which were translated into Latin and used by Dante for his *Divine Comedy*. He was a defender of MAIMONIDES.

iconography

Art of illustrated manuscripts. Because of the commandment against making graven images, there is little iconography from Jews living in Muslim countries. No doubt influenced by their Christian neighbours, manuscripts from Europe are often illustrated by biblical and AGGADIC scenes, and vary according to the community of origin. In particular, illustrations can be found in the HAGGADAH, MAḤZOR and Siddur manuscripts.

idolatry

Worship of idols. Idolatry is forbidden in the TORAH, and is grouped with wrath, murder and incest as sins that should not be committed even to save life. However, idol worship persisted in ancient Israel – the cults of BAAL and Asherah were condemned by the PROPHETS. The Bible gives instances of child sacrifice to Moloch (2 Kgs.), star worship (Amos 5:26), and sacred prostitution (Ezek. 16:17). The reforms of King HEZEKIAH and JOSIAH should be understood in this context. Rabbinic scholars forbade any contact with idolaters; food must not be shared with idol worshippers, and no houses in the land of ISRAEL may be leased or sold to an idolater.

ikkarim

See PRINCIPLES OF FAITH.

illegitimacy

According to Jewish LAW, the status of a child who is the offspring of any union prohibited in the Bible. Such an individual is designated a MAMZER: he or she may not marry an Israelite (or Jew), except one of the same status. However, such a person is allowed to marry a PROSELYTE. Children of *mamzerim* share the same prohibition with regard to marrying a true Israelite. These restrictions are still in force in ORTHODOX Jewish circles.

image of God

The notion that all human beings were created in God's image is based on Genesis 1:25 ('So God created man in his own image; in the image of God created he him; male and female created he them'). Jewish commentators differ as to the meaning of this verse; some, including the 12th-century Jewish philosopher Moses MAIMONIDES, argue that since God has no body, this text should not be understood literally.

imitation of God

The requirement to imitate God. According to GENESIS, humanity is made in the image of God, and DEUTERONOMY (10:12) teaches that human beings are commanded to 'walk in his ways'. Rabbinic scholars explain the meaning of this verse by emphasizing that human beings should imitate God by such activities as VISITING THE SICK and clothing the naked. MAIMONIDES lists the emulation of God in all his ways as one of the essential commandments.

immersion

The statement 'He shall bathe his flesh in water', (Lev. 15:16) is traditionally interpreted as referring to the total immersion of the body in a MIKVEH (ritual bath). In all cases the body must be scrupulously clean before immersion takes place. ORTHODOX practice stipulates that women of childbearing age should practise immersion after menstruating. Further, PROSELYTES should immerse themselves as a sign of adopting the Jewish faith. Among the pious, it is the custom to prepare for FESTIVALS by immersion, and some groups practise it daily before the MORNING PRAYER. Vessels that have become unclean also require cleansing through immersion, as do new or used vessels which have been purchased from a non-Jew.

immortality

The eternal existence of the soul after death. In Scripture the dead are described as living a shadow-like existence in Sheol. According to rabbinic sources, human beings are portrayed as having a body and a soul; these are parted at death but reunited when the resurrection of the dead takes place. After the Day of Judgement, the righteous will enter into heaven (Gan Eden), and the wicked will be punished everlastingly in hell (Gehenna). In modern times the traditional view of physical resurrection, reward and punishment has been largely replaced by belief in the immortality of the soul.

incense

Gum, spice or other substance which produces a sweet smell when burned. During the biblical period the burning of incense accompanied all SACRIFICES in the TEMPLE, except the SIN OFFERING of the poor and the meat offering of the leper. It was burned by the HIGH PRIEST in the HOLY OF HOLIES on the DAY OF ATONEMENT. Exodus specifies its ingredients (Exo. 30:34–8), which were later elaborated in the TALMUD.

incest

Sexual relationships between close kindred. LEV. 18:6–18 specifies prohibited sexual relationships between members of a family. The TALMUD added other sexual unions to those already defined as incestuous. The offspring of incestuous (as well as adulterous) relationships are classed as *mamzerim*. Incest, idolatry and murder are the three offences which must never be committed even to save life.

ingathering of the exiles

See EXILES, INGATHERING OF.

inheritance

According to the RABBIS, the order of legal heirs is: (1) sons and their descendants (with the first-born receiving a double portion); (2) daughters and their descendants; (3) the father; (4) brothers and their descendants; (5) sisters and their descendants; (6) father's fathers; (7) paternal uncles and their descendants; (8) paternal aunts and their descendants; (9) paternal great-grandfathers, etc.

initiation

See CIRCUMCISION; MIKVEH; PROSELYTE.

Inquisition

Ecclesiastical tribunal of the Catholic Church. It was dedicated to investigating and suppressing heretical views. Established in the 13th century under Innocent III, the Inquisition was initially concerned only incidentally with Jews, yet from 1478 in Spain it focused on the MARRANO community.

insanity

According to rabbinic tradition, an insane person is exempt from all religious obligations and punishments. His dealings have no legal authority, and he cannot marry. Any person who becomes insane after MARRIAGE cannot give his wife a bill of DIVORCE. However, a woman who becomes insane after marriage can be divorced (although the RABBIS forbade such an act on humanitarian grounds).

intermarriage

MARRIAGE between a Jew and a gentile. Since the time of EZRA, intermarriage has been condemned by the Jewish community as leading to APOSTASY and IDOLATRY. It was rare before the 19th century. However, with EMANCIPATION and equal access to university and the professions, it has become increasingly common. Although no ORTHODOX rabbi will officiate at an intermarriage, some PROGRESSIVE rabbis in the United States are prepared to participate in such marriages.

Irgun Tzevai Leumi

Jewish underground organization in PALESTINE. Known as the Irgun, it was founded in 1937 by members of the Betar and REVISIONISTS in the HAGANAH. Its purpose was to retaliate against Arab attacks on Jews. When the White Paper advocating joint Jewish–Arab rule in Palestine was published in 1939, the Irgun attacked the British. It was subsequently outlawed by the Mandatory government. The Jewish Agency dissociated itself from the activities of the organization. Its leader, David Raziel, was killed in 1941; he was succeeded by Menahem

BEGIN. In 1944 the Irgun renewed its anti-British activities; later it carried out attacks on Arab villages. When the State of ISRAEL was proclaimed, its members joined the Haganah.

Isaac (fl. ?16th century BCE)

Israelite, son of ABRAHAM and SARAH. According to Genesis, he was born when Abraham was 100 (Gen. 21:5). He was the heir of the Abrahamic tradition and COVENANT (Gen. 17:19; 21:12). In order to test Abraham, God commanded that he sacrifice his son Isaac, but the youth was saved at the final moment (Gen. 22). Isaac married REBEKAH, who bore two sons, ESAU and JACOB.

Isaiah, Ascension of

Early Christian APOCALYPTIC work. It contains the Jewish apocryphon, the Martyrdom of ISAIAH. In this text Isaiah's death is seen as foreshadowing the coming of Jesus, and the early history of the Church. The later part of the book portrays the scenes witnessed by Isaiah during his ascent to the seven heavens.

Isaiah, Book of

Biblical book, one of the books of the LATTER PROPHETS. The first part (chapters 1–39) contains an account of Isaiah's ministry; he prophesied in JERUSALEM from the death of UZZIAH until the middle of HEZEKIAH's reign (740–701 BCE). He protested against unrighteousness and demanded justice for the poor and oppressed. He opposed all treaties with neighbouring peoples and insisted that the Jewish nation should put their trust in God. He proclaimed that the Jewish people would be punished through Assyrian conquest, but that a remnant would return and continue the COVENANT. Most scholars believe that the Book of Isaiah should be divided into two sections, chapters 1–39 and chapters 40–66, which are believed to have been written by different authors, Isaiah and Deutero-Isaiah. Deutero-Isaiah was an unknown prophet writing during the time of the EXILE in Babylon. It is possible that more than one writer contributed to chapters 40–66.

Ishmael ben Elisha (fl. 2nd century)

PALESTINIAN TANNA. He lived at Kephar Aziz, south of HEBRON. He engaged in disputations with AKIVA about HALAKHIC and AGGADIC matters, and expanded to 13 the seven HERMENEUTICAL rules of HILLEL. He was one of the leading aggadists of his era. According to tradition, he was martyred during the persecutions that followed the BAR KOKHBA rebellion against Rome in the second century. Many mystical statements and literary works were ascribed to him.

Israel, Land of (Hebrew: *Eretz Israel*)

Land promised by God to ABRAHAM and his descendants. The area is specified in the PATRIARCHAL COVENANT (Gen. 15:18–19). Other boundaries are described in Numbers 34:2–12 and other biblical books as well as talmudic sources. It is viewed as a divine gift to the Jewish people. Love of the land is expressed in Scripture, the TALMUD, the liturgy, religious thought and Jewish LAW. See map on p. 17).

Israel, State of

From the beginning of the Second World War, the establishment of a Jewish homeland was the primary aim of the ZIONISTS. Although the BALFOUR DECLARATION of 1917 supported the creation of a Jewish homeland in PALESTINE, the White Paper of 1939 effectively rejected this proposal. After the end of the war, the United Nations discussed the Palestinian problem. A plan to partition Palestine into an area for Arabs

(Jordan) and one for Jews (Israel) was endorsed by the General Assembly of the United Nations on 29 November 1946. On 14 May 1948 in TEL AVIV, David BEN-GURION read out the Israeli Scroll of Independence. In the years that followed Israel was constantly at war with its Arab neighbours, which did not recognize the legitimacy of the state. See map on p. 17.

Israel ben Eliezer (1700–60)

Polish spiritual leader, founder of ḤASIDISM. Known as the Baal Shem Tov, or Besht, he was born in Podolia and lived in the Carpathian mountains. He was a healer and spiritual leader; he travelled about curing the sick and expelling demons and evil spirits. In the course of his journeys his influence grew. PRAYER rather than study was the foundation of his approach to God. He attracted a wide circle of followers, and remains the inspiration for Ḥasidim to the present day. His teachings were based on the KABBALAH, and stressed the importance of individual salvation. He emphasized the importance of joy in prayer and worship and discouraged melancholy and FASTS. In addition, he advocated study of the TORAH and used GEMATRIA as a tool. He was also the originator of the doctrine of the ZADDIK.

Israel Independence Day
(Hebrew: *Yom Haatzmaut*)

Festival commemorating ISRAEL'S declaration of independence. It takes place on Iyyar 5.

isser ve-hetter

Legal rulings about forbidden food. During the middle ages, many books were composed dealing with the laws and customs of forbidden food. (*See also* DIETARY LAWS.)

Isserles, Moses (*c.*1530–72)

HALAKHIST. One of the great legal authorities of his day, he was known as the 'MAIMONIDES of Polish Jewry'. His supplement to the SHULḤAN ARUKH of Joseph CARO was made so that this code would be acceptable to ASHKENAZI Jewry.

J

Jabneh

Ancient city located on the coastal plain to the south of Jaffa. Jabneh was fortified by Uzziah as a barrier against the Philistines (2 Chr. 26:6). During the Second Temple period it was Hellenized; by the time of the accession of Alexander Yannai (103 BCE), it was a Hasmonean city. Pompey sought to revive the city as a gentile town in 63 BCE, and it became the seat of an imperial procurator. In the first Jewish war, it was occupied by Vespasian. However, after the fall of Jerusalem in 70 CE, the Sanhedrin was reconstituted at Jabneh under Johanan ben Zakkai. The city prospered as the centre of Jewish life in Palestine until the time of the Bar Kokhba revolt.

Jabotinsky, Vladimir
(1880–1940)

Russian Zionist leader, soldier and writer. Born in Odessa, he worked as a foreign correspondent in Berne and Rome. After returning to Odessa, he established a Jewish self-defence group there. During the First World War he advocated the recruitment of Jewish regiments to fight on the Palestinian front. After the war, he supported the maintainance of a Jewish legion in Palestine to defend Jews from Arab attack. In 1920 he organized a Jewish self-defence unit in Jerusalem, for which he was arrested, tried and punished by the British. In 1925

he established the World Union of Zionist Revisionists, and from 1936 he urged the evacuation of East European Jews to Palestine. He was the spiritual father and head of the Jewish underground movement Irgun Tzevai Leumi, created in 1936. Besides his political activities, he was a translator, writer and poet.

Jacob (fl. ?16th century BCE)

Israelite, son of Isaac and Rebekah. He bought the birthright of his brother Esau for food. Later he succeeded in securing the blessing Isaac intended to give to Esau. Fearing his brother's wrath, Jacob left home and travelled to Haran, where he married Leah and then Rachel, the daughters of his uncle Laban. By them and their handmaids, Bilhah and Zilpah, he had 12 sons and a daughter. After many years he went back to Canaan; during the journey he wrestled with an angel at a ford on the River Jabbok. As an old man, he was reunited with his youngest son Joseph, who had been sold into slavery by his brothers and had become Pharaoh's chief minister in Egypt (Gen. 25–50).

Jacob ben Asher (c.1270–c.1343)

Spanish codifier, son of Asher ben Jehiel. Known as Baal ha-Turim, he was born in Germany and settled in Spain in 1303. He lived first in Barcelona, subsequently in Toledo. His code, Arbaah Turim, contains decisions found in both

TALMUDS, and those of the geonim (*see* GAON), as well as those given in earlier commentaries and codes. The work is divided into four parts: Oraḥ Ḥayyim deals with daily conduct, including PRAYERS, SABBATHS and holidays; Yoreh Deah lays down DIETARY LAWS; Even ha-Ezer covers personal and family matters; and Ḥoshen Mishpat describes civil law and administration.

Jacob Joseph of Polonnoye
(d. 1782)

Ukrainian ḤASIDIC scholar. He served as RABBI at Shargorod, later becoming a follower of the Baal Shem Tov (ISRAEL BEN ELIEZER). He subsequently was a rabbi at Rashkov, Nemirov and Polonnoye. His *Toledot Yaakov Yoseph* is an important source for the teachings of the Baal Shem Tov.

Jacobson, Israel (1768–1828)

German REFORM leader. Born in Halberstadt, he became president of the Jewish consistory in Westphalia, where he worked for the reform of Jewish education and the SYNAGOGUE liturgy. In 1801 he established the Jacobson School for Jewish and Christian pupils in Seesen, Braunschweig. In 1810 he created a Reform synagogue in Seesen. Later he settled in BERLIN, where he held Reform services in his home.

Jashar, Book of

Ancient work, one of the lost books mentioned in Scripture (Josh. 10–13; 2 Sam. 1:18; 1 Kgs. 8:53). It contains poems about individuals and events dating from the time of JOSHUA to the beginning of the monarchy (1250–1000 BCE). A medieval composition of biblical legends, based on MIDRASHIM to the PENTATEUCH, was known by the same title.

Jehu (fl. 9th century BCE)

King of Israel (*c.*842–814 BCE). He was commander-in-chief to Jehoram.

Nonetheless, he conspired with the army against the king. With the help of ELISHA, he eliminated the royal family including Jehoram, Ahaziah of Judah and JEZEBEL, as well as the priests of BAAL. He fought unsuccessfully against Aram and paid tribute to Shalmaneser III of Assyria for protection from the Arameans. His dynasty continued for 100 years (2 Kgs. 9–11).

Jeremiah, Book of:

Biblical book, one of the books of the LATTER PROPHETS. It contains 32 chapters. Chapters 1–18 contain prophecies from the time of JOSIAH; chapters 19–36 record prophecies and narrative from the reigns of Jehoiakim, Jehoiachin and Zedekiah; chapters 37–44 consist of prophecies concerning other nations; and chapter 52 recapitulates the Books of KINGS. When Jeremiah first emerged as a PROPHET he rebuked the nation for IDOLATRY. After the religious revivial during the reign of Josiah, he warned the people to keep the newly made COVENANT with God. When NEBUCHADNEZZAR became king in BABYLONIA, Jeremiah prophesied that he would conquer JUDAH. Subsequently he foretold the defeat of Zedekiah and his anti-Babylonian alliance, and advocated surrender. After the fall of JERUSALEM, he went to EGYPT, where he condemned Egyptian Jews for idol-worship.

Jeremy, Epistle of

PSEUDEPIGRAPHIC book, supposed to be a letter from JEREMIAH to the BABYLONIAN exiles. In the Latin Vulgate, it is placed in the APOCRYPHA attached to the Book of BARUCH.

Jericho

Ancient city in the southern Jordan valley, 15 miles north-east of JERUSALEM. A royal city (Deut. 32:49), it was destroyed by JOSHUA (Josh. 6). Left desolate, it was revived during the reign of AHAB by Hiel the Bethelite (1 Kgs. 16:34).

Jeroboam (fl. 10th century BCE)

King of Israel from *c*.928 to 907 BCE. During the reign of SOLOMON, he was superintendent of forced labour; during this time he led a revolt against the monarchy. After Solomon's death, he led a group representing the northern tribes to meet REHOBOAM at SHECHEM. The delegation demanded changes in the system of labour; when its request was turned down, the northern tribes rebelled and appointed Jeroboam king. He first made his capital at Shechem; it was later moved to Penuel. He established new shrines at BETHEL and Dan, centred on the worship of golden calves (1 Kgs. 11–15; 2 Chr. 10, 13).

Jerusalem

Capital of ISRAEL. During the time of JOSHUA, Adonizedek, King of Israel, was defeated by the Israelites at Aijalon (Josh. 10). Yet his city remained an independent enclave between the tribal areas of Benjamin and JUDAH. It was subsequently captured by DAVID and became the capital of a united Israel (2 Sam. 5:6–8; 1 Chr. 11:4–6). By transferring the ARK OF THE COVENANT there, David made it the religious centre of Israel. SOLOMON enlarged the city by adding a palace and the TEMPLE. After his death, Jerusalem remained the capital of Judah until it was destroyed by the Babylonians in the 6th century BCE. Later, Jewish exiles returned and rebuilt the Temple. The Temple and the city were devastated by the Romans in the first century CE. In modern times Jerusalem became the capital of the State of Israel.

Jesus (fl. first century CE)

Palestinian religious leader, founder of Christianity. According to the New Testament, he grew up in GALILEE and was baptized by John the Baptist. He performed various miracles and declared the coming of the Kingdom of God. He was arrested and crucified by

Jerusalem: This photograph shows the Wailing Wall, the remains of the second Temple, with the dome of the Mosque of Omar behind. This mosque marks the traditional site of Abraham's intended sacrifice of his son.

order of Pontius Pilate. His followers believed that he rose from the dead and ascended to heaven. They formed the core of the early Church and actively spread the good news about Jesus whom they regarded as the MESSIAH. According to Christian belief, Jesus was God Incarnate and is restored to the Godhead in the form of the Trinity.

Jew

Member of the Jewish community. The word is derived from the Latin *Judaeus*, which itself is from the Hebrew *Yehudah*, meaning Judah. Traditionally

Jewish identity is dependent on maternal descent or CONVERSION to Judaism. Recently the REFORM movement has also accepted patrilineal descent as a basis for Jewish identity. The term is also employed to denote ethnic origin without reference to religious observance.

Jewish War

Rebellion against Roman rule in the first century BCE. The Jewish War was led by the ZEALOTS and is described in detail by JOSEPHUS. It led to the siege of JERUSALEM, and the almost complete destruction of the TEMPLE in 70 CE. The centre of Jewish life then moved to JABNEH under JOHANAN BEN ZAKKAI, but the ancient institutions of PRIESTHOOD, SACRIFICE and Temple observance were lost. The war ended with the capture of MASADA. The Roman triumph is portrayed on the triumphal arch of Titus in Rome.

Jezebel (fl. 9th century CE)

Israelite woman of Sidonite origin. She was the wife of AHAB and daughter of Ethbaal, King of Sidon. She attempted to introduce her native cult of BAAL worship, thereby exciting the anger of ELIJAH. In 1 and 2 Kings she is depicted as a callous person who unjustly brought about the death of Naboth and persecuted the PROPHETS (1 Kgs. 16–2 Kgs. 9). She was killed in JEHU's revolt against the monarchy.

Job, Book of

Biblical book, part of the HAGIOGRAPHA. It recounts the story of Job, a righteous man, who challenged God's justice in allowing him to suffer. Job's friends argued that his suffering was a punishment for wickedness, but Job refused to accept this explanation. Eventually God spoke from a whirlwind and emphasized Job's finite knowledge compared with his own designs for the universe.

Joel, Book of

Biblical book, one of the 12 MINOR PROPHETS. It depicts a plague of locusts (chapters 1–2) and describes the DAY OF THE LORD, when God will rescue the Jewish people from captivity and punish their enemies in the Valley of Jehoshaphat (chapters 3–4).

Johanan ben Zakkai
(fl. first century CE)

Palestinian TANNA. He was the leading scholar at the end of the Second TEMPLE period and during the years following the destruction of the Temple. During the Jewish revolt against Rome (66–77), he was one of the peace party in JERUSALEM. According to tradition, he was carried out of the city in a coffin. When he confronted Vespasian, he predicted his accession to the imperial throne; as a reward, he was allowed to continue his teaching. He founded an academy at JABNEH, which became the seat of the SANHEDRIN after the destruction of Jerusalem.

John Hyrcanus
(fl. second century BCE)

HIGH PRIEST and ethnarch (135–104 BCE), son of Simon the HASMONEAN. After the murder of his father and brothers by Ptolemy, he fled to JERUSALEM. In 135–134 BCE Antiochus Sidetes captured Jerusalem, and John Hyrcanus became High Priest. Later he threw off Syrian domination, attacked the SAMARITANS, destroying their temple on MOUNT GERIZIM, and compelled the Idumeans to convert to Judaism. Although initially he was an ally of the PHARISEES, he subsequently drew closer to the SADDUCEES.

Jonah, Book of

Biblical book, one of the 12 MINOR PROPHETS. It recounts God's command to Jonah, son of Amittai, to go to NINEVEH and pronounce judgement upon its inhabitants for their wickedness. On a sea voyage Jonah was swallowed by a great fish. He was eventually spewed out on dry land. He then travelled to Nineveh, and prophesied against its inhabitants. As a result, the population repented of their evil ways.

Joseph (fl. ?16th century BCE)

Israelite, son of JACOB and first-born of RACHEL. He was his father's favourite son; as a result he aroused the wrath of his brothers, who sold him into slavery in EGYPT. He was bought by Potiphar as a slave. Later he was imprisoned on a false charge made by Potiphar's wife. After interpreting Pharaoh's dreams, he was appointed to high office in Egypt. Eventually he was reconciled with his brothers, and reunited with his father. His family then settled in the Goshen region (Gen. 37–50).

Josephus, Flavius
(c.38–after 100 CE)

PALESTINIAN historian and soldier. Born in JERUSALEM, he went to Rome in 64 on a mission to secure the release of several priests. At the outset of the JEWISH WAR against Rome in 66, he was appointed commander of GALILEE. When the Romans attacked the province in 67, he directed the resistance. He surrendered to the Romans after Jotapata was captured, and accompanied Vespasian and Titus during the siege of Jerusalem. After the Roman victory, he lived in Rome. His works include *The Jewish War*, *The Antiquities of the Jews*, *Against Apion* and *An Autobiography*.

Joshua, Book of

Biblical book, one of the FORMER PROPHETS. It depicts Joshua's conquests and the division of the land of CANAAN among the 12 tribes. As MOSES' successor, Joshua was assigned the task of leading the Jewish people in the conquest of Canaan. He commanded the Israelites in the war with the Amalekites (Exod.

17:14–16). Subsequently he was one of the 12 spies sent to reconnoitre the land of Canaan. After the Israelites crossed the river Jordan, he led them to victory over the alliance of southern and northern kings. He brought the TABERNACLE to SHILOH and divided the territory among the 12 tribes.

Josiah (fl. seventh century BCE)

King of JUDAH (640–609 BCE), son of Amnon. He became king while still a child after his father was assassinated. His reign was marked by a great religious revival. He removed foreign cults and re-established MONOTHEISM. During the restoration of the TEMPLE, the HIGH PRIEST announced the discovery of a Book of the Law. This persuaded Josiah to convene an assembly of the people, during which he made a COVENANT with God. He also discontinued worship in the HIGH PLACES and centralized the cult in the Jerusalem Temple.

Josippon

Hebrew historical narrative. It describes the period of the Second TEMPLE. Composed in southern Italy in the 10th century, it was ascribed to Joseph ben Gorion. It is based on JOSEPHUS' writings.

Jubilee

Seventh SABBATICAL YEAR. Lev. 25 decrees that every seventh year should be a sabbatical year, when no agricultural work should be done, and all debts should be forgiven. Every seventh sabbatical year is a jubilee year, when slaves are freed, and land bought since the previous jubilee should be returned. Laws concerning the jubilee year are contained in the TALMUDIC tractate Sheviit and only ever applied to the land of ISRAEL.

Jubilees, Book of

PSEUDEPIGRAPHIC work. Composed during the middle of the Second TEMPLE period, it contains the secret revelations of the ANGEL of the Divine Presence to MOSES on his second ascent to MOUNT SINAI. According to some scholars, it originated in an early ESSENE group.

Judah (fl. ?16th century BCE)

Israelite, fourth son of JACOB and LEAH. When the sons of Jacob turned against JOSEPH, Judah persuaded them to sell Joseph to travelling Ishmaelites rather than let him die in a pit (Gen. 37). Judah later received Jacob's blessing (Gen. 49:8). DAVID was a member of the tribe of Judah. When the Israelite kingdom split after the death of SOLOMON, the tribe of Judah supported REHOBOAM and became predominant in the south.

Judah, Kingdom of

The southern of the two kingdoms into which the HOLY LAND was divided after JEROBOAM's revolt against REHOBOAM in 930 BCE. The monarchy passed peacefully from father to son in the Davidic house, except during the usurpation of Athaliah in the ninth century BCE. In the eighth century BCE the reigns of HEZEKIAH and JOSIAH were marked by religious revival. In 586 BCE the Kingdom of Judah was conquered by the BABYLONIANS. Later in the century a number of Babylonian exiles returned to Judah to rebuild the TEMPLE.

Judah Halevi (before 1075–1141)

Spanish Hebrew poet and philosopher. Born in TOLEDO, he dwelt in various towns in Christian and Muslim Spain, where he was a physician. Subsequently he left for PALESTINE. He composed about 800 poems, including eulogies and laments, dealing with such topics as love, Jewish FESTIVALS, personal religious experience and longing for ZION. His *Kuzari* is a philosophical work depicting a disputation before the King of the Khazars by a RABBI, a Christian, a Muslim and an Aristotelian philosopher.

Judah Ha-Nasi
(fl. *c.* second or third century)

PALESTINIAN leader, son of Simeon ben Gamaliel. He lived in GALILEE, first at Bet Shearim and then at SEPPHORIS. Known as 'Rabbenu ha-Kadosh' (our holy teacher), he is referred to in rabbinic sources as 'Rabbi'. He was the political and religious head of the Jewish community in PALESTINE. He was responsible for the redaction of the MISHNAH.

Judah Maccabee
(fl. second century BCE)

PALESTINIAN military leader, son of Matthias the HASMONEAN. He succeeded his father as the leader of the rebellion against ANTIOCHUS IV EPIPHANES. After occupying JERUSALEM in 164 BCE, he purified the TEMPLE and assisted Jewish communities in Transjordan and GALILEE. Later he was killed in battle at Elasa. (*See also* ḤANUKKAH.)

Judaism

The Jewish religion originated with God's call to ABRAHAM (Gen. 22). The Jewish faith has undergone numerous developments. Throughout its history various groups including the SADDUCEES, PHARISEES, KARAITES, ḤASIDIM, CONSERVATIVE Jews and REFORM Jews have claimed that their beliefs and practices are authentically Jewish. During the middle ages MAIMONIDES formulated THIRTEEN PRINCIPLES of the Jewish faith, which are widely acknowledged as the central tenets of Judaism. In modern times the Jewish community is fragmented along religious lines. Groups ranging from the ultra-ORTHODOX to the most liberal all claim to represent valid manifestations of Judaism.

Judea

Latin form of the name JUDAH. It was the name of the vassal kingdom in PALESTINE which came under Roman rule in 63

BCE. The kingdom was renamed Palestina in 135. The name Judea is also applied to the southern part of Palestine.

judge

Before the settlement in CANAAN, Israelite ELDERS acted as judges. Subsequently leaders, PRIESTS and PROPHETS took on this role. The prophet SAMUEL administered justice (1 Sam. 7:15–17). However, after the creation of the monarchy this role passed to the king (2 Sam. 12:1–16; 15:2). According to the First Book of CHRONICLES, David appointed 6,000 LEVITES as officers and judges (1 Chr. 23:4). Jehoshaphat's court in JERUSALEM consisted of judges selected from among the priests, Levites and heads of houses (2 Chr. 19:8–11). During the Second TEMPLE period the GREAT SANHEDRIN in Jerusalem consisted of 71 judges. In addition, lesser Sanhedrins of 23 judges met in towns. Courts of three judges also settled civil disputes. During the middle ages and later, tribunals of RABBIS sat as judges in religious cases.

judgement (Hebrew: *din*)

Legal decision. The term is normally used in the context of a lawsuit or legal dispute.

judgement of the law
(Hebrew: *din Torah*)

Legal hearing. It is conducted in accordance with the provisions of Jewish LAW.

Judges, Book of

Biblical book, one of the books of the FORMER PROPHETS. It depicts the period of the JUDGES from the death of JOSHUA until before the time of Eli and SAMUEL. Chapters 1–3:6 consist of an introduction; chapters 3:7–16:31 recount stories about the judges (particularly Othniel, Ehud, DEBORAH, GIDEON, Jephthah and SAMSON); and chapters 17–21 relate the incident of the statue stolen by the Danites, and the story of the concubine of Gibeah.

Judith, Book of

APOCRYPHAL book. It recounts the story of Judith, a Simeonite woman, living in Bethulia in northern SAMARIA. During the siege of the city by the Assyrian forces, she succeeded in beheading their general, Holophernes. As a consequence, the besieging army took flight.

justice

According to Scripture, justice is a fundamental principle. As Deuteronomy declares: 'Justice, justice shall you pursue (Deut. 16:20). In rabbinic sources, the divine name Elohim denotes the attribute of justice.

justification

The Jewish faith teaches that righteousness is the only way to attain justification in the eyes of God. Hence the prophet MICAH declared: 'What does the Lord require of you, but to do justice and to love mercy and to walk humbly with thy God.' Because it was understood that human beings are incapable of perfect righteousness, SACRIFICE was instituted as a means of ATONEMENT. Once the sacrificial system disappeared with the destruction of the Second TEMPLE, PRAYER and FASTING served as the means by which the divine–human relationship could be restored.

K

kabbalah

Mystical teachings. *Kabbalah* refers to Jewish esoteric teachings which have evolved since the period of the Second TEMPLE. Traditionally it was believed to have been revealed in its full perfection either to the first man, ADAM, or as a secret part of the ORAL LAW to MOSES on MOUNT SINAI. The goal of *kabbalah* was to uncover the hidden life of God and the secrets of his relationship with his creation. Characteristic kabbalistic doctrines include the transmigration of souls, cosmic repair (TIKKUN), the *sefirot* (DIVINE EMANATIONS) and the activities of supernatural powers. These ideas were later absorbed into folk belief and popular customs. (*See also* ADAM KADMON; BAHIR, BOOK OF; CHARIOT MYSTICISM; DEVEKUT; EN SOF; GEMATRIA; ḤASIDISM; LURIA, ISAAC; METATRON; SEFER YETZIRAH; SHABBETAIANS; ZADDIK; ZIMZUM; ZOHAR.)

kabbalat Shabbat

See RECEPTION OF THE SABBATH.

kabronim (Hebrew, 'buriers')

Community gravediggers.

kaddish (Aramaic, 'holy')

Doxology in ARAMAIC recited to conclude the sections of the liturgical services. There are four forms: (1) the complete *kaddish*, which is said at the end of the AMIDAH, except in the MORNING SERVICE; (2) the half *kaddish*, which connects the sections of the service; (3) the scholars' *kaddish* (*kaddish de-rabbanan*), which is said by MOURNERS after study; and (4) the mourner's *kaddish* recited by mourners at the end of the SYNAGOGUE service. All four forms of the *kaddish* are recited standing, facing JERUSALEM. In some communities the entire congregation stands; in others, only the MOURNERS. The prayer consists of praise and glorification of God, and expresses the hope for the creation of God's kingdom on earth. The mourners' *kaddish* is said every day for eleven months after the death of a parent, spouse, child or sibling, and subsequently on each anniversary after death. (*See also* YAHRZEIT.)

Kairouan

Town in North Africa. Jews settled there after it was founded in the seventh century. It later served as the leading Jewish intellectual centre in the West. After the rise of the Almohades in the 12th century, the Jewish community in Kairouan went into decline.

kal va-ḥomer (Hebrew, 'light and heavy')

The first principle of rabbinic HERMENEUTICS in the systems of HILLEL and ISHMAEL BEN ELISHA. It consists of an *a fortiori* argument.

Kalischer, Zevi Hirsch
(1795–1874)

German RABBI and ZIONIST pioneer. Born in Lissa, in the Posen district, he settled in Thorn in 1824. As an opponent of REFORM JUDAISM, he advocated Jewish settlement in PALESTINE, and in his *Derishat Zion* pressed for the establishment of a Jewish agricultural society there. In 1864 he became responsible for the creation in BERLIN of the Central Committee for Palestine Colonization. He argued that Jewish redemption will come about through human efforts before the advent of the MESSIAH. His publications deal with rabbinic subjects and Zionism.

kallah

During the TALMUDIC and GAONIC periods, the KALLAH was a course of study which took place at the BABYLONIAN ACADEMIES of SURA and PUMBEDITA during the months of Elul and Adar. During each *kallah* month a specific TRACTATE of the Talmud was studied.

Kallir, Eleazar (fl. seventh century)

Hebrew poet. He lived in TIBERIAS and was the greatest and most prolific of the composers of PIYYUTIM. He wrote *piyyutim* for all the FESTIVALS, special SABBATHS, weekdays of festive character and FASTS.

Kanah, Book of

KABBALISTIC text dealing with the commandments. It was composed in Spain during the 14th century. It consists of a commentary on the commandments, containing the author's own mystical interpretation.

Kaplan, Mordecai (1881–1983)

American RABBI and founder of RECONSTRUCTIONIST JUDAISM. Born in Lithuania, he moved to the USA and became a rabbi in New York. In 1909 he was appointed dean of the Teacher's Institute of the Jewish Theological Seminary of America. Subsequently he developed a concept of Judaism known as Reconstructionist Judaism, and in 1922 the Society for the Advancement of Judaism was established. He also founded the Jewish Reconstructionist Foundation which published *The Reconstructionist* magazine. His writings include *Judaism as a Civilization*.

kapparah (Hebrew, 'atonement')

The custom of transferring the sins of a person symbolically to a bird. In a ceremony which takes place on the eve of the DAY OF ATONEMENT, a fowl is swung over the head of a person, who prays that its death will serve as a substitute and bear his sins. The following prayer is recited during the ceremony: 'This is my substitute, my vicarious offering, my atonement; this cock [or hen] shall meet death, but I shall find a long and pleasant life of peace.'

Karaites

Jewish sect established at the beginning of the eighth century. It was active in and around Persia. The Karaites rejected the rabbinic tradition. The most ancient Karaite text is the *Sefer ha-Mitzvot* of ANAN BEN DAVID, the founder of the movement. In this work he interpreted the Bible literally and sought to produce a code of life without reference to the ORAL LAW. During the following centuries Karaite groups existed in Persia, BABYLONIA, PALESTINE, EGYPT, and elsewhere. Karaite scholars wrote polemical works, grammars, Bible commentaries and codes. From the 12th century the movement went into decline.

karet (Hebrew, 'extirpation')

Divine punishment. The MISHNAH lists 36 offences which merit *karet*.

kashrut

See DIETARY LAWS.

kavod

See GLORY.

kavvanah

See DEVOTION.

kedushah

See HOLINESS.

kehillah

Congregation: the term may apply to the Jewish community or to the congregation in a synagogue.

kelal Israel

(Hebrew, 'community of Israel')

The interrelatedness of all Jews. Traditionally it was taught that all Jews were present at Mount Sinai. Today, the notion of *kelal Israel* is invoked to encourage ORTHODOX, PROGRESSIVE and secular Jews to work together on communal projects.

keneset Israel

(Hebrew, 'congregation of Israel')

In rabbinic sources the phrase refers to the entire Jewish community. In modern times it was used as a title by the Jewish community in PALESTINE when it was organized as a corporate entity in 1927. When the provisional council of the State of ISRAEL was convened in 1948, the Keneset Israel was abandoned and its powers transferred to the state.

keriah

See RENDING OF THE GARMENTS.

kerovah

Several types of PIYYUTIM which form part of the AMIDAH prayer. There were composed for SABBATHS, FESTIVALS, PURIM and FAST days. During the Sabbath and festivals they generally extend over the first three blessings. At times they extend over all the EIGHTEEN BENEDICTIONS.

keter malkut

(Hebrew, 'crown of royalty')

Mark of the sovereignty of God, recognized by ANGELS and men in worshipping him. It was the name given by Solomon ibn GABIROL to his poem in praise of God. It is recited after the EVENING SERVICE on the DAY OF ATONEMENT.

keter torah

(Hebrew, 'crown of law')

Symbol of learning in the form of a crown. The cover of the SCROLLS OF THE LAW is often embellished with a silver crown.

ketubbah

See MARRIAGE CONTRACT.

Ketuvim   (Hebrew, 'Writings')

HAGIOGRAPHA. The Ketuvim consists of the third section of the Hebrew Scriptures. It contains the books of PSALMS, PROVERBS, JOB, the SONG OF SONGS, RUTH, LAMENTATIONS, ECCLESIASTES, ESTHER, DANIEL, EZRA, NEHEMIAH, and 1 and 2 CHRONICLES.

Khazars

Turkish or Finnish tribe in the lower Volga region. From the eighth to the 10th century the Khazar state extended westward as far as Kiev. During the eighth century a Judaizing movement manifested itself among the people. Led by the king, Bulan, thousands of nobles converted to the Jewish faith. The central theme of the *Kuzari* (*Khazari*) by JUDAH HALEVI is the legendary disputation which brought about this conversion. Ḥasdai ibn Shaprut argued that the Khazars were one of the TEN LOST TRIBES of Israel. According to tradition, he entered into correspondence with their king, Joseph, in the 10th century.

kibbutz   (Hebrew, 'gathering in')

Collective village in ISRAEL. It originated during the Third ALIYAH from 1918 to

Pepper picking on the Quetara kibbutz, Israel.

1921. At this time the *kevutzah* (cooperative agricultural group) was broadened to incorporate industry, wage labour and the removal of restrictions on the size of the group. Inspired by social ideas, the kibbutz movement played a prominent role in the economic, political and cultural activities of the country. In addition, it contributed significantly to Israeli national security.

kiddush (Hebrew, 'sanctification')

Prayer recited over a cup of wine in the home or SYNAGOGUE to consecrate the SABBATH or a FESTIVAL.

kiddush ha-Shem (Hebrew, 'sanctification of the Divine Name')

The term originally referred to acts of MARTYRDOM. Subsequently it was applied to other acts of righteousness that reflect well on Jews and Judaism in the eyes of gentiles. When a Jew suffers death rather than violate the commandments, he achieves *kiddush ha-Shem*. If he fails to do this, he is guilty of *hillul ha-Shem* (PROFANATION OF THE DIVINE NAME).

kidnapping

Scripture views kidnapping as a capital offence (Exod. 21:16; Deut. 24:7). According to the TALMUD, the eighth commandment of the Decalogue (TEN COMMANDMENTS) refers to kidnapping rather than stealing. To be liable to capital punishment, four conditions must be met: the kidnapper must have taken the captive person into his possession or domain; he must have sold him as a slave; he must have sold him to a stranger; and he must have treated his victim as a slave before selling him. Each condition must have been attested to by at least two witnesses.

kike

An offensive term for a Jew.

Kimhi, David (?1160–1235)

French grammarian and exegete. Known as Redak, he was a teacher in Narbonne, Provence where he was active in public life. During the MAIMONIDEAN CONTROVERSY in 1232, he went on a journey to TOLEDO to gain the support of

Judah ibn Alfakhar for the adherents of MAIMONIDES. His *Mikhol* consists of a HEBREW grammar and biblical dictionary. He also composed biblical commentaries, which combine Spanish speculative, philological and philosophical traditons with the MIDRASHIC method of exegesis and the interpretations of RASHI.

kinah
See POEM OF MOURNING.

kindling of lights
See CANDLES.

kingdom of heaven
ESCHATOLOGICAL concept. It concerns the future perfection of the world. After divine judgement, the sinful order of the world will end and God will create a new HEAVEN and a new earth, in which all creatures will be at peace (Dan. 7:13–14). Eventually this notion was linked to the concept of the messianic redemption. (*See also* MESSIAH.)

Kings, Books of
Name of two biblical books which form part of the FORMER PROPHETS. They relate the history of ISRAEL and JUDAH from the death of DAVID until the liberation of Jehoiachin during the BABYLONIAN captivity.

kingship
The Israelite monarchy replaced the tribal chiefs of the earlier period. From the 11th to the 10th century BCE, kings ruled over the entire nation. In 931 BCE the nation divided into two kingdoms (JUDAH and Israel), with their own dynasties. When these kingdoms were destroyed (Israel in 722 BCE and Judah in 586 BCE), Israelite kingship came to an end. Under the HASMONEANS (second–first century BCE), the monarchy was restored, but Jewish movements of the first and second century CE produced claimants to MESSIANIC kingship. The

positions, rights and limitations of the king are described in the MISHNAH (Sanhedrin 2:2–5) as well as in Maimonides' MISHNEH TORAH.

kipah
See YARMULKE.

kittel
See GOWN.

Knesset (Hebrew, 'Assembly')
Parliament of ISRAEL. It conists of a single chamber of 120 members, who are elected by proportional representation for a four-year term. It is the supreme authority in the state. Established in 1949, the Knesset first met in TEL AVIV, but was later transferred to JERUSALEM.

Kohelet
See ECCLESIASTES.

Kohler, Kaufmann (1843–1926)
American Reform RABBI. Born in Fürth in Bavaria, he emigrated to the USA in 1869. He served as rabbi in Detroit, Chicago and New York. He was a leading figure at the Pittsburgh Conference of Reform Rabbis in 1885, at which the Pittsburgh Platform (a statement of the principles of REFORM JUDAISM) was adopted. In 1903 he became president of the Hebrew Union College. His writings include *Jewish Theology*.

Kol Bo (Hebrew, 'Compendium')
Anonymous medieval Jewish legal codification. It contains 148 sections dealing with such subjects as BLESSINGS, PRAYER, the SYNAGOGUE, the meal, the SABBATH, FESTIVALS, MARRIAGE, money, VOWS, OATHS, laws relevant to the land of ISRAEL, forbidden foods, the REDEMPTION OF THE FIRST-BORN son, VISITING THE SICK and MOURNING.

kol nidrei (Hebrew, 'all vows')
Opening words of the formula for the cancellation of vows; it is recited on Yom Kippur eve. The custom of annulling

personal vows and oaths made unwittingly or rashly during the year originated in the early GAONIC period. This practice gave rise to the charge among non-Jews that a Jewish oath was not to be trusted. In the 13th century Jacob TAM changed the formula to refer to vows of this type that might be made in the forthcoming year.

kollel

Advanced YESHIVAH.

Kook, Abraham Isaac
(1865–1935)

Palestinian rabbinic scholar of Latvian origin. Born in Greiva, Latvia, he was RABBI of Zaumel and Bauska before emigrating to PALESTINE in 1904. He served as CHIEF RABBI of the ASHKENAZI community. In his view the return to Palestine marked the begining of divine redemption. His writings include *Orot* (on holiness in the new-born nationalism), *Orot ha-Teshuvah* (on repentance), and *Halakhah Berurah* (on halakhic matters).

korban

Sacrificing all property to God. This custom is mentioned in the New Testament as a means of escaping the duty of supporting parents. It disappeared with the destruction of the TEMPLE in Jerusalem in 70 CE.

kosher (Hebrew, 'ritually fit')

Term applied to food which it is permissible to eat. The laws enumerated in the Bible were developed in the oral traditon and by rabbinic legislation. In the TALMUD the TRACTATE Hullin deals with the DIETARY LAWS, as does the section Yoreh Deah in the SHULHAN ARUKH. Only food which is ritually prepared in accordance with Jewish LAW may be consumed. Food which is *terefah* (unfit) is forbidden. The laws of *kashrut* deal with animals that are fit for consumption, methods of slaughter, the preparation of meat, the eating of milk and meat products together, vegetable foodstuffs, PASSOVER regulations and so forth.

Kotsk, Menahem Mendel of
(1787–1859)

HASIDIC master. Initially he was a follower of Simhah Buneh of Przysucha. On the latter's death, he became the leader of the Kotsker branch of Hasidism. About 20 years before his death, he went into seclusion.

Krochmal, Nahmun (1785–1840)

Galician philosopher and historian. Born in Brody, he lived in Zolkiew in Galicia. Subsequently he returned to Brody; eventually he moved to Tarnopol. He was a leading figure of the HASKALAH and the founder of WISSENSCHAFT DES JUDENTUMS.

kuppah (Hebrew, 'charity box')

There is a *kuppah* in every religious home and synagogue, and money is put into it on sad, joyful and solemn occasions to be distributed to the poor. (*See also* CHARITY.)

Kuzari

See JUDAH HALEVI.

L

Ladino

Judeo-Spanish dialect. Spoken by SEPHARDI and Mediterranean Jews, it is written in HEBREW script.

Lag Ba-Omer

Thirty-third day of the OMER period. It takes place on 18 Iyyar. According to tradition, a plague among the pupils of AKIVA ended on this date; thus it is called the 'Scholars' Feast'. It has been celebrated as a semi-holiday since the time of the geonim (see GAON). KABBALISTS observed this day as the anniversary of the death of SIMEON BEN YOHAI.

lamed vav zaddikim

Thirty-six righteous men. According to tradition, 36 righteous men live in every generation. The world depends on their continued existence. Each one is referred to as a *lamed-vovnik* or *nistar* (secret saint).

Lamentations, Book of

Biblical book, the third of the five scrolls in the HAGIOGRAPHA. It contains elegies and mourning over the destruction of JUDAH, JERUSALEM and the TEMPLE by the BABYLONIANS. It is read in the SYNAGOGUE on the NINTH OF AV.

lamps

Lamps and light play a major part in the Jewish tradition. During the biblical period a candelabrum (MENORAH) was placed in the TABERNACLE and the TEMPLE. Smaller lamps were used for houses and public buildings. The eight-branched HANUKKAH lamp was produced in a variety of forms from the middle ages. In the SYNAGOGUE the *ner tamid* (ETERNAL LIGHT) is kept constantly burning before the ARK. The practice of lighting a lamp during mourning and on the anniversary of a parent's death is based on Proverbs 20:27. (*See also* CANDLES; SABBATH LAMP.)

Landau, Ezekiel (1713–93)

Bohemian HALAKHIC authority. Born in Opataów, Poland, he was a DAYYAN of Brody and RABBI of Yampol. In 1754 he became rabbi of PRAGUE and the whole of Bohemia. He sought to mitigate the conflict between Jacob EMDEN and Jonathan EIBESCHÜTZ, fought against the SHABBETAIANS and opposed the HASIDIM.

lashanah habaah bi-Yerushalayim (Hebrew, 'next year in Jerusalem')

Concluding words of the PASSOVER SEDER. In some communities it is used as the conclusion to the service on Yom Kippur. Its purpose is to remind Jews of the coming era of the MESSIAH, when all the Jewish people will return to JERUSALEM.

latter prophets

The books of the latter prophets are divided into the MAJOR PROPHETS (ISAIAH, JEREMIAH and EZEKIEL) and the 12 MINOR PROPHETS (HOSEA, JOEL, AMOS, OBADIAH, JONAH, MICAH, NAHUM, HABAKKUK, ZEPHANIAH, HAGGAI, ZECHARIAH and MALACHI).

laver

Basin for ritual ABLUTIONS required of PRIESTS. During the biblical period lavers were provided in the TENT OF MEETING and the TEMPLE. They are used for washing the priests' hands before the PRIESTLY BLESSING in some SYNAGOGUES.

law

Rules by which Jewish life is regulated. The ultimate source of law is the PENTATEUCH (Five Books of MOSES); according to tradition, they contain 613 commandments. In addition, the ORAL LAW was passed on from generation to generation. Discussions of the law are recorded in the MISHNAH and TALMUD, and decisions concerning the law are collected in various CODES. Later decisions based on individual laws are known as RESPONSA. (*See also* WRITTEN LAW.)

Law of Return

Law of the State of ISRAEL; passed in 1950, which gives every Jew the right to immigrate to Israel. At present the ORTHODOX establishment is seeking to change the law so that it applies only to those recognized as Jews by the Orthodox.

Leah   (fl. ?16th century BCE)

Israelite woman, elder daughter of Laban and wife of JACOB. She was married to Jacob as a result of Laban's trickery in substituting her for her sister RACHEL (Gen. 29:23–5).

leaven   (Hebrew: *ḥametz*)

Fermenting dough. It is made from flour and used as a raising agent for bread. It was forbidden for use as a meal offering in most of the TEMPLE SACRIFICES. Leaven is prohibited during PASSOVER.

lekhah dodi

(Hebrew, 'come, my beloved')

Opening words of a song of greeting for the SABBATH. It was written by Solomon Alkabetz in the early 16th century in SAFED. While reciting the final verse, it is customary to turn towards the SYNAGOGUE entrance and bow.

leku nerananah

(Hebrew, 'O come, let us exult')

Opening words of Psalm 95; it refers to a group of six PSALMS (95–9 and 29). They are recited in the ASHKENAZI rite for the inauguration of the SABBATH at the beginning of the Friday EVENING SERVICE. They describe God's grandeur in nature as well as his righteous judgement of the world. The custom of reciting these psalms was introduced by KABBALISTS in the 16th century in SAFED.

lel shimmurim

See NIGHT OF WATCHING.

Leon, Moses ben Shem Tov de
(1250–1305)

Spanish KABBALIST. He lived in Guadalajara, eventually settling in Avila. He composed a variety of kabbalistic works. Although the ZOHAR was attributed to SIMEON BEN YOHAI, most scholars regard Moses de Leon as the author.

Leontopolis

Ancient Egyptian city, located six miles north of Cairo. Under the HIGH PRIEST Onias IV, Jewish scholars were stationed there after the MACCABEAN revolt. Onias constructed a temple in the city; it was closed by the Romans in 73 CE.

leprosy

In Scripture the term *tzoraat* denotes an affliction of the skin which renders the person unclean; the word is also applied to a blemish on the surface of an object which makes it unfit for ritual or sacred use. Signs of leprosy are listed in Lev. 13. A person declared leprous by a PRIEST is quarantined. When cured, the leper must undergo a service of cleansing and bring offerings to the TEMPLE. According to the RABBIS, the disease results from scandalmongering and evil talk. The laws regarding leprosy are found in the TRACTATE Negaim in the TALMUD.

leshon hara

See SLANDER.

letter mysticism

See GEMATRIA.

Levi (fl. ?16th century BCE)

Israelite, son of JACOB and LEAH. He founded the tribe of LEVITES. He and his brother Simeon killed the men of Shechem who raped their sister, Dinah (Gen. 34). Because of this act, they were rebuked by Jacob who predicted that their descendants would be scattered throughout ISRAEL (Gen. 49:7).

Levi ben Gershon (1288–1344)

French philosopher, mathematician, astronomer, biblical scholar and TAL-MUDIST. Known as Gersonides, he was born at Bagnols-sur-Ceze and lived in Orange and Avignon. His *Milhamot Adonai* deals with the IMMORTALITY OF THE SOUL, PROPHECY, omnipotence, PROVIDENCE, astronomy, CREATION and MIRACLES. He also wrote a study of the 13 HERMENEUTICAL rules of ISHMAEL, as well as works on arithmetic, geometry, harmonic numbers and trigonometry. In addition, he produced commentaries on Aristotle, Averroes and Scripture.

Leviathan

Sea monster. It is depicted in Job 40–1. The AGGADAH and APOCRYPHA identify it

with the male and female sea animals made by God on the fifth day of CREATION. When they threatened to destroy the world, God emasculated the male but preserved the female. In the future God will wage war against Leviathan and the righteous will participate in the struggle. A similar legend is found in UGARITIC sources.

levirate marriage

The marriage of a man with his brother's childless widow. Such a marriage is prescribed in Scripture if the deceased brother has left no offspring (Deut. 25:5). Release from this obligation may be obtained through performance of the ceremony of *ḥalitzah* (Deut. 25:7–10). It involves the woman removing her brother-in-law's shoe and reciting the formula: 'So shall be done to the man who will not build his brother's house.' Regulations governing levirate marriage are found in the TRACTATE Yevamot in the TALMUD.

Levite

Descendant of the tribe of LEVI. MOSES consecrated the Levites to serve in the TABERNACLE and teach the people. They were therefore in attendance upon the PRIESTS. Each family of Levites was assigned particular duties. The First Book of CHRONICLES narrates that DAVID divided them into separate groups with different roles in the TEMPLE. According to Jewish LAW, a Levite is viewed as second only to the priest in the line of those who may read the law.

levitical cities

Forty-eight towns which God commanded MOSES to set apart for the tribe of LEVI (Num. 35). They included the six CITIES OF REFUGE. Joshua 21 relates the decisions made by each of the other 11 tribes as to which cities should be assigned to the Levites.

Leviticus

Third book of the PENTATEUCH. It contains the laws concerning sacrifice, the sanctuary, impurity and holiness.

libation

Drink offering or SACRIFICE. During the biblical period oil and wine were used in most sacrifical ceremonies. Oil was usually employed with the meal offering. Every animal oblation was accompanied by a wine libation. Different measures were prescribed for the various types of animals (Num. 15: 1–16).

Liberal Judaism

See REFORM JUDAISM.

light

Symbol of life, blessing, peace, knowledge, understanding, redemption, the SOUL and goodness. According to Scripture, it was God's first CREATION (Gen. 1:3–4). In KABBALISTIC mysticism, it plays a significant role.

Lights, Festival of

See HANUKKAH.

Lilith

Female DEMON. Referred to in ISAIAH 34:14, she is depicted as having a human face, long hair and wings. In mystical literature, she was the queen of demons and the consort of SATAN–Samael. KABBALISTIC sources portray her as the symbol of lust and temptation. It was a common practice to protect women who were giving birth from her power by fixing AMULETS to their beds.

liturgy

The Jewish liturgy dates back to TEMPLE worship when PRAYERS were recited during the sacrificial ritual. During the BABYLONIAN exile, SACRIFICE was replaced by prayers recited in public gatherings. In time the Jewish liturgy

followed a fixed pattern: *shaharit* (MORNING SERVICE), *minhah* (AFTERNOON SERVICE) and *maariv* (EVENING SERVICE). An ADDITIONAL PRAYER (*musaf*) was recited on SABBATHS and FESTIVALS. In addition, a special prayer (NEILAH) was recited at the conclusion of the service on Yom Kippur. The central prayers of the Jewish liturgy are the SHEMA and the AMIDAH. Prayers recited on weekdays and the Sabbath are contained in the *siddur* (PRAYER BOOK). Those recited on festivals are found in the *mazhor* (festival prayer book). There are two versions of the liturgy: the ASHKENAZI, which is used by East European Jewry, and the SEPHARDI, used by Jews of Spanish and Portuguese origin, as well as a number of oriental communities.

Litvak

Lithuanian Jew.

Liubavitch

Russian village near Mohilev. It became the centre of HABAD HASIDISM. DOV BAER, the successor of SHNEOUR ZALMAN of Lyady, settled there. He was eventually succeeded as leader of the sect by Menahem Mendel Shneersohn (also known as Menahem Mendel of Liubavitch), whose descendants lived there until 1916. In that year Shalom Dov Shneersohn went to Rostov-na-Donu.

loans

According to Jewish LAW, anyone who borrows money must return it at a fixed time. Otherwise, the lender may recover the value of the loan in the form of the borrower's property. If a loan is made by a promissory note, it may even be recovered from the property sold by the debtor after the date of the note. Originally a SABBATICAL YEAR cancelled a debt, but the sage HILLEL instituted a PROSBUL, a legal document which allowed the collection of debts to be postponed until after the sabbatical year. Scripture decrees that loans with interest are forbidden; nonetheless, permission was given to charge interest under certain conditions.

lost tribes

See TEN LOST TRIBES.

Lots, Feast of

See PURIM.

love of neighbour

According to Scripture, it is obligatory to love one's neighbour: 'Thou shalt not avenge, nor bear any grudge against the children of thy people, but thou shalt love thy neighbour as thyself' (Lev. 19:18).

Love of Zion

(Hebrew: Ḥibbat Zion)

ZIONIST movement. It emerged in the 1860s and served as the focus of early Zionist aspirations before the creation of political Zionism. It appealed to the Jewish masses of Russia and Romania, and similar groups were established in Western Europe and the USA. Its adherents (called Ḥovevei Zion) provided Theodor HERZL with support for his policies. When the World Zionist Organization was founded in 1897, the members of Ḥibbat Zion joined the new movement.

Luria, Isaac ben Solomon

(1534–72)

PALESTINIAN KABBALIST. Known as Ari, he was born in JERUSALEM and educated in EGYPT. From 1570 he lived in SAFED. His teachings were received by his disciples orally; they were later recorded by his pupil Hayyim VITAL in *Etz hayyim, Peri etz hayyim* and *Sefer ha-gilgulim*. His kabbalistic ideas profoundly influenced the evolution of Jewish mysticism. In his teaching he propounded theories about divine contraction (ZIMZUM), the shattering of the vessels (*shevirat ha-kelim*) and cosmic repair (TIKKUN).

Luzzatto, Moses Ḥayyim

(1707–46)

Italian KABBALIST, Hebrew poet and writer. Known as Ramhal, he was born in Padua. He engaged in mystical exercises and gathered around himself a group of followers. He believed he was in communion with a MAGGID who dictated secret doctrines to him. His MESSIANIC claims provoked the hostility of the rabbinic establishment. Forced to leave Italy, he settled in AMSTERDAM and later went to PALESTINE. He composed kabbalistic studies, ethical works, theological investigations, poetry and verse drama. He is viewed as the father of modern HEBREW literature.

Luzzatto, Samuel David

(1800–65)

Italian philosopher, biblical commentator and translator. Known as Shadal, he served as professor at the Padua Rabbinical College from 1829. He composed works dealing with the Bible, HEBREW grammar and philology, Jewish liturgy, Hebrew poetry and philosophy. In addition, he edited the poems of JUDAH HALEVI, translated parts of the Bible into Italian, and wrote poetry in Hebrew in the traditional Italian style. He was opposed to the KABBALAH and criticized a number of Jewish philosophers, including MAIMONIDES and SPINOZA. His correspondence with other Jewish scholars is of historical importance.

LXX

See SEPTUAGINT.

M

ma'amadot

See COURSES, PRIESTLY.

maaravot

Arrangement of PIYYUTIM. The *maaravot piyyutim* are recited in addition to the usual prayers in the EVENING SERVICE.

Maarekhet Ha-Elohut

(Hebrew, 'The Order of God')

KABBALISTIC work. It is an attempt to present the teachings of the kabbalah systematically. It was composed in the 13th century by an unknown author.

maariv

see EVENING SERVICE.

Maaseh Bereshit

(Hebrew, 'Work of Creation')

Mystical tradition about creation. Based on Genesis 1, it depicts the formation of the universe according to mystical doctrines. These views are expressed in the SEFER YETZIRAH; here the cosmos is said to have been created out of 32 secret paths of wisdom, consisting of 10 *sefirot* (DIVINE EMANATIONS) and the 22 letters of the HEBREW alphabet.

Maaseh Book

Name given to various collections of mostly miraculous stories, which offer ethical instruction. Written in YIDDISH, they were derived from the TALMUD as well as medieval folklore. An English edition of these stories was published in 1934 by Moses Gaster. Similar collections were found among Mediterranean SEPHARDI communities under the title *Maaseh Nissim*.

Maaseh Merkavah

(Hebrew, 'Work of the Chariot')

Mystical doctrine based on the vision of the divine CHARIOT in Ezek. 1. It depicts the mystic's ascent to HEAVEN, his visions of the divine palaces and personal religious experience. It formed the basis for a complex of speculative material consisting of homilies, sermons and visions of the throne of glory and the divine chariot.

maaser

See TITHES.

Maccabees

Name of four APOCRYPHAL works. 1 Maccabees covers the period of 40 years from the accession of ANTIOCHUS IV EPIPHANES in 175 BCE to the death of Simeon the HASMONEAN in 135 BCE. 2 Maccabees focuses on the life and times of JUDAH MACCABEE. 3 Maccabees is unrelated in content to the other books: it explains why Egyptian Jews have a PURIM-like celebration in the summer. Possibly it was grouped with 1 and 2 Maccabees because it relates a persecution of the Jews by a HELLENISTIC king and their deliverance. 4 Maccabees relates the story of the MARTYRS of the persecution preceding the Maccabean revolt in 168 BCE. It is a philosophical sermon dealing with the theme of pious reason.

Machpelah

Site near Hebron consisting of a field containing a cave. It was purchased by ABRAHAM from Ephron the Hittite as a burial plot for SARAH (Gen. 23). Abraham, ISSAC, REBEKAH, JACOB and LEAH were also interred there.

Magen David

See STAR OF DAVID.

maggid (Hebrew, 'preacher')

Popular preacher. Such figures spoke on SABBATHS and on weekdays. Often they described the torments of HELL in order to bring their congregations to REPENTANCE. They also preached words of comfort and hope and the promise of MESSIANIC redemption. The Ḥasidim, in particular, produced such preachers who helped to spread the teachings of the movement in Poland and Russia.

magic

Art of influencing events by the occult control of natural and spiritual forces. In Scripture sorcery, witchcraft and magic are forbidden (Exod. 22:17). Nevertheless the Bible, TALMUD and later rabbinic sources abound with examples of magical practices. Magical activities connected with divine NAMES, the names of ANGELS, permutations and combinations of HEBREW letters, and scriptural quotations flourished under the influence of KABBALISTIC thought. In the middle ages Jewish magicians were widely known.

Mah Nishtannah

(Hebrew, 'Why is it different?')
First of the four questions recited at the PASSOVER SEDER.

Maharel of Prague (d. 1609)

TALMUDIST and theologian. Acronym for Morenu Harav Rabbi Laib. He served as RABBI of PRAGUE, and is known as the creator of the GOLEM.

mahamad

Among SEPHARDIM the name is given to the governing body of the congregation of the SYNAGOGUE. During the 18th and 19th centuries the term was also applied to the executive body of an autonomous Jewish community. The word is an alternative transliteration of the Hebrew word more often rendered *maamad*.

mahloket (Hebrew, 'division')

Used figuratively, the term signifies discussion as well as difference of opinion. Dissension was condemned by the RABBIS, yet differences of opinion based on principle were a central feature of rabbinic debate.

maḥzor (Hebrew, 'cycle')

The prayer book for FESTIVALS, in contrast to the SIDDUR, which is used every day.

Maḥzor Vitry

Oldest prayer book. Both the ASHKENAZI and SEPHARDI versions of the PRAYER BOOK are based on the *Maḥzor Vitry*. It was compiled in the 11th century by Simḥah ben Samuel of Vitry, a pupil of RASHI.

Maimon, Solomon (1754–1800)

Polish philosopher. Born in Sukoviboeg, Poland, he was a child prodigy. He supported his family by working as a tutor, but in his spare time he studied Jewish philosophy and KABBALAH. He adopted the name Maimon in honour of MAIMONIDES. He subsequently went to BERLIN where he became a member of Moses MENDELSSOHN's circle. He then lived in various cities, returning to Berlin in 1786. His work was praised by Immanuel Kant, and he published a number of studies on philosophical topics.

Maimonidean Controversy

After the publication of MAIMONIDES' *Guide for the Perplexed*, a controversy ensued which lasted for a century. The work was accused by a number of scholars of excessive rationalism, which might lead to HERESY; other scholars, however, supported Maimonides' views.

Maimonides (1135–1204)

North African philosopher and HALAKHIST. His real name was Moses ben Maimon (he was also known as Rambam). Born in CÓRDOBA, he left the city with his family in 1148 when it was captured by the Almohades. After years of wandering, he eventually settled in FEZ. During this period Maimonides wrote treatises on the Jewish calendar, logic and *halakhah*. In 1168 he completed his commentary on the MISHNAH. From 1170 to 1180 he worked on the MISHNEH TORAH, a compilation of Jewish law. In 1190 he completed his philosophical study, the GUIDE FOR THE PERPLEXED. He also composed medical studies and became physician to the Sultan of EGYPT. Maimonides exerted a profound influence on Jewish studies: his codification of Jewish law remained a standard guide to *halakhah*. He is viewed as the most important philosopher of this period.

Maimuna

Celebration of the last day of PASSOVER. It is marked with picnics in many Eastern communities.

major prophets

In the Jewish CANON of Scripture the major prophets are considered to be ISAIAH, JEREMIAH and EZEKIEL, in contrast to the shorter books of the MINOR PROPHETS.

majority

According to Scripture, the decision of the majority does not excuse a person for wrongdoing; an individual should not follow the majority in doing evil (Exod. 23:2). On this basis, rabbinic scholars emphasize that a majority should be followed only in doing good.

Malachi, Book of

Biblical book, one of the books of the MINOR PROPHETS. It records the prophecies of the fifth-century BCE PROPHET Malachi, who protested against the transgression of ritual laws concerning SACRIFICE and TITHES, and also condemned INTERMARRIAGE and DIVORCE. His ESCHATOLOGY embraced a vision of the DAY OF THE LORD, preceded by the coming of ELIJAH. According to rabbinic sages, he was the last of the prophets.

Malbim (1809–79)

Acronym of Meir Laib Ben Yehiel Michal, Russian RABBI and biblical exegete. He served as rabbi of Bucharest, but was compelled to give up his post after falling out with the leaders of the community because of his strict standards. His commentary on the Bible was widely used by ORTHODOX Jews.

Malkuyyot (Hebrew, 'Sovereignty')

Name of the first of the three sections of the additional AMIDAH service on Rosh Ha-Shanah (NEW YEAR); the others are Zikhronot and Shofarot. It deals with the theme of God's sovereignty.

mamzer (Hebrew, 'bastard')

Offspring of any sexual relationship forbidden in Jewish LAW (that is, incest or sexual intercourse between a married woman and a man who is not her husband). The offspring of an unmarried woman is not a *mamzer*. A marriage between a *mamzer* and a legitimate Jew is prohibited, but two *mamzerim* may marry. The offspring of a *mamzer* and a legitimate Jew is a also a *mamzer*.

Manasseh (fl. seventh century BCE)

King of JUDAH (698–643). The son of HEZEKIAH, he ascended to the throne at the age of 12 (2 Kgs. 21:1). He revoked his father's reforms and reintroduced pagan worship. According to 2 Kings. 21:11–17, the destruction of the TEMPLE was due to his wickedness. He paid tribute to Esarhaddon and Assurbanipal of Assyria; 2 Chronicles 33:11–19 relates that he was taken captive to BABYLON.

Manasseh, Prayer of

APOCRYPHAL book. It consists of a penitential psalm supposedly by MANASSEH, King of JUDAH. According to 2 Chronicles 33:11ff, Manasseh repented of his sins when he was taken to BABYLON. In this prayer he praises God's mercy for the repentant. The prayer was composed by an unknown author before the beginning of the Common Era.

manna

Food eaten by the Israelites in the desert (Exod. 16:4–35). It was discovered on the ground every morning except the SABBATH. A double portion was left on the day before the Sabbath. It was thin and white and tasted like honey cake.

Manual of Discipline

DEAD SEA SCROLL text. It describes the rules and customs of the monastic community of QUMRAN.

maot ḥittim

(Hebrew, 'wheat monies')

Collections made before PASSOVER to ensure that there is a supply of flour for UNLEAVENED BREAD for the poor. The maot ḥittim was a compulsory community tax from the period of the TALMUD. In modern times the term refers to a collection of charitable donations to provide for the needs of the poor at Passover. (See also CHARITY.)

Maoz Tzur (Hebrew, 'O fortress, rock [of my salvation]')

Opening words of a hymn sung in the ASHKENAZI rite in the SYNAGOGUE as well as at home after kindling the ḤANUKKAH lights. The song originated in Germany in the 13th century and was composed by a poet named Mordecai.

maphtir

(Hebrew, 'one who concludes')

Term referring to a person who concludes the reading in the SYNAGOGUE and to the reading itself. The maphtir first reads a portion of the TORAH (usually a repetition of the last three verses of the portion assigned for the day) and then the HAFTARAH.

mappah (Hebrew, 'cloth')

Fabric strip used as a binder round a TORAH SCROLL. The term also refers to the decorated cover of the reading desk in the SYNAGOGUE. The term was used by Moses ISSERLES as the title of his commentary on the SHULḤAN ARUKH.

mar (Hebrew, 'master')

Title given to some BABYLONIAN AMORAIM and especially to EXILARCHS.

Mari

Ancient Mesopotamian city. Its site is close to the modern town of Tell Ḥariri. Archaeological and epigraphical discoveries made there cast light on the history of Mesopotamia and Upper Syria as well as the early period of Israelite history.

maror

See BITTER HERBS.

marranos (Hebrew: Anusim)

Term applied in Spain and Portugal to the descendants of baptized Jews who were suspected of adhering to Judaism. They were numerous in Spain after the Jewish massacres of 1391 and after the

Dominican campaign at the beginning of the 15th century. It was partly to deal with such persons that the INQUISITION was introduced in Spain in 1480. Similarly, in Portugal FORCED CONVERSIONS in 1497 led to an increase in the number of marranos. Their heretical tendencies were suppressed by the Inquisition introduced in 1540. Many marranos fled to Italy, North Africa and Turkey; large groups later settled in the Netherlands, the West Indies and North America.

marriage

The Bible decrees that it is necessary for the human race to reproduce in order to ensure its continuation. Hence the first commandment in Scripture is 'be fruitful and multiply' (Gen. 1:22). Men are obligated to marry and fulfil this command. According to Judaism, there are two stages in the marriage ceremony: BETROTHAL (*erusim* or *kiddushin*) and marriage itself (*nissuim*). Betrothal is the ceremony when a woman is promised as the wife of the betrother. The ceremony must occur before witnesses, and it can be contracted in three ways: by money, by deed, or by sexual intercourse. The second stage involves bringing the woman into the home in order to live a marital life. Until the 10th century, when monogamy became legally binding, Jews practised polygamy. In modern Judaism marriage continues to be a social, moral and religious ideal.

marriage canopy

(Hebrew: *ḥuppah*)

Weddings are conducted under the *ḥuppah,* which symbolizes the marriage chamber. A *ḥuppah* is open at the sides; it can be anything from a simple TALLIT held over the bridal party to an elaborate bower of flowers.

marriage contract

(Hebrew: *ketubbah*)

Document which records the financial obligations undertaken by a bridegroom

Jewish marriage: A Jewish wedding taking place under the canopy.

towards his bride. Written in ARAMAIC, it contains clauses which follow a sterotyped formula. The TRACTATE Ketubbot in the TALMUD deals with the document and its preparation. It was frequently written on parchment with illuminated borders. The art of illuminating *ketubbot* is particularly associated with Italy. (*See also* MARRIAGE.)

marriages, forbidden

The list of forbidden marriages is found in Lev. 18:16–30; 20:9–22.

marshalik (Yiddish, 'jester')

The jester at East European weddings.

martyr

Among early Jewish martyrs were the seven sons of Hannah who were killed by ANTIOCHUS IV EPIPHANES during the HASMONEAN revolt (166–164 BCE). In the early rabbinic period the TEN MARTYRS were killed during the BAR KOKHBA revolt of 132 BCE. According to rabbinic traditon, a martyr is someone who dies willingly for the faith and thereby achieves the sanctification of the divine name (KIDDUSH HA-SHEM). During the middle ages regulations concerning the ways in which martyrs should conduct themselves and the BENEDICTIONS they are to recite were formulated by the sages.

Marx, Karl (1818–83)

German social philosopher. Born in Trier, he converted to Christianity at the age of six. He served as editor of the Cologne daily, the *Rheinische Zeitung*. Later he moved to Paris, and then to Brussels. In 1848 he and Friedrich Engels published *The Communist Manifesto*. In 1849 he settled in London where he wrote *Das Kapital*. In his writings he expressed antipathy towards Jews and Judaism.

Masada

Stronghold on a rock near the Dead Sea. It served as the refuge of HEROD the Great in 40 BCE, when it was unsuccessfully besieged by Antigonus Mattathias. Later Herod built a palace there. In the JEWISH WAR against Rome in 66–70 CE and afterwards, it served as a ZEALOT fortress. In 73 CE a garrison of nearly 1,000 Jews committed suicide there rather than be captured by the Romans.

mashal

See FABLE.

mashiaḥ

See MESSIAH.

maskilim

Proponents of the 18th- and 19th-century ENLIGHTENMENT, or Haskalah.

masorah

Rules, principles and traditions developed from the sixth to ninth centuries by textual scholars known as *masoretes*.

The *masoretes* divided the biblical text into words, sentences and segments of verse length. They also added vowel signs to the HEBREW words as well as CANTILLATION marks indicating the articulation and inflection of the text for chanting. Further, they indicated those cases where the written form of the word (*ketiv*) differs from the pronunciation or even the actual word used when the text is read aloud (*keri*). They also corrected spellings. The accepted text of the Bible is that determined by Aaron ben Asher of the TIBERIAS school of *masoretes*.

masoret (Aramaic, 'tradition')

Jewish custom, law, history and folk beliefs.

masoretes

See MASORAH.

massekhet

See TRACTATE.

mastema

Name of the DEVIL in the Book of JUBILEES. According to Jubilees, Mastema is the chief of the evil spirits who tested ABRAHAM and killed the firstborn of the Egyptians.

matchmaker (Hebrew: *shadkhan*)

Marriage broker. The *shadkhan* negotiated MARRIAGES, settlements and DOWRIES. The institution originated in antiquity; in the middle ages it played an important role in Jewish life. It is still part of Jewish social custom in some communities.

matmid (Hebrew, 'one who persists')

A scholar devoted to the study of the TALMUD.

matriarchs

The wives of the three PATRIARCHS: SARAH, REBEKAH, LEAH and RACHEL.

mattan torah

See GIVING OF THE LAW.

matzah

See UNLEAVENED BREAD.

mazal tov (Hebrew, 'good luck')

Phrase used as a greeting on festive occasions.

mazevah

Gravestone or monument.

meditation

The practice of contemplating spiritual matters. The KABBALISTS sought to attain a contemplative vision of the divine, and instructions on methods of meditation were widespread. In the modern world meditation is an important aspect of ḤASIDIC prayer and was influenced by the kabbalists of SAFED. (*See also* DEVOTION.)

megillah

Scroll. In ancient times parchment scrolls were the form of books. Letters were also written on scrolls. Biblical books used in the SYNAGOGUE continue to take this form, notably the scroll of the law from which the TORAH portion is read. Its plural form, *megillot*, is used specifically to refer to the five biblical books SONG OF SONGS, RUTH, LAMENTATIONS, ECCLESIASTES and ESTHER. The term *megillah* also refers to the tenth TRACTATE in the MISHNAH order of MOED. It deals with the reading of the Scroll of Esther on PURIM, and enumerates scriptural readings for special SABBATHS, FESTIVALS and FAST days. In addition, it contains regulations for the care of synagogues and holy objects.

Megillat Taanit
(Hebrew, 'Scroll of the Fast')

Early TANNAITIC work compiled at the beginning of the first century. It relates the 36 days that commemorate miracles and joyous events, and on which it is forbidden to FAST.

meḥitzah (Hebrew, 'partition')

Screen in the SYNAGOGUE which separates men from women during public PRAYER. In Jewish LAW, it is also a technical term for the partition, fence or wall which creates a separate domain.

meil (Hebrew, 'mantle')

Term used for the embroidered cloth covering in which a SCROLL OF THE LAW is wrapped.

Meir (fl. second century CE)

PALESTINIAN TANNA. He was a pupil of AKIVA; subsequently he served as a member of the SANHEDRIN at USHA after the Hadrianic persecutions. He was sometimes known as RABBI Meir Baal Ha-Nes. His MISHNAH was one of the main sources of the Mishnah of JUDAH HA-NASI. His wife, Beruriah, was also an outstanding scholar.

Meir, Golda (1898–1978)

Israeli politician. Born in Kiev, she emigrated to the USA in 1906. In 1921 she settled in PALESTINE. Active in Labour

Golda Meir: This portrait was taken in 1973, one year before her resignation as Prime Minister of Israel.

ZIONISM, she held important positions in the Histadrut (federation of Israeli trade unions) and the Jewish Agency. After the establishment of the State of ISRAEL in 1948, she was appointed minister to Moscow. In 1949 she was elected to the KNESSET as a member for the Mapai party. Later she was minister of labour in successive governments, and from 1956 to 1966 she served as foreign minister. She was prime minister from 1969 to 1974.

mekhilta (Hebrew, 'measure')

Term applied to various MIDRASHIC works. It is also used as a synonym for *masekhet* (TRACTATE of the MISHNAH or TALMUD).

melammed (Yiddish, 'teacher')

Private teacher or assistant in a HEDER.

melavveh malkah

Meal eaten at the close of the SABBATH. KABBALISTIC and ḤASIDIC influence has led to the practice of prolonging the meal (and thereby delaying the end of the Sabbath) by the singing of melodies.

Melchizedek
(fl. ?16th century BCE)

King of Salem (Gen. 14:18–20). After ABRAHAM's victory over the four kings who had captured Lot, Melchizedek welcomed Abraham, gave him bread and wine, and blessed him.

meldar

SEPHARDI term for the reading of sacred literature.

memorbuch
(German, 'book of memory')

Type of community PRAYER BOOK, once common in Jewish communities in Central Europe. It consists of a collection of prayers, a necrology of distinguished persons and a martyrology.

memorial prayers

See KADDISH; YAHRZEIT; YIZKOR.

memra (Aramaic, 'word')

Creative word of God. The *memra* is the agent by which God created the world.

Mendelssohn, Moses (1729–86)

German philosopher. Born in Dessau, he lived in BERLIN where he studied philosophy, mathematics, Latin, French and English. He became a partner in a silk factory. In 1754, with the help of Gotthold Ephraim Lessing, he began to publish philosophical studies; in 1763 he was awarded the first prize of the Prussian Royal Academy of Sciences for his philosophical work. He became embroiled in a controversy about Judaism, and from 1769 devoted his literary work to issues dealing with the Jewish faith. He published a German translation of the PENTATEUCH with a Hebrew commentary (*Biur*). His *Jerusalem* is an analysis of Judaism and a defence of tolerance.

menorah (Hebrew, 'candelabrum')

The seven-branched candlestick. It stood in the TABERNACLE and in the Jerusalem TEMPLE. According to Exod. 25:40 its pattern was a divine gift to MOSES. The eight-branched CANDLE-holder used at ḤANUKKAH is also described as a *menorah*.

mensh (Yiddish, 'human being')

An honourable person, someone of consequence.

menstruation

See NIDDAH.

mercy seat

See ARK OF THE COVENANT.

merits of the fathers

According to Jewish tradition, the blessings secured for their descendants by parents who perform worthy deeds. In particular, the merits of the PATRIARCHS (Abraham, Isaac and Jacob) are believed to have obtained benefits for future generations.

Merkavah Mysticism

See CHARIOT MYSTICISM.

meshullah

See EMISSARY.

meshummad

See APOSTATE.

messiah

Anointed one. In Scripture the term refers to kings, HIGH PRIESTS, and any individual who has a divine mission. After the EXILE, the prophetic vision of God's kingdom was associated with the ingathering of Israel under an anointed scion of the House of DAVID. During the period of Roman rule, the expectation of a messiah who would deliver the Jewish people gained prominence. During this period various false messiahs appeared, including Jesus whom the Jews refused to accept because he did not fulfil the prophecies of messianic redemption contained in the Hebrew Bible. In the second century Simeon BAR KOKHBA was viewed as the messiah. In the fifth century a pseudo-messiah, Moses, appeared in Crete. Other messianic figures included Abu Issa al-Isfahani (eighth century), Serene (eighth century), Yudghan (eighth century), David ALROY (12th century), Abraham ABULAFIA (11th–12th century), Moses Botarel (14th century), Asher Lamlein (16th century), Solomon Molcho (16th century), SHABBETAI ZEVI (17th century) and Jacob FRANK (18th century).

Metatron

Angel in AGGADIC and KABBALISTIC literature. He was identified with the Angel of the Presence and with ENOCH after he ascended into HEAVEN. He served as the scribe of the divine court, the keeper of celestial secrets and the heavenly archetype of man.

metempsychosis (Hebre: *gilgul*)

Migration of a SOUL from one body after its death to another. In KABBALISTIC Judaism the doctrine of transmigration of souls is found in the Book of BAHIR and the ZOHAR. Eventually it became a commonly accepted belief among mystics. It played an important role in HASIDISM.

meturgeman
(Aramaic, 'interpreter')

The spokesman for a scholar. When giving lectures, the SAGES used to speak to the *meturgeman*, who delivered the message to the listeners.

Mezhirech

Village in Volhynia, Russia. It served as the residence of DOV BAER of Mezhirech in the 18th century. After the death of the Baal Shem Tov (ISRAEL BEN ELIEZER) in 1760, it was the centre of HASIDISM.

mezumman

The word is used to refer to one of the quorum of three people whose presence is necessary for the public recitation of GRACE AFTER MEALS.

mezuzah (Hebrew, 'doorpost')

Parchment scroll placed in a container which is attached to the doorpost of a room in a Jewish house. Every doorway in the house carries a *mezuzah*. On the scroll are written verses from DEUTERONOMY (6:4–9 and 11:13–21). The practice is prescribed by Deuteronomy 11:20: 'You shall write [these words] upon the doorposts of your house and upon your gates.' The term also refers to one of the seven minor talmudic TRACTATES dealing with the writing and use of the *mezuzah*.

Mezuzah on a doorpost containing text from Deuteronomy.

mi she-berakah

(Hebrew, 'he who blessed')

Opening words of a BENEDICTION recited on behalf of a person called up for the reading of the TORAH. After each reading, it is customary for the CANTOR to ask God's blessing on the reader, his family, and anyone he wishes to have mentioned. In many congregations the person called up for the Torah reading makes an offering for the SYNAGOGUE or CHARITY. Additional forms of this prayer are recited after the birth of a son, the birth and naming of a daughter, by the bridegroom before his wedding, and on behalf of a sick person.

Micah, Book of

Biblical book, one of the books of the 12 MINOR PROPHETS. It records the prophecies of Micah, an eighth-century BCE Israelite PROPHET. He lived in JUDAH where he defended the people against the oppression of the ruling classes. He prophesied the destruction of the country

and exile to BABYLONIA. In addition, he predicted the coming of a king of the House of DAVID who would bring peace to the world.

Michael

Archangel. Together with GABRIEL he is the only ANGEL mentioned by name in Scripture (Dan. 10:13). He is a divine messenger who carries out God's judgements. In the APOCRYPHA and AGGADIC sources he is the guardian angel of ISRAEL, the chief opponent of SATAN and the keeper of the celestial keys.

midrash (Hebrew, 'exposition')

Interpretation of Scripture. The interpretative approach known as *midrash halakah* seeks to define the full meaning of biblical law. *Midrash aggadah*, on the other hand, aims to derive a moral principle, lesson or theological concept from the biblical text. Rabbinic scholars formulated various rules to deduce hidden or new meanings.

Midrash Rabbah

Collection of AGGADIC MIDRASHIM on the PENTATEUCH and the five MEGILLOT. It consists of: Genesis Rabbah, Exodus Rabbah, Leviticus Rabbah, Numbers Rabbah, Deuteronomy Rabbah, Song of Songs Rabbah, Ruth Rabbah, Lamentations Rabbah, Ecclesiastes Rabbah and Esther Rabbah.

midrashic literature

The body of rabbinic writings concerning the interpretation of biblical texts. It dates from the beginning of the TANNAITIC period (*c.*100 BCE). Of works connected with Scripture, the best-known is MIDRASH RABBAH on the PENTATEUCH and the five MEGILLOT. The TANHUMA contains discourses on the portion of the law read weekly in the SYNAGOGUE. Other homiletical works on the Bible include *Shoher Tov* on PSALMS, and works on PROVERBS and SAMUEL. *Midrashim* concerning FESTIVALS and special SABBATHS are called *pesiktot*. The *Pesikta de-Rav Kahana* and *Pesikta Rabbati* contain homilies for special occasions. *Avot de-Rabbi Nathan* is an expansion of the MISHNAIC tractate AVOT. *Derekh Eretz Rabbah* deals with ethical teachings, and *Derekh Eretz Zuta* advises scholars about religious and pedagogic duties. The *Tanna de-ve Elayhu* contains moral advice. *Seder Olam* is a work of historical AGGADAH, and *Pirke De-Rabbi Eliezer* contains numerous stories about biblical events. The *Yalkut Shimoni* is a collection of AGGADIC literature. In addition, there are large numbers of separate *midrashim* on books of the Bible, and short *midrashim* on various subjects.

mikveh

Ritual bath. According to Jewish law, individuals as well as various objects must be immersed and ritually cleansed on certain occasions. The water in the *mikveh* should come from a natural spring or river. Such immersion renders a person ritually clean who has had contact with the dead or a defiled object, or who has become impure through an unclean flow from the body (it is, for example, practised by women after menstruation). In addition, ritual bathing is undertaken by pious individuals to add to their spirituality; it is also prescribed for CONVERTS. Ritual cleansing is used for vessels as well. (*See also* IMMERSION.)

milah

See CIRCUMCISION.

milk

According to Jewish LAW, milk should be drawn only from a permitted animal. Milk or milk products should not be mixed or cooked with meat or meat products.

min

See APIKOROS.

minhag

See CUSTOM.

minḥah

See AFTERNOON SERVICE.

minor prophets

Collection of shorter prophetic books in the Bible. The minor PROPHETS are HOSEA, JOEL, AMOS, OBADIAH, JONAH, MICAH, NAḤUM, ZEPHANIAH, ḤAGGAI, ZECHARIAH and MALACHI.

minyan (Hebrew, 'number')

Term applied to the group of ten male Jews (13 years or older) who constitute the minimum number for communal worship.

minyan man

A Jew who, for payment, attends SYNAGOGUE services to ensure that there is a MINYAN.

miracle

Extraordinary event due to divine intervention. In the Bible such occurrences are referred to as 'signs' and 'wonders'. The TALMUD records miracles performed by men of God on account of their merits. In Jewish philosophy attempts were made to provide a rational account of miraculous events.

Miriam (fl. ?13th century BCE)

Israelite woman, sister of MOSES. Exod. 2:2–8 relates that she advised Pharaoh's daughter, who had discovered the hiding place of the baby Moses, to call a Hebrew nurse for Moses and succeeded in having his mother engaged to care for him. Subsequently, when she and AARON challenged Moses' exclusive right to speak in the name of the Lord (Num. 12), she was stricken with LEPROSY, but she was healed by Moses, who interceded on her behalf.

mishmarot

See COURSES, PRIESTLY.

Mishnah

Early rabbinic legal code. It was compiled by JUDAH HA-NASI in the second century. It is divided into six orders: (1) ZERAIM (Seeds), dealing with laws regarding agriculture; (2) MOED (Set Feast), regarding the laws of the SABBATH and FESTIVALS; (3) NASHIM (Women), describing the laws of MARRIAGE, DIVORCE and VOWS; (4) NEZIKIN, (Damages), treating civil and criminal violations; (51) KODASHIM (Holy Things), setting out the laws concerning ritual SLAUGHTER, SACRIFICES, and consecrated objects; and (6) TOHOROT (Purities), dealing with the laws of ceremonial PURITY.

Mishneh Torah

Compilation of HALAKHAH written by MAIMONIDES. It is also referred to as Yad Ḥazakah.

Mishpat Ivri

(Hebrew, 'Hebrew Law')

HALAKHAH which parallels secular law. It arose in the 20th century. In the State of ISRAEL, the *halakhah* applies in all matters of MARRIAGE and DIVORCE. When legislating on difficulties of personal status, Article 46 of the Israeli constitution demands that traditional Jewish law must be explored before the final legislation is formulated.

mitnagdim (Hebrew, 'opponents')

Opponents of ḤASIDISM. The Vilna Gaon, ELIJAH BEN SOLOMON ZALMAN, led the opposition to Ḥasidism. He insisted that Judaism rests on disciplined study and ORTHODOX practice. However, later in the 19th century the *mitnagdim* joined forces with the Ḥasidim to resist secularism, assimilation and the HASKALAH. Nonetheless, the *mitnagdim* follow a different rite from Ḥasidic Jews: they use the ASHKENAZI Polish liturgy, while the Ḥasidim use the SEPHARDI PRAYER BOOK of Isaac LURIA.

mitzvah (Hebrew, 'commandment')

In Jewish LAW commandments are either positive (*mitzvah aseh*) or negative (*mitzvah lo taaseh*). According to tradition, there are 613 commandments in the TORAH. The TALMUD differentiates between two types of commandment: *mishpatim*, ordinances that would have been deducible even if the Hebrew Bible had not prescribed them, and *ḥukkim*, commandments that could not have been logically derived. Medieval scholars referred to the first type as rational (*sikhliyyot*), and the second as revealed (*shimiyot*). The term *mitzvah* is also applied to a good deed.

mixed marriage

See INTERMARRIAGE.

mizraḥ (Hebrew, 'east')

Decorated parchment or metal plate. For the purpose of PRAYER, it is hung on a wall to indicate the direction of JERUSALEM.

Mizraḥi

Religious ZIONIST organization. Founded in 1902, its first conference took place in Pressburg. It encouraged a programme of religious Zionism within the framework of the Zionist movement. Since the creation of a Jewish state, it has formed part of successive Israeli governments. It also engaged in religious education at all levels, founded an organization for YESHIVOT, established the Mosad ha-Rav Kook publishing society, maintained economic enterprises including banks and a house-building company, and ran an organization to deal with religious RABBIS. Its women's section sponsored kindergartens, social welfare and children's homes in ISRAEL. In 1955 it joined with

Ha-Poel ha-Mizraḥi to form the National Religious Party. The World Centre of Mizraḥi and Ha-Poel ha-Mizraḥi is the highest body of the religious Zionist movement and acts as an executive for both organizations.

moadim le-simḥah
(Hebrew, 'holidays for rejoicing')

Greeting used by SEPHARDIM on religious holidays. The reply is 'Ḥagim u-zemanim le-sason' ('Festivals and festal period for joy').

modeh ani   (Hebrew, 'I give thanks')

Opening words of the PRAYER recited upon waking in the morning.

Moed   (Hebrew, 'Set Feast')

Second order of the MISHNAH dealing with laws concerning the SABBATH, FESTIVALS and FAST days.

mohel

Person who carries out a CIRCUMCISION.

monarchy

See KINGSHIP.

monasticism

Although Judaism does not have a monastic tradition, ASCETIC groups such as the ESSENES and NAZIRITES led quasi-monastic lives.

monotheism

The belief that there is only one God. Jewish monotheism is expressed in the SHEMA prayer: 'Hear, O Israel, the Lord our God, the Lord is one' (Deut. 6:4). The doctrine of Jewish monotheism depicts God as holy, transcendent, immanent, eternal, omnipresent, omniscient, omnipotent and all-good. As creator of the universe, he is also a redeemer of humanity, just, compassionate, merciful and ready to answer the prayers of humankind. In the middle ages Jewish theologians discussed a wide

range of issues connected with this concept of God.

Montefiore, Claude   (1858–1938)

English theologian and leader of Liberal Judaism. He studied at Balliol College, Oxford and the Hochschule für WISSENSCHAFT DES JUDENTUMS in BERLIN. In 1888 he founded the *Jewish Quarterly Review*. He was a founder of the Jewish Religious Union in 1902, which led to the creation in 1926 of the Liberal Jewish Synagogue in London. In 1926 he became president of the World Union for PROGRESSIVE JUDAISM. His writings include *Aspects of Judaism*, *The Synoptic Gospels*, *Liberal Judaism*, *Outlines of Liberal Judaism* and *Rabbinic Literature and Gospel Teaching*.

Montefiore, Moses   (1784–1855)

British communal leader. Born in Livorno, he grew up in London where he worked as a broker. In 1837 he became sheriff of the City of London, and he was the first Jew to be knighted in Britain. He went on a mission to the Levant with Isaac-Adolphe Crémieux in 1840 at the time of the DAMASCUS AFFAIR, and he intervened with their governments on behalf of the Jews of Russia, Morocco and Romania. He visited PALESTINE on several occasions and worked to improve the conditions under which the Jewish community lived there.

months

The months of the Jewish year are Nisan, Iyyar, Sivan, Tammuz, Av, Elul, Tishri, Ḥeshvan, Kislev, Tevet, Shevat, and Adar. (*See also* CALENDAR.)

Moon, Blessing of the
(Hebrew: *Kiddush Levenah*)

Prayer of thanksgiving which is recited at the appearance of the new moon. According to tradition, a MINYAN of ten adult men is required to perform this rite. It usually takes place at the close of the SABBATH in the SYNAGOGUE courtyard on any day between the 3rd and 15th days of the lunar month (when the moon is waxing).

More Judaico

OATH imposed on Jews involved in legal proceedings with non-Jews. Used in Central and Eastern Europe from the middle ages, it was abolished in Germany in 1846. The oath was sworn on the TORAH and CURSES were invoked on those who broke it.

Moreh Nevukhim

See GUIDE FOR THE PERPLEXED.

morenu (Hebrew, 'our teacher')

Title bestowed upon distinguished RABBIS in the middle ages and later.

morning service
(Hebrew: *shaharit*)

Service of the morning PRAYER. It consists of the dawn BENEDICTIONS, biblical verses related to the SACRIFICAL system, passages of rabbinic writings for study, the Pesuke de-Zimra with their benedictions, the SHEMA with its benedictions, the AMIDAH, the TAHANUN, and concluding prayers, including the ALENU.

moser (Yiddish, 'betrayer')

An informer who denounces fellow Jews.

Moses (fl. ?13th century BCE)

Lawgiver, leader of the Israelites and PROPHET. Born in EGYPT to Amram and Jochebed, who hid him in a basket among the reeds of the Nile in order to escape Pharaoh's decree to slaughter all new-born Jewish males. He was found by Pharaoh's daugher, who raised him in the royal household. In early manhood he killed an Egyptian whom he discovered beating a Hebrew. After fleeing to Midian, he became a shepherd to the local priest Jethro and married his daughter, Zipporah. While tending Jethro's sheep on Mount Horeb, he encountered God, who spoke to him from the burning bush and commanded him to free the Hebrew slaves. He interceded with Pharaoh, who eventually released the Hebrews after ten plagues had afflicted Egypt. Moses led the people across the Red Sea, which miraculously parted so that they could cross, and guided them for 40 years in the desert. Moses received God's revelation of the law on MOUNT SINAI, embodied in the TEN COMMANDMENTS written on tablets of stone. Before his death he appointed JOSHUA his successor.

Moses, Assumption of

Apocryphal work. It relates the address given by MOSES to JOSHUA in the form of a prophecy. It also includes the history of ISRAEL to the time of HEROD. In an additional section, the death of Moses and the war between SATAN and the archangel MICHAEL over his body are depicted.

Moses, Blessing of

Title given to Deut. 33, which records the blessing of the tribes of Israel by MOSES before his death. Poetic in form, this text consists of a blessing for each tribe, except Simeon, and a blessing for the entire people.

Moses ben Maimon

See MAIMONIDES.

Moses ben Nahman

See NAHMANIDES.

mother

According to Scripture and the TALMUD, the mother has equal rights with the father in the moral and ethical sphere with regard to the respect and deference of her children. The duty of honouring both parents is prescribed by the TEN COMMANDMENTS. Similarly, the punishment for smiting or cursing parents applies to such actions against the mother as well as against the father. In valid Jewish marriages, the child is accorded the status of the father. However, in mixed marriages (between a Jew and non-Jew), the child receives the status of the mother. The child of an unmarried Jewish woman is viewed as Jewish in all respects. The concept of bastardy applies only to the doctrine of prohibited relationships. The mother is the symbol of home and FAMILY, for which she is responsible.

Mount Carmel

Mountain ridge in north-west ISRAEL. It runs from the Samarian Hills to the Mediterranean. It was the site of ELIJAH's victory over the PROPHETS of BAAL (1 Kgs. 18:19ff), and of his residence (2 Kgs. 4:25).

Mount Gerizim

Mountain in the Hills of Ephraim, 30 miles north of JERUSALEM. When the Israelites entered CANAAN, a ceremony was held there. The assembled gathering blessed all those who observed the law, while those opposite on Mount Ebal cursed those who violated it (Deut. 11:29–30; 27:11–13; Josh. 8:30–5). Mount Gerizim was venerated by the SAMARITANS and Sanballat built a temple there, which constituted their religious and political centre. Later ANTIOCHUS IV EPIPHANES converted the temple to the worship of Zeus. It was destroyed by JOHN HYRCANUS in 129 BCE.

Mount Sinai

Mountain in the wilderness of Horeb on the Sinai peninsula. According to the Book of DEUTERONOMY, Mount Sinai was identified with Mount Horeb. The Israelites camped at the foot of Mount Sinai after the EXODUS from Egypt (Exod. 19:1), and MOSES ascended the

The Sinai mountains in the early morning.

mountain to receive the TEN COMMANDMENTS (Exod. 20:1–24:8). According to rabbinic tradition, Moses received both the WRITTEN LAW and the ORAL LAW on Mount Sinai.

Mourners for Zion
(Hebrew: *Avele Zion*)

Jews who mourned the destruction of the TEMPLE and prayed for the redemption of Zion. In the TALMUD they are referred to as *perushim* (abstainers) because they refused meat and wine. After the rise of KARAISM, they became important in Jewish life.

mourning (Hebrew: *avelut*)

Mourning customs during the biblical period involved RENDING GARMENTS, wearing sackcloth, sitting on the ground, putting earth and dust on the head, and weeping. Other practices were added during the TALMUDIC period. In contemporary practice, mourning begins after the BURIAL of a close relative. The bereaved person wears special garments, takes off his shoes, remains in the home for seven days of mourning sitting on a low stool, refrains from attending the SYNAGOGUE except on the SABBATH, and reads Scripture. No work may be done and sexual intercourse is forbidden. It is the duty of friends and relations to visit the mourner during this period. Persons are mourned intensively for 30 days; during this time the hair and beard are left uncut and no weddings or joyful celebrations may take place. A lesser state of mourning continues until 12 months after the burial. In post-talmudic times some alterations to these customs occurred, but most continued to be observed. A major innovation was the kindling of a lamp during the mourning period, and the recitation of the KADDISH prayer for 11 months after the burial of a parent or child, and each

year on the anniversary of the death. (*See also* SHIVAH; SHELOSHIM.)

muktzeh
See SET ASIDE THINGS.

mumar
See APOSTASY.

murder

According to Jewish legislation, the penalty for premeditated murder, witnessed by two individuals who warned the perpetrator of the seriousness of the crime before it was committed, is beheading. Yet the law requires such meticulous proof of the details of the act that, for practical pursposes, it became impossible to impose CAPITAL PUNISHMENT. Under such circumstances, the guilty person was sentenced to imprisonment. When the murder was not premeditated, the killer could flee to one of the CITIES OF REFUGE.

musaf
See ADDITIONAL SERVICE.

musar

In biblical Hebrew, the word is used variously to mean punishment or chastisement and instruction. Later it came to signify morals, ethics and moral instruction. During the middle ages a distinct branch of literature emerged, known as '*musar* literature'. It dealt with moral and ethical matters. In the modern world the word has connotations of sermonizing and denotes a type of literature of edification.

Musar movement

Movement for ethical education in the spirit of the HALAKHAH. It emerged in the 19th century among ORTHODOX groups in Lithuania. Its founder, Israel SALANTER, emphasized the need to develop inner piety. His followers encouraged the study of traditional ethical literature. Throughout Lithuania *musar* institutions were created, and the movement became influential among the YESHIVOT. A number of *yeshivot* were established by leaders of the movement at Chelm, Slobodka and Novahardok.

music

In early biblical history music and musical instruments were frequently mentioned. In the TEMPLE, the LEVITES organized the performance of the service and trained singers, players and conductors. After the Babylonian EXILE, a decline in instrumental music occurred. With the destruction of the Second Temple, Jewish music was restricted to chanting in the SYNAGOGUE. Services were sung in a traditional chant by the HAZZAN who might, however, embellish the melodies. Jewish musical life in Eastern Europe culminated in the worship of the HASIDIM, who placed emphasis on ecstatic religious music. In modern times there has been a renewed interest in the development of music in the Jewish world. Many works have been written for the concert hall that take Jewish events as their subjects, or use HEBREW words or melodies.

myrtle

One of the four species of plant, branches of which are waved on the feast of SUKKOT.

mysticism

See KABBALAH.

nagid (Hebrew, 'prince')

Head of the Jewish community in Islamic lands (except under Abbasid rule from 750 to 1258, when the Jews were led by the EXILARCH). There was a *nagid* from the 10th century in Spain, Kairouan, Egypt and Yemen, and from the 16th century to the 19th century in Morocco, Algeria and Tunisia. The office disappeared in the 19th century.

nahalat

See YAHRZEIT.

Naḥman of Bratslav
(1772–1811)

Ukrainian ḤASIDIC leader, great-grandson of ISRAEL BEN ELIEZER, the Baal Shem Tov. Born in Medzhibozh, he lived in Medvedevka where he attracted numerous disciples. In 1798 he travelled to PALESTINE, but he subsequently settled in Zlatopol where he engaged in controversy with Aryeh Leib of Spola. In 1802 he moved to Bratslav. His journeys are described in works by his disciple Nathan Sternhartz. In 1810 he settled in the Ukrainian city of Uman. In his teachings he emphasized simple faith and prayer, and propounded the theory of the ZADDIK as the intermediary between God and man.

Naḥmanides (1194–1270)

Spanish TALMUDIST, KABBALIST and biblical commentator. Known as Naḥmanides,

his Hebrew name was Moses ben Naḥman. He served as RABBI of Gerona. In 1263 he was challenged by Pablo Christiani to a religious disputation; this took place in BARCELONA in the presence of King James I. Later he was tried for blasphemy and forced to flee from Spain. From 1267 he lived in Palestine, settling in Acre. Naḥmanides was the foremost Spanish talmudist of his day. His works include *Torat ha-Adam*, which deals with the rites of mourning, and a popular Bible commentary.

Nahum, Book of

Biblical book, one of the books of the 12 MINOR PROPHETS. It narrates the prophecies of the Israelite PROPHET Nahum (fl. seventh century BCE) concerning the fall of NINEVEH.

nakdanim (Hebrew, 'punctuators')

Name of a group of scholars who were active from the 9th to the 14th century; they provided biblical manuscripts with vowels and accents. Successors of the MASORETES, they dwelt in the Orient and in England, France and Germany.

name, change of

In Scripture, names were changed to mark a significant event, e.g. Abrahm to ABRAHAM, JACOB to Israel. The TALMUD records that if a person's name is changed when they are ill, this might mislead the Angel of Death, who would turn his attention elsewhere. The change of name is normally accomplished during a short service in which renewed life is asked for the person newly named.

names of God

See GOD, NAMES OF.

nashim (Hebrew, 'women')

Third order of the MISHNAH. It deals with BETROTHAL, MARRIAGE, DIVORCE, the relationship between husband and wife, VOWS and the law of the NAZIRITE.

nasi (Hebrew, 'prince')

Title accorded in the TALMUD to the president of the SANHEDRIN. He served as spiritual head and, later, political representative of the Jewish nation. The second in authority to the *nasi* was the AV BET DIN (president of the court). From the second century CE the *nasi* was recognized by Roman authorities as PATRIARCH of the Jews. Subsequently the title was employed in some lands to designate the lay leader of the Jewish community.

Nasi, Joseph (*c*.1524–79)

Portuguese statesman, active in Turkey. Born a MARRANO in Portugal, he accompanied his aunt Gracia Mendes when she went from Lisbon to Antwerp in 1537. However, when in 1545 she fled to Italy, he remained behind to settle her affairs. In 1554 he joined her in Constantinople, where he embraced Judaism and married her daughter, Reyna. He became an intimate of Selim, the heir to the Turkish throne. In 1561 he obtained the lease of TIBERIAS from the sultan and control of an adjacent area which he developed as a Jewish centre. He was eventually created duke of Naxos and the Cyclades.

Nathan of Gaza (1643–80)

Palestinian religious leader, disciple of SHABBETAI ZEVI. Born in JERUSALEM, he lived in Gaza, where he engaged in KABBALISTIC study and practices. He met Shabbetai Zevi in Gaza and proclaimed him the long-awaited MESSIAH. After Shabbetai Zevi converted to Islam, Nathan travelled throughout the Balkans and Italy; there he developed and preached the theology of SHABBATEANISM, which was based on LURIANIC KABBALAH. He was expelled by the rabbis of VENICE, and returned to the Balkans. He died at Uskub near Salonica.

nature

Although biblical writers acknowledged the regular workings of nature (as in Ps. 104 and 148), they were primarily concerned with God's supervision of the universe. In the view of the rabbis, the regularity of natural phenomena is an expression of God's providence, just as are miraculous occurrences.

nazirite

Jewish ASCETIC bound by a VOW. He is prohibited from drinking wine, cutting his hair and contracting impurity through contact with the dead (Numb. 6:2). The vow was normally taken for a limited period, but it could also be for life (as in the case of Samuel and Samson). Taking the Nazirite vow was common in biblical times, but the practice eventually disappeared.

Nebuchadnezzar
(fl. seventh/sixth century BCE)

King of BABYLON (605–562 BCE). Ater his victory over the Assyrian–Egyptian alliance, he conquered lands from the Euphrates to the Egyptian frontier, including JUDAH. After Judah rebelled, he took JERUSALEM in 597 BCE. He replaced king Jehoiachim with Zedekiah, and took captives back to

Babylonia. Subsequently Zedekiah rebelled, and Nebuchadnezzar invaded Judah again. In 586 BCE he captured and destroyed the TEMPLE, and expelled the Jews from Jerusalem (2 Kgs. 24–5).

nefesh

See SOUL.

Nehardea

BABYLONIAN town located on the Euphrates at its junction with the Malka River. It was created by the Jews exiled to Babylonia during the time of Jehoiakim in the sixth century BCE. They built a SYNAGOGUE there called Shaf Yeyativ. Nehardea became the seat of a famous ACADEMY as well as of the EXI-LARCH and his BET DIN. In 259 the academy was destroyed; most of its scholars moved to the academy at PUMBEDITA.

Nehemiah, Book of

Biblical book, part of the HAGIOGRAPHA. It recounts the events of the life of Nehemiah and includes part of the story of the PROPHET EZRA. Nehemiah was a cup-bearer to the Persian king, Artaxerxes I, of whom he sought permission to go to JERUSALEM. The king agreed, and appointed him Governor of JUDAH. Nehemiah organized the repair of the walls of Jerusalem, and organized various social and religious reforms. Subsequently he returned to Susa, but later settled in Jerusalem. He and Ezra took steps to discourage the Israelites from contracting mixed marriages (*see* INTERMARRIAGE).

neilah (Hebrew, 'closing')

PRAYER originally recited daily one hour before sunset and the closing of the TEMPLE. It was also recited on public FAST days and the DAY OF ATONEMENT. It now survives only as a service on the Day of Atonement. The Neilah concludes the rite for the day, symbolizing the closing of the gates of HEAVEN after the DAY OF JUDGEMENT.

neo-Orthodoxy

Modernist movement within ORTHO-DOXY. It was founded in the late 19th century by Samson Raphael HIRSCH. Accommodation with modern society was accepted, including a full secular education, alongside adherence to the Jewish tradition.

neo-Platonism

Late Greek philosophy which combines Platonism with Oriental elements. It was expounded by Plotinus, Porphyry and Proclus. During the middle ages it exerted a profound influence on the writings of Jewish theologians including Isaac Israel, Solomon ibn GABIROL, Baḥya ibn PAKUDA, Abraham bar Ḥiyya, Joseph ibn Zaddik, and Abraham ibn Ezra. The KABBALAH was also influenced by Neoplatonic ideas.

ner tamid

See ETERNAL LIGHT.

nesekh

Wine intended or used for heathen worship. By extension, the term refers to any wine made by a gentile. Wine produced by a non-Jew was always suspected of having been sanctified for a libation or a similar act. In contemporary society the ban on drinking gentile wine is still binding. The prohibition also extends to unbottled wine that is no more than touched by a gentile. Wine which has not been touched by a gentile before the bottle was sealed is KOSHER.

neshamah yeterah

See ADDITIONAL SOUL.

Neturei Karta

(Aramaic, 'Guardians of the City')
Strictly observant Jews who do not recognize the State of ISRAEL. The Neturei

Karta consists of a group of families living in the Mea Shearim quarter of JERUSALEM. They take no part in Israeli society, carry no identity card and vote in no elections.

Neviim

See PROPHET.

New Christians

See MARRANOS.

new moon

See ROSH HODESH.

New Year
(Hebrew: Rosh Ha-Shanah)

The Jewish New Year begins on the first day of Tishri. It marks the start of the TEN DAYS OF PENITENCE, which end on the DAY OF ATONEMENT. In the Bible, Rosh Ha-Shanah is referred to as falling on the first day of the seventh month (Lev. 23:24). During rabbinic times, it came to be regarded as a day of judgement for the entire world, on which each person's fate is inscribed in the BOOK OF LIFE. During the festival service, which is traditionally observed in white vestments, the SHOFAR is blown and other rituals are introduced. Traditionally it is observed for two days.

New York

American city on the eastern seaboard of the United States. Its Jewish community dates from the 17th century. In the 1820s and 1830s European immigrants increased the size of the Jewish population. By the end of the century 250,000 Jews resided there; by 1940, a million. New York now has the largest Jewish community of any city in the USA, with a vibrant religious and cultural life.

Next Year in Jerusalem

See LASHANAH HABAAH
BI-YERUSHALAYIM.

nezikin (Hebrew, 'damages')

Fourth order of the MISHNAH. It deals with money matters, damages decided by courts, criminal law and OATHS. It also contains an ethical treatise, *Pirke Avot*.

niddah
(Hebrew, 'menstruous woman')

Seventh TRACTATE in the MISHNAH order of TOHOROT. It deals with the ritual uncleanliness created by menstruation (Lev. 15:19–24) and childbirth (Lev. 12:1–5).

Night of Watching
(Hebrew: *lel shimmurim*)

First night of PASSOVER. Because it was believed that no danger could take place on this night, it was the custom to leave doors unbolted and omit the recital of the NIGHT PRAYER.

night prayer
(Hebrew: *keriat shema al ha-mittah*)

Prayer recited before going to sleep. The main part of the prayer is the first paragraph of the SHEMA. The rest consists of blessings and prayers from the EVENING SERVICE. TALMUDISTS and later authorities, including KABBALISTS, added other prayers and scriptural texts to the Shema to form the night prayer LITURGY. The substance of the night prayer is based on a saying by Joshua ben Levi that he who wishes to sleep should recite a certain portion of the Shema and the blessing to God.

nikkur

See SEPARATING THE FAT.

Nineveh

Ancient city located on the left bank of the Tigris, capital of the Assyrian Empire. JONAH was sent there by God, and persuaded its citizens to repent.

Ninth of Av (Hebrew: *Tisha b'Av*)

FAST day. It commemorates the destruction of the First and Second TEMPLES and other Jewish tragedies. The Book of LAMENTATIONS is read during the service in the SYNAGOGUE and dirges (*kinot*) are recited. A three-week period of mourning, including the nine days of penitential observance, lead up to the fast day.

nishmat (Hebrew, 'the breath of every living thing')

Opening word of the doxology which is recited at the end of the PESUKE DE-ZIMRA on SABBATHS and FESTIVALS. It is referred to as the Birkat ha-Shir (Blessing of the Song) in TALMUDIC literature. During MISHNAIC times it was recited after the Hallel at the PASSOVER SEDER. It consists of three parts: the section known in mishnaic days; a section which served as a thanksgiving for rain; and a GAONIC addition. According to medieval legend, it was ascribed to the apostle Peter.

Noah

Son of Lamech, father of Shem, Ham and Japheth (Gen. 5:28–9; 6:10; 1 Chr. 1:4). In Scripture he is described as a righteous and blameless man who walked with God (Gen. 6:9). At God's behest he built an ark, and placed in it members of his family, and representatives of the animal kingdom. When a great FLOOD came, they were saved to perpetuate humankind and the animals. After the Flood, Noah disembarked from the ark and offered SACRIFICES to God, who blessed him and his sons and established a COVENANT with them (Gen. 6–9).

Noachide laws

Series of laws, derived from Gen. 9:4–7, which in rabbinic Judaism are binding on all human beings. They prohibit IDOLATRY, BLASPHEMY, MURDER, ADULTERY, robbery, and the eating of flesh cut from a living animal. They also require the creation of courts of justice. According to tradition, gentiles can enter into the afterlife if they observe these commandments.

Northern Kingdom

Known as ISRAEL, it was created when the ten northern tribes rebelled against the Davidic monarchy in 930 BCE and established their own kingdom. It was conquered by the Assyrians in 721 BCE, and the tribes were exiled.

notarikon

System of abbreviation by shortening words or writing only one letter of a word. The term is derived from the system of shorthand which was used by the *notarii* in Roman courts. In Hebrew studies *notarikon* is one of the methods of interpreting Scripture. It is the 30th of the 32 HERMENEUTICAL rules laid down in the BARAITA of 32 rules.

numbers

In HEBREW the letters of the alphabet stand for numbers. This attribute of the language has given rise to the significance of numbers in Jewish thought. Although Scripture does not generally attribute particular significance to numbers, TALMUDIC literature uses numbers mnemonically. Further, rabbinic sources regard the occurrence of the same number in different contexts or events as indicating a connection between them. This concept was developed in the tradition of biblical exegesis known as GEMATRIA. In KABBALISTIC literature numbers were viewed as having creative powers. The concept of the magical significance and uses of numbers was developed in the Jewish and Christian traditions of the KABBALAH.

Numbers, Book of

Fourth book of the PENTATEUCH. It traces the history of the Israelites in the desert after the EXODUS.

nusakh (Hebrew, 'version)

Different rites used in the various Jewish communities. The term can also refer to the different traditions of melody used in SYNAGOGUES.

Nuzi

Ancient city in Mesopotamia. Excavations there have cast light on biblical traditions.

oath

Self-curse if obligations or conditions are not fulfilled. The Bible records various instances of oaths being taken, and fake oaths were strongly condemned. According to the TALMUD, oaths can be used as evidence in civil cases; however, the oaths of minors, the insane, the deaf and known liars are not acceptable. Taking an oath involved touching a TORAH SCROLL and swearing by God or by one of his attributes. By the 14th century, witnesses swore oaths that they were speaking the truth, although this was not a practice for which there was universal approval.

Obadiah, Book of

Biblical book of prophecy, one of the 12 books of the MINOR PROPHETS. The Book of Obadiah is generally dated in the late seventh/early sixth century BCE. It includes oracles of woe against Edom, especially for the Edomites' support of the BABYLONIANS. The final section, which is possibly a later addition, promises the future triumph of the Israelites.

Odel (fl. 18th century)

Polish matriarch, daughter of ISRAEL BEN ELIEZER, the Baal Shem Tov. She was the mother of various ZADDIKIM. In Ḥasidic literature she is portrayed as the ideal of womanhood.

ohel

Structure over a grave. The ḤASIDIM venerate the tombs of their ZADDIKIM, visiting them on the anniversary of the death. An *ohel* was erected over the grave and a *ner tamid* (GENERAL LIGHT) is kept burning at its foot. It was formerly the practice to prostrate oneself upon the grave and place a note there asking for help.

oil

Oil plays an important role in the ritual, ceremonial and SACRIFICIAL practices of Judaism. Pure olive oil was used in both the SANCTUARY and the TEMPLE (Exod. 27:20). Among Oriental Jews this is still the only oil that may be used to fuel the ETERNAL LIGHT in the SYNAGOGUE. According to Rabbi Tarphon, a 1st-century scholar, only olive oil can be used for SABBATH lamps, but the general ruling is that any oil may be used. Oil was also used to anoint the HIGH PRIEST as well as kings, and formed part of certain sacrificial offerings.

olam ha-Ba
(Hebrew, 'world to come')

The hereafter. *Olam ha-Ba* will begin with the resurrection of the dead and a final judgement. The righteous will be rewarded and the wicked punished.

Old Testament

See BIBLE.

oleh (Hebrew, 'one who ascends')

The word is used specifically of an immigrant to ISRAEL. It also refers to a person visiting the HOLY LAND as a PIL-GRIM for the observance of PASSOVER, SHAVUOT and SUKKOT (Exod. 23:14–17).

omer (Hebrew, 'sheaf')

First sheaf cut during the barley harvest; it was offered in the TEMPLE on the second day of PASSOVER (Lev. 23:15). Until the SACRIFICE had been offered, it was forbidden to eat the new grain. The period of seven weeks between the second day of Passover and SHAVUOT is known as the counting of the omer.

omer, counting of the

The counting of the 49 days from the second day of PASSOVER, when the first sheaf (OMER) of the barley harvest was offered in the TEMPLE, until the feast of SHAVUOT. The time of counting is referred to as the Sephirah period, during which MOURNING customs are practised and MARRIAGES are prohibited. The KABBALISTS viewed the 49 days of the counting of the omer as having mystical significance.

onanism

Interrupted sexual intercourse or masturbation. In GENESIS 38, Onan was condemned for spilling his seed on the ground. On the basis of this text, most RABBIS condemn any form of contraception which creates a barrier to semen. Other methods (such as the contraceptive pill) are accepted only for medical reasons.

oneg shabbat
(Hebrew, 'Sabbath delight')

Name given to an educational or cultural gathering that takes place on Saturday afternoon. The term has come to refer to any celebration during the SABBATH.

Onkelos (fl. second century BCE)

PALESTINIAN proselyte. He was a contemporary of Rabban GAMALIEL II. He translated the PENTATEUCH into ARAMAIC. (*See also* TARGUM.)

oracle

See URIM AND THUMMIM.

oral law

According to the Jewish tradition, the oral law was given to MOSES on MOUNT SINAI together with the WRITTEN LAW. During the period of the Second TEMPLE, the oral law was upheld by the PHARISEES in opposition to the SADDUCEES. Eventually it was studied in the ACADEMIES, and was written down in the MISHNAH which was compiled by JUDAH HA-NASI in the second century. After centuries of discussion, the oral law was recorded in the TALMUD. After the redaction of the Talmud in the sixth century, it was further studied in talmudic academies. In the GAONIC period, the KARAITES rejected the authority of the oral law. Modern non-ORTHODOX Judaism rejects the belief that the oral law was revealed to Moses on Mount Sinai; instead it is viewed as originating through discussion and interpretation over the centuries.

ordination (Hebrew: *semikhah*)

In Jewish usage, the conferring of the title RABBI on a person learned in Jewish law. Traditionally, teachers granted the title to learned pupils. The TALMUD traces the origin of the institution to MOSES. Initially, ordination was confined to PALESTINE; in BABYLONIA scholars were referred to as RAV. A new form of ordination was created in the 14th century in Germany by Meir ha-Levi of Vienna. In modern times a candidate for the rabbinate undergoes a lengthy period of study at the end of which he is given the certificate of *hattarat horaah* (permission to lay down a decision).

This usually includes the phrase '*yoreh yoreh, yadin yadin*' (he may surely give a decision and may surely judge). In some seminaries the graduation ceremony is described as 'ordination' and may involve the laying on of hands (*see* HANDS, LAYING ON OF).

organ

According to the TALMUD, there was an organ of ten pipes in the Second TEMPLE. In the 17th to 19th centuries an organ was used in the principal SYNAGOGUE in PRAGUE. During the 19th century the use of the organ in synagogues became a point of controversy between REFORM and ORTHODOX Judaism. Within Orthodox circles, the organ is forbidden under the general ban on instrumental MUSIC in worship outside the Temple. Its use also contravenes the rabbinic decree against playing a musical instrument on the SABBATH. Currently the organ is used in services in Reform and CONSERVATIVE synagogues.

original sin

Christian doctrine that all human beings live in a state of sin due to ADAM's disobedience. According to this view, humanity can be redeemed only through JESUS' atoning death. Judaism, however, stresses that human beings are not born in a state of sinfulness but rather that each person is motivated by innate evil and good inclinations. (*see also* GOOD INCLINATION; EVIL INCLINATION.)

orphan

According to Scripture, caring for orphans is an act of CHARITY and a duty (Deut. 14:29; 24:19–21). Rabbinic law provides for the support of orphans and grants them special privileges. During the middle ages, the number of orphans increased due to frequent massacres of the Jewish community. Many communities organized special bodies to look after their welfare. In the 19th century orphanages were founded in many Jewish centres.

Orthodoxy

Applied to a particular strand of religious thought and practice in Judaism, the term was first used in 1795. From the beginning of the 19th century it passed into common usage to refer to traditional Judaism, which adheres to the belief in the divine origin of the WRITTEN LAW and ORAL LAW, and insists on strict adherence to the laws contained in the code of Jewish law, the SHULḤAN ARUKH.

ownerless property
(Hebrew: *hefker*)

Property which has no apparent owner. Such property is exempt from the laws of TITHE.

P

pacifism

See PEACE; WAR.

pais

See EARLOCKS.

Pakuda, Baḥya ibn
(fl. 11th century)

Spanish moral philosopher. His *Duties of the Heart* describes the inner life. This work draws on Islamic mysticism and NEO-PLATONISM.

Palestine

One of the names of the territory known as ISRAEL. The name is derived from the HEBREW name 'Peleshet'; in classical antiquity Palestine was called 'Palestinian Syria', but in time 'Syria' was omitted and the first element of the name adjusted. It is likely that the Romans imposed the name Palestine on the country because of the Jewish associations connected with the name JUDEA. In the modern world the name Palestine was changed to Israel with the establishment of the Jewish state in 1948.

Palestinian Talmud

See TALMUD.

pantheism

The doctrine that the universe is God and God the universe. All forms of pantheism are opposed to classical theism, which affirms the belief in a creator and created order. KABBALISTIC doctrines are often pantheistic in character.

parable

Comparison. Parables are frequently stories which make a moral or religious point through a comparison. They were employed by the PROPHETS and many are found in AGGADIC literature.

paradise

See HEAVEN.

parashah (Hebrew, 'section')

Term applied to the weekly portion (*sidrah*) of the TORAH which is read in the SYNAGOGUE on the SABBATH. It also refers to one of the shorter passages into which the *sidrah* is divided, each of which is read by a different person.

parents

The obligation of children to respect their parents is specified by the TEN COMMANDMENTS (Exod. 20:12; Lev. 19:3) and emphasized in rabbinic teaching. According to Jewish LAW, parents should be obeyed unless they demand that their children violate the TORAH, or disagree with a son about his choice of a wife. The TALMUD declares that a son should not stand or sit in his father's place or contradict him; he should provide for his father's material needs in old age and take him where he needs to go. A father has the responsibility to support his children up to the age of six. He is permitted to chastise them, but only while they are minors. Both the father and mother are equal with respect to the duties which are owed them by their children.

Paris

Capital of France. Jews settled there in Roman times, and a Jewish community existed there throughout the early middle ages. From the 12th century Parisian Jews faced persecution and between 1182 and 1198 the Jewish community was banished from France. In 1240 the Disputation of Paris was followed by a burning of the TALMUD. Further expulsions of the Jewish population took place in 1306 and 1394. In the 17th century Jews from Bordeaux, Avignon and Alsace settled in Paris. A major influx of Jews occurred in the next century. At the end of the 19th century the DREYFUS AFFAIR caused consternation among Jews and Christians alike and exerted an important effect on French political life.

parnas (Hebrew, 'provider')

Head of the Jewish community. Originally he was a lay leader; later (particularly among the ASHKENAZIM from the middle ages onwards) he was elected as president of the community or SYNAGOGUE. Election was normally for a term of one or three years, but it could occasionally be for life. During the middle ages and the early modern period, a system existed whereby several *parnasim* led the community in rotation. In modern times the term refers to the president of a community or congregation.

parokhet

Curtain used to veil the sanctuary of the TABERNACLE which served as a temple for the Israelites during their wanderings in the wilderness. It was made by BEZALEL of scarlet, purple and fine linen with a woven design (Exod. 26:31). In modern times the term is used among the ASHKENAZIM to refer to the curtain which hangs before the ARK in the SYNAGOGUE.

partition

See MEHIZAH.

parveh (Yiddish, 'neutral')

Food which is viewed as neutral in relation to milk and meat, and which can thus be eaten with either.

paschal lamb

Name given to the lamb which was sacrificed during the TEMPLE period on the eve of PASSOVER (14 Nisan). After the SACRIFICE the animal was roasted whole and eaten by the community (Exod. 12:1–28; 43–9; Deut. 16:1–8).

Passover (Hebrew: *Pesach*)

First of three PILGRIM FESTIVALS, beginning on 15 Nisan. It commemorates the EXODUS from Egypt. The festival is observed for seven days. The first and seventh day are feast days. All LEAVEN is removed from the house in the evening before the festival. During Passover it is forbidden to eat or possess leaven, and only UNLEAVENED BREAD (*matzah*) is eaten. During the period of the First and Second TEMPLES, the PASCHAL LAMB was SACRIFICED on the eve of the festival. After the destruction of the Temple, a home celebration (SEDER) was instituted: this takes place on the first night of Passover and the Passover HAGGADAH is read.

Passover meal

See SEDER.

patriarchs

The biblical ancestors of the Jewish people: ABRAHAM, ISAAC and JACOB. Their stories are recorded in the Book of GENESIS. According to the RABBIS, because of their

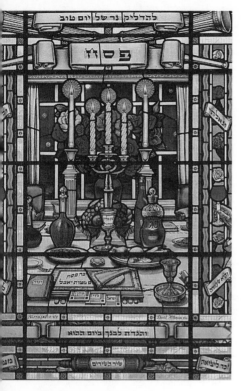

Passover: The Pesach-Seder table, Central Synagogue, London.

merits God hastened the liberation of the Israelites from slavery in EGYPT.

peace (Hebrew: *shalom*)

The Hebrew word *shalom* carries connotations of wholeness. The ideal of peace was proclaimed by the PROPHETS, and the MESSIAH was hailed as the bringer of peace. The last of the EIGHTEEN BENEDICTIONS is a prayer for peace. However, pacifism is not obligatory since WAR is justified in certain circumstances.

peace offering

SACRIFICE of cattle or sheep given as a thanksgiving in fulfilment of a VOW or as a free-will offering (Lev. 3; 7:11). The PRIESTS sprinkled the blood of the animal on the ALTAR, sacrificed parts of the fat, and took their own portion. Those making the sacrifice then ate the remains.

peah (Hebrew, 'corner')

Term used to refer to the corner of a field, in connection with the rules on GLEANING. Gleanings are one of the obligatory gifts for the poor (Lev. 19:9–10; 23:22). The Bible decrees that they should be left at the corners of a field that is being harvested. The rabbis taught that at least one-sixtieth of the harvest should be left. In the event of a good crop or a large number of poor gleaners, the proportion should be increased.

Penitence, Ten Days of
(Hebrew: *Aseret Yeme Teshuvah*)

Name given to the first ten days of Tishri, from the beginning of the NEW YEAR to the close of the DAY OF ATONEMENT. According to tradition, individuals are judged at the New Year, and judgement is proclaimed on the Day of Atonement. Clemency may be obtained through REPENTANCE during the Ten Days of Penitence. PENITENTIAL PRAYERS are said daily, FASTS take place, and there are changes to the LITURGY which stress God's kingship.

penitential prayers
(Hebrew: *selihot*)

Prayers recited during the HIGH HOLY DAY period as well as on FAST days. Some date from the first century, but the majority were composed by the Hebrew poets of Spain or by the liturgical poets of the 12th and 13th centuries. They deal with suffering, MARTYRDOM, the destruction of the TEMPLE, human weakness, confession, and God's forgiveness and mercy.

Pentateuch

The Five Books of MOSES (GENESIS, EXODUS, LEVITICUS, NUMBERS and DEUTERONOMY), also known as the TORAH. It covers the history of the

Israelites from the creation of the world until the death of Moses. According to the rabbis, the Five Books of Moses were given by God to Moses on MOUNT SINAI. In modern times non-ORTHODOX Judaism has denied this central principle of the Jewish tradition, insisting that the Torah is a composite work reflecting the views of Jews living in different historical circumstances.

Pentecost

See SHAVUOT.

peot (Yiddish, 'sidecurls')

Long ringlets of hair worn in front of the ears by ORTHODOX, Yemenite and ḤASIDIC Jewish men. The practice is based on Lev. 19:27.

perek shirah
(Hebrew, 'chapter of song')

Anonymous collection of hymns of praise. It dates from as early as the 11th century BCE. It is occasionally recited after the MORNING SERVICE.

Peres, Shimon (b. 1923)

Israeli politician. Born in Poland, he went to PALESTINE in 1934. He served as chairman of the Labour Party from 1977 and became acting prime minister; he served as prime minister of Israel 1984–6. His publications include *From These Men, Tomorrow is Now* and *The Next Phase*.

persecution

See ANTI-SEMITISM; HOLOCAUST; POGROM.

perush

RASHI's commentary as printed in editions of the TALMUD.

Perushim

See PHARISEES.

Pesach

See PASSOVER.

peshat

Literal meaning of a text; it is frequently set in contrast with DERASH, the symbolic interpretation. This distinction was used by RASHI in his commentaries.

pesher (Hebrew, 'interpretation')

The application of prophecy to future events. In particular, pesher is the name given to various biblical commentaries among the DEAD SEA SCROLLS.

Peshitta (Syriac, 'simple')

Syriac translation of the Bible. The Peshitta dates from the late first century CE.

pesuke de-zimrah
(Hebrew, 'passages of songs')

Name given to a section of the *shaḥarit* PRAYER recited between the morning blessings and the prayer that precedes the SHEMA. The order of these elements accords with the dictum that praise of God should precede prayer. The pesuke de-zimrah consists of Psalms 145–50, various verses, and the Song of Moses (Exod. 14:30–15:18). Among the SEPHARDIM the pesuke de-zimrah are referred to as the ZEMIROT. In the Sephardi rite a different ordering is observed, and on SABBATHS and FESTIVALS more psalms are added.

petiḥah (Hebrew, 'opening')

Ritual of opening the ARK in the SYNAGOGUE. *Petihah* is performed to take out or replace the TORAH SCROLLS, or when reciting solemn prayers. It is usual to stand when the ark is opened.

Pharisees (Hebrew: *Perushim*)

Religious sect of the Second TEMPLE period. The Pharisees are first mentioned *c.*160 BCE. Their name means 'the separated ones', and they were scrupulous in their observance of the WRITTEN and ORAL LAW. They taught in the SYNA-GOGUES and their beliefs, particularly in the RESURRECTION of the dead and the coming of the MESSIAH, influenced the majority of the Jewish nation. At times they came into conflict with the SADDUCEES, and at one stage they were excluded from the SANHEDRIN. After the destruction of the Temple in 70 CE, the SACRIFICIAL system came to an end, and the Pharisees became the dominant group in the Jewish community.

Philo (c.25 BCE–40 CE)

HELLENISTIC philosopher. He lived in Alexandria. In his writings Philo combined Hellenistic thought with the belief in Scripture. His writings include a legal exposition, philosophical interpretation and commentary on the TORAH. In 40 CE he was a member of the Jewish deputation which travelled to Rome and met with the Emperor Caligula concerning anti-Jewish riots in Alexandria.

philosophy

Jewish philosophical activity began with the first-century thinker PHILO who interpreted Judaism in NEOPLATONIC terms. Later Jewish thinkers were influenced by the revival of Greek philosophy by the Arabs. Prominent among such medieval philosophers were SAADIAH GAON, Solomon ibn GABIROL, Baḥya ibn PAKUDA, Abraham ibn Daud, MAIMONIDES, Gersonides (LEVI BEN GERSHON), Ḥasdai CRESCAS, Joseph ALBO and Isaac ABRABANEL. The modern period of Jewish philosophy began with Moses MENDELSSOHN, who was followed by such writers as Solomon FORMSTECHER, Samuel HIRSCH, Naḥman Krochmal, Solomon Ludwig STEINHEIM, Hermann COHEN, Franz ROSENZWEIG, Leo BAECK, Martin BUBER, Abraham HESCHEL and Mordecai KAPLAN.

phylactery

See TEFILLIN.

pidyon ha-ben

See REDEMPTION OF THE FIRST-BORN.

pikkuah nefesh

See REGARD FOR HUMAN LIFE.

pilgrim festivals

According to the Bible, male Israelites were enjoined to make a pilgrimage to JERUSALEM during the festivals of PASSOVER, SHAVUOT and SUKKOT (Exod. 23:17; Deut. 16:16), which became known as 'pilgrim festivals'. All pilgrims were to offer a SACRIFICE and give the TEMPLE the second TITHE of their produce, which had to be consumed in Jerusalem. In modern times there is no longer an obligation to go to Jerusalem on the pilgrim festivals. Special prayers are recited in the SYNAGOGUE, and each festival has its own special liturgical characteristics, ceremonies and customs.

pilgrimage

Journey to a holy city or site for the benefit of the traveller. Jews made pilgrimage to JERUSALEM for the FESTIVALS of PASSOVER, SHAVUOT and SUKKOT during TEMPLE times. In the middle ages, the institution was revived largely through the influence of the KARAITES. Special PRAYERS were composed for pilgrims to recite in Jerusalem, as well as on visits to the graves of biblical figures and rabbinic sages.

pilpul (Hebrew, 'fine distinctions')

Tradition of interpretation of the ORAL LAW. It was occasionally carried to extremes of legal casuistry, and its unrestrained use evoked the disapproval of various scholars. Neverthless, the method of *pilpul* was developed by TOSAFISTS and in YESHIVOT.

Pinsker, Leon (1821–91)

Russian ZIONIST. Born in Tomaszów, Poland, he was one of the first Jews to enrol at Odessa University. Later he studied medicine at the University of Moscow, returning to Odessa to set up in practice. He was a founder of the first Russian Jewish weekly, *Dawn*. Intially he was an advocate of the HASKALAH, but after the POGROMS of 1881, he called for the rebirth of the Jewish nation. In his pamphlet *Auto-Emancipation* he proposed the establishment of a Jewish territory, where Jews could govern themselves. In 1884 he convened the Katowitz Conference of Ḥovevei Zion where he was elected president of ḤIBBAT ZION's presidium (*see* LOVE OF ZION).

pioneer (Hebrew: *ḥalutz*)

Term used to refer to a Jewish settler in PALESTINE before the establishment of the State of ISRAEL.

Pirke Avot

See AVOT.

Pirke de-Rabbi Eliezer

TANNAITIC MIDRASH on GENESIS and the first chapters of EXODUS. The first two chapters consist of biographical details concerning the first-century Palestinian scholar Eliezer ben Hyrcanus.

piyyut

Liturgical poem. Originating in PALESTINE possibly in the fifth century, *piyyutim* were also composed in BABYLONIA, Germany, France, Spain and Italy. The oldest authors of such poems are Yose ben Yose, Yannai and Eleazar Kallir. Later important writers included SAADIAH GAON, Meshullam ben Kalonymos, Amittai ben Shephatiah, RASHI, Solomon ibn GABIROL, JUDAH HALEVI, Solomon ben Judah ha-Bavli, Moses ben Kalonymos, Jekuthiel ben Moses and Meir ben Baruch of Rothenburg. The chief groups of *piyyutim* are: the *yotzer*, inserted in the first blessing before the SHEMA in the MORNING SERVICE; the *ophan*, inserted in the middle of the same blessing; the *zulat*,

inserted in the Emet ve-Yatziv prayer recited after the *Shema* in the morning service; and the *kerovah*, which accompanies the first three blessings of the AMIDAH. *Piyyutim* for the EVENING SERVICE are known as MAARAVOT. Special groups of *piyyutim* were written for the DAY OF ATONEMENT and the NINTH OF AV.

Poale Zion
(Hebrew, 'Workers of Zion')

Socialist ZIONIST movement, originating in Russia at the beginning of the 20th century. The World Confederation of Poale Zion was established in 1907. In Palestine it formed collective settlements, co-operatives and the Histadrut (Israeli federation of trade unions). Eventually three groupings of socialist Zionists emerged.

poem of mourning
(Hebrew: *kinah*)

Dirge for the dead, recited at FUNERALS and on other days of MOURNING in biblical, MISHNAIC and TALMUDIC times. In the middle ages the term was applied to a special type of PIYYUT for the NINTH OF AV dealing with the destruction of the TEMPLE and national independence, contemporary persecutions, and the hope for messianic redemption.

pogrom

Massacre of a body of people. The term has come to be used to denote attacks against the Jews, notably those carried out by the Christian population, especially in Russia, between 1881 and 1921. Three waves of pogroms took place, in 1881–4, 1903–6 and 1917–21. Such attacks involved destruction of property, looting, rape and murder.

polemic

Controversial theological discussion. In TALMUDIC literature there are references to Jewish polemics in the discussions between RABBIS and HERETICS. Christians also composed polemical material aimed at persuading Jews of the truths of Christianity. In the middle ages anti-Jewish polemics were encouraged by the Dominicans, and various disputations took place, including the Disputation of PARIS (1240) and the Disputation of BARCELONA (1263). In addition, Jewish writers composed polemics on various subjects.

polygamy

In the biblical period Jewish society was polygamous; however, certain biblical passages appear to reflect the values of a monogamous community. In the TALMUD, monogamy is extolled. The TAKKANAH of Gershom ben Judah (*c*.1000) forbids polygamy, and thereby provided a formal sanction to the state of affairs that already existed among ASHKENAZI Jewry. Among Spanish and Oriental Jews polygamy continued to be accepted under religious law, although in modern times it has been forbidden by civil law.

posekim

Religious leaders who interpreted the meaning of the law in practice and thus contributed to its codification.

poverty

According to the Bible, poverty is an ever-present misfortune (Deut. 15:11); its relief is a religious duty. Various institutions have been founded throughout history to sustain the poor, and the giving of alms is enshrined in Jewish LAW and practice. The Jewish tradition emphasizes that the aim of charitable giving and social welfare should be to help the poor to become self-supporting. (*See also* CHARITY; GLEANING.)

practical kabbalah

See KABBALAH.

Prague

Capital of Czechoslovakia and the modern Czech Republic. Jews settled there in the 10th century. From as early as the 11th century, they were subject to attacks. During the 14th and 15th centuries the Jewish community in Prague was repeatedly persecuted and eventually expelled. However, in the 16th century the position of Jewry improved and over the next 200 years the city had one of the largest Jewish populations in Europe. In 1848 Jews were granted full equality and the GHETTO was abolished four years later.

prayer

Offering of public devotion, petition, confession, adoration or thanksgiving to God. In the Bible prayers are mentioned as being made by individuals as well as in a cultic context. At the commencement of the Second TEMPLE period, a formal pattern of daily worship was determined by the GREAT ASSEMBLY. Following the pattern of SACRIFICE, it took place in the morning, afternoon and evening. An additional prayer was recited on SABBATHS and FESTIVALS. On the DAY OF ATONEMENT a further prayer was added. The original version of the prayer service included the EIGHTEEN BENEDICTIONS (AMIDAH) and the SHEMA. Over the centuries other prayers were added. From the GAONIC period compilations of prayers were made in the daily and festival PRAYER BOOK.

prayer book

Book containing the text of set prayers. Prior to the GAONIC era, all prayers were known by heart and prayer books appear not to have existed. A book containing the daily prayers is known as a *siddur*, and one containing the FESTIVAL prayers as a MAḤZOR. The earliest prayer book, that of Rav Amram Gaon, dates from the ninth century. The ASHKENAZIM use four main types of prayer book: *Ha-Maḥzor ha-Gadol* ('the Great Festival Prayer Book'), which contains all the yearly prayers; the *maḥzor*, which contains the prayers for each individual festival; the *siddur* for individual daily use;

Traditional Jewish man praying at the Wailing Wall, Jerusalem.

and the fuller *Ha-Siddur ha-Shalom*. The SEPHARDIM use the *Tefillat ha-Ḥodesh* for daily and SABBATH prayer and individual books for festivals. The ḤASIDIM and the PROGRESSIVE movement have their own prayer books.

prayer for the dead

See KADDISH; YAHRZEIT.

prayer shawl

See TALLIT.

preacher

See MAGGID.

pride

In the Jewish tradition pride is considered one of the most serious vices. For this reason, the TALMUD condemns such an attitude in the most forceful terms. Whatever talents a person possesses are to be regarded as a divine gift.

priest (Hebrew: *cohen*)

In Judaism the position of priest is hereditary, based on descent from the family of AARON. The duties of priests were originally connected with the SACRIFICIAL service in the TEMPLE of JERUSALEM. The HIGH PRIEST served as the spiritual head of the people; in some cases he was also the secular head of the community. After the destruction of the Temple in 70 CE, the duties of the priest were limited to pronouncing the PRIESTLY blessing on FESTIVAL days, redeeming first-born males on the 31st day after birth (*see* REDEMPTION OF THE FIRST-BORN), and taking precedence at functions such as the reading of the TORAH. While the priesthood continues to exist, the identity of those entitled to claim membership of this group is obscure.

priestly blessing

Formula of words ordained by God and given to the PRIESTS by MOSES for the blessing of ISRAEL (Num. 6:24–6): 'The Lord bless you and keep you; the Lord make his face to shine upon you and be gracious to you; the Lord lift up his countenance upon you and grant you peace.' It was recited by the priests in the

TEMPLE each day; eventually it became part of the SYNAGOGUE LITURGY.

primordial man
(Hebrew: *Adam Kadmon*)

Adam Kadmon first appeared in 13th-century texts. According to KABBALISTIC literature, he is the spiritual prototype of man created by God. In the ZOHAR he is portrayed as a manifestation of the *sefirot* (DIVINE EMANATIONS). LURIANIC kabbalah depicts him as a mediator between the EN SOF and the *sefirot*. Adam Kadmon came to be identified with the MESSIAH and was contrasted with the Devil Adam Beliyyaal (Hebrew, 'the evil man').

principles of faith
(Hebrew: *ikkarim*)

Articles of faith. Various authorities have formulated the principles of the Jewish faith. PHILO spoke of eight essential principles; MAIMONIDES set out THIRTEEN PRINCIPLES; and Joseph ALBO argued for three *ikkarim* (existence of God, the divine origin of TORAH, and REWARD AND PUNISHMENT). The tradition continued into the modern period with such thinkers as Moses MENDELSSOHN. Nonetheless, every Jew is part of the COVENANT of Israel, independent of his or her attachment to dogma. The most important Jewish belief is expressed by the SHEMA ('Hear, O Israel, the Lord our God, the Lord is One').

printing

During the middle ages, books were produced by hand. The invention of printing, however, made texts of Jewish sources widely available. Thus editions of the TALMUD, the MIDRASHIM, the CODES, commentaries, philosophical studies and works of mysticism as well as the Bible and PRAYER BOOK became available to a large audience.

procreation

According to rabbinic Judaism, the first commandment in the TORAH is to be fruitful and multiply (Gen. 1:28; 9:1). Procreation is one of the central aims of marriage. This is the basis for opposition to birth control. The tradition maintains that the obligation to have children is a duty which devolves upon men rather than women.

profanation

Desecration of holy things. Anyone committing such an act was obliged to bring a SACRIFICE and pay for the value of whatever was profaned with an increment of a fifth (Lev. 5:14). If an animal donated for sacrifice was discovered to be unfit through a physical blemish, the donor could redeem it by paying the value of the animal plus an increment. A house which had been consecrated to the SANCTUARY could also be redeemed (Lev. 26:13–15). The priestly order was consecrated, and a PRIEST was not allowed to marry a divorcee or harlot. The term is also used in a wider, non-cultic context, in such expressions as 'profanation of the name' (ḤILLUL HA-SHEM) and 'profanation of the SABBATH'.

profanation of the name

See ḤILLUL HA-SHEM.

Progressive Judaism

Non-ORTHODOX movements within Judaism. Progressive Judaism is the product of the Enlightenment (*see* HASKALAH) and embraces REFORM JUDAISM, CONSERVATIVE JUDAISM, RECONSTRUCTIONIST JUDAISM and HUMANISTIC JUDAISM.

promised land

Land promised to the PATRIARCH ABRAHAM. According to Scripture, God promised Abraham that the land would belong to his offspring for ever. (*See also* CANAAN; ISRAEL, LAND OF.)

prophet (Hebrew: *navi*)

One who speaks the word of God. The early prophets (*Neviim*) are depicted in

Scripture as 'seers' or 'men of God'. Prominent among the pre-classical prophets were SAMUEL, Nathan, ELIJAH and ELISHA. Also mentioned are groups of prophets who dwelt together in bands. The early prophets gave advice, predicted future events and were involved with the political life of the nation. The classical prophets are those whose words are recorded in the Bible. They include the MAJOR PROPHETS (ISAIAH, JEREMIAH and EZEKIEL) and the 12 MINOR PROPHETS (HOSEA, JOEL, AMOS, OBADIAH, JONAH, MICAH, NAHUM, HABAKKUK, ZEPHANIAH, HAGGAI, ZECHARIAH and MALACHI).

prosbul

Legal formula for reclaiming debts after the SABBATICAL YEAR. The *prosbul* was introduced by HILLEL; however, in the middle ages it was abandoned because the sabbatical year was no longer operative.

proselyte (Hebrew: *ger*)

Convert to Judaism. Conversion to Judaism appears to have been common in the Second TEMPLE period, and a fixed procedure was established by the TANNAIM. The disadvantages of becoming Jewish were explained to the candidate; if he or she replied, 'I know of this and am not worthy,' the person was to be accepted immediately. CIRCUMCISION and ritual IMMERSION were required for male converts; ritual immersion alone for female. Once converted, the proselyte was given a new name as 'son' or 'daughter of ABRAHAM'. He or she must be regarded as a Jew in every respect except that a female convert may not marry a COHEN, and, unlike a born Jew, may marry a MAMZER. In modern times, conversion to Judaism has become more common, particularly within the non-Orthodox movements. The ORTHODOX, however, recognize the validity only of their own conversions.

prostitution, sacred

Sexual intercourse as part of the cult. Sacred prostitution was common in ancient Middle Eastern religions, but was associated with IDOLATRY. It was strictly forbidden by the Book of DEUTERONOMY and condemned by the PROPHETS.

prostration

Lying face down in submission. It was practised in the TEMPLE during the Yom Kippur service, and this tradition has been continued by the ASHKENAZIM.

Proverbs, Book of

Biblical book and part of the HAGIOGRAPHA. It consists of a collection of moral maxims. The first section (chapters 1–9) contains an introduction and a depiction of wisdom. The second section (10:1–22:16) and the fifth (25–39) are ascribed to Solomon and consist of collections of sayings. The third section (22:17–24:22) and the fourth (24:23–24) consist of long stanzas on various themes. The sixth section (chapter 30), attributed to Agur ben Jakeh, contains riddles, the sayings of King Lemuel and a poem praising a virtuous wife.

providence

God's foreseeing care for his creatures. According to the Bible, God directs the course of human affairs and the destiny of the Jewish people. During the medieval period Jewish philosophers such as SAADIAH GAON, JUDAH HALEVI and MAIMONIDES discussed various issues connected with this doctrine.

Psalms, Book of

Biblical book, part of the HAGIOGRAPHA. It contains 150 songs. It is subdivided into five books, beginning respectively with Psalms 1, 42, 78, 90 and 107. Each section concludes with a benediction of thanksgiving. The psalms include poems of thanksgiving and praise, didactic songs, songs in honour of kings, war songs, songs connected with FESTIVALS and historical events, and songs concerning events in individuals' lives. According to tradition, they are attributed to DAVID.

Pseudepigrapha

Title of a group of works of Jewish religious literature written between the second century BCE and the second century CE. Like the APOCRYPHA, these works were not included in the CANON of Scripture. They are generally APOCALYPTIC in character and comprise the Psalms of SOLOMON, the Testament of the Twelve Patriarchs, the Book of JUBILEES, the Apocalypse of BARUCH, the Book of ENOCH, the Assumption of MOSES, the Ascension of Isaiah and the Sibylline Oracles.

Pumbedita

Town in BABYLONIA on the bank of the River Euphrates. The Jewish community was established there in the Second TEMPLE period and the town became a centre for TORAH study. After NEHARDEA was devastated in 259, an ACADEMY was established at Pumbedita. It became the central religious authority for Babylonian Jewry until the middle of the fourth century. After the death of RAVA in 352, and until the beginning of the ninth century, the academy was second in importance to that at SURA. It eventually moved to Baghdad. Under Sherira Gaon and his son Hai Gaon, the Pumbedita academy gained distinction in the 10th and 11th centuries. It closed in 1038.

punishment

Biblical law prescribes various penalties for crime and wrongdoing. Physical penalties include stoning, burning, beheading, strangulation and flogging as well as EXILE. Material penalties incude restitution, reparation for loss and financial compensation. All these penalties were supplemented by rabbinic law.

purification after childbirth

After chidbirth, a woman is ritually unclean for 33 days if she has a boy and 66 if she has a girl. After this period, the Book of LEVITICUS prescribes that a SACRIFICE of purification be made. In modern times it is customary for a woman to visit the SYNAGOGUE once her period of ritual impurity is finished. (*See also* NIDDAH.)

Purim (Hebrew, 'Lots')

The Feast of ESTHER. Purim commemorates the deliverance of the Jews by Esther and Mordecai from HAMAN's plot to destroy them. It is celebrated on 15 Adar, and the Book of Esther is read in the SYNAGOGUE.

Purim, Special

Annual celebrations instituted by particular Jewish communities to commemorate times when they were delivered from danger. Examples include the Purim of Narbonne (21 Adar), the Purim of Cairo (23 Adar), the Purim of Buda (10 Elul) and the Purim of Livorno (22 Shevat).

purity

State of ritual acceptability. According to tradition, the three causes of ritual impurity are LEPROSY, sexual emission and contact with the dead. The Book of LEVITICUS lays down provisions for the purification of lepers; however, these laws are no longer observed since modern leprosy is not viewed as the same disease as that mentioned in the Bible. Contact with the dead renders an individual ritually impure for seven days, and cohenim (PRIESTS) are instructed to avoid all contact with the dead. The laws of ritual purity are enumerated in the MISHNAH, but many have fallen into disuse. PROGRESSIVE JUDAISM has abandoned such laws. (*See also* MIKVEH; NIDDAH.)

Qumran

Ancient settlement on the north-west shore of the Dead Sea. Archaeological finds have revealed buildings which appear to have been occupied by the community that produced the DEAD SEA SCROLLS.

R

rabbi (Hebrew, 'my master')

Title used during the first century to refer to ordained members of the SANHEDRIN. It was used only in PALESTINE until the fifth century; scholars in BABYLONIA were addressed by the title RAV. Subsequently Jews distinguished in learning were referred to as 'rabbi'. The title was also conferred on the spiritual heads of Jewish communities. Rabbis were not salaried until the 15th century. In large communities they maintained YESHIVOT, and various functions were performed under their supervision: DAYYANIM adjudicated lawsuits and arranged divorces, the SHOHET was in charge of ritual SLAUGHTER, and members of the community were purified by ritual bathing. In modern times rabbis have adopted pastoral, social and educational duties. A rabbi is appointed by his congregation to act as its spiritual leader, organize services, supervise the religious education of the young, visit the sick and bereaved, and preside over life-cycle events.

rabbinical conferences

Gatherings of RABBIS convened to make authoritative rulings. From the mid-19th century PROGRESSIVE rabbis met together to provide definitive guidance for the emerging REFORM Jewish community. Such decisions were bitterly opposed by ORTHODOX critics who maintained that traditional beliefs and practices must be observed. These synods were held first in Europe; subsequently Reform rabbis gathered together in the USA on a regular basis. In 1887 the Pittsburgh Platform was adopted; this was followed in 1937 by the Columbus Platform, and in 1976 by the San Francisco Platform. In 1961 the Federation of RECONSTRUCTIONIST Congregations also laid down its programme at a conference. Since the founding of the State of ISRAEL, there has been some agitation among the Orthodox for the restoration of the SANHEDRIN.

rabbinical seminaries

After the emancipation of Jewry, seminaries for RABBIS were established in European countries: in Italy in 1829; France in 1829; the Netherlands in 1834 and 1837, Lithuania in 1847; the Ukraine in 1847; England in 1855; Germany in 1854, 1872 and 1873; Hungary in 1877; Austria in 1893; Turkey in 1898; and Poland in 1928. In the USA the following seminaries were founded from the late 19th century: Maimonides College, 1867; the Hebrew Union College, 1875; the Jewish Theological Seminary of America, 1886; the Isaac Elḥanan Yeshiva 1896; the Jewish Institute of Religion 1922; and the Reconstructionist Rabbinical College 1968. In addition, numerous YESHIVOT have been established in the USA, Israel and elsewhere to train ORTHODOX rabbis.

Rabbinites

Opponents of the KARAITES.

Rabin, Yitzḥak (1922–95)

Israeli soldier and diplomat. Born in JERUSALEM, he joined the Palmaḥ in 1940 and participated in undergound activities against the British Mandatory government. In 1947 he became deupty commander of the Palmaḥ, and later chief of operations of the Southern Command. From 1956 to 1959 he served as chief of operations of the Northern Command. He later became head of the General Staff Branch, deputy chief of staff and eventually chief of staff. In 1968 he was appointed Israeli ambassador to the USA. In 1992 he became prime minister of Israel. In 1995 he was assassinated by an Israeli Jewish student, Yigal Amir.

Prime Minister of Israel, Yitzḥak Rabin

rain, prayers for

Prayers for rain are an important feature of congregational worship, and an entire TRACTATE of the MISHNAH (Taanit) is largely devoted to prayers for rain. In the TALMUD this tractate contains various tales of MIRACLE workers whose prayers for rain were efficacious.

ransom

It is the duty of a Jew to ransom a fellow Jew captured by slave dealers or robbers, or unjustly put in prison. According to Jewish law, there are a number of rules for the ransoming of captives: (1) women should be given preference over men; (2) a person captured with his father and teacher may ransom himself first, but he is then bound to ransom his teacher, and then his father; (3) preference should be given to a scholar; (4) the court has the power to compel a husband to ransom his wife; (5) money set aside for charity or the building of a SYNAGOGUE may be used to ransom captives; (6) a person who delays ransoming a captive is viewed as if he spilled the captive's blood.

rape

TALMUDIC law concerning rape is based on Deut. 22:22–8.

Raphael

Archangel and divine messenger. First mentioned in the Books of ENOCH and TOBIT, he has the special function of healing. In the TALMUD he is named as one of the three ANGELS who visited ABRAHAM after he had CIRCUMCISED himself. Jewish traditions concerning Raphael were taken over into Christian angelology and syncretistic MAGIC.

Rapoport, Solomon Judah (1790–1867)

Galician RABBI. Born in Lemberg, he was a rabbi in Tarnopol from 1837 to 1840, when he became CHIEF RABBI of PRAGUE. He was attacked by the ḤASIDIM and the ultra-ORTHODOX for his enlightened approach to Jewish study. He wrote works dealing with Jewish scholars of the GAONIC period, commenced a TALMUDIC encyclopedia, and translated European poetry into Hebrew.

Ras Shamra

Site of archaeological excavations in modern Syria. The city of UGARIT was located here, and excavations at this site have greatly added to our knowledge of CANAANITE customs.

Rashi (1040–1105)

French rabbinic scholar. Also known as Solomon ben Isaac, he was born in Troyes and studied in the Rhineland. He later returned to Troyes where he established a school. He published RESPONSA, composed penitential hymns and wrote commentaries on the Bible and TALMUD. His commentary on the Talmud established the correct text, defined numerous terms, and explained unusual words and phrases. His Bible commentary was the basis for later interpretations of Scripture.

rav

BABYLONIAN title for RABBI in the TALMUDIC period.

Rav (fl. third century)

BABYLONIAN AMORA. Born in Kafri in southern Babylonia, he went to PALESTINE; later he returned to Babylonia. Founder of the ACADEMY at SURA.

Rava (fl. fourth century)

BABYLONIAN AMORA. Born in Maḥoza, he created an ACADEMY there when ABBAYE became head of the academy at PUMBEDITA. After Abbaye's death, Rava succeeded him at Pumbedita, which he amalgamated with Maḥoza. His controversies with Abbaye were famous: with six exceptions, the ordinances of HALAKHAH were decided in accordance with his views.

Raziel, Book of

Collection of mystical, cosmological and MAGICAL Hebrew texts. It contains mystical teachings, letter mysticism, descriptions of the heavens, angelology, magical recipes, and formulas for AMULETS.

reading of the Torah

See TORAH, READING OF THE.

rebbe (Yiddish)

Rabbi. The title is also given to a teacher; among the ḤASIDIM it refers to their spiritual leader.

Rebekah
(fl. ?16th century BCE)

Israelite woman, wife of ISAAC. When ABRAHAM sent his servant Eliezer to Aram Naharaim to seek a wife for his son Isaac, Eliezer chose Rebekah. She bore him twin sons, ESAU and JACOB (Gen. 24–8).

rebuke

The basis for offering reproof to one's neighbour is Lev. 19:17: 'Thou shalt not hate thy brother in thine heart: thou shalt surely rebuke thy neighbour and not suffer sin because of him.' According to rabbinic Judaism, one should reprove sinners until they repent (unless they become aggressive and resort to violence).

reception of the Sabbath
(Hebrew: *kabbalat Shabbat*)

Evening SYNAGOGUE service greeting the SABBATH. Normally one puts on fresh clothes and recites particular hymns.

Rechabites

Ancient Jewish sect mentioned in JEREMIAH 35. They were descended from Jehonadab (or Jonadab) ben Rechab (2 Kgs. 10:15–17). According to the precepts established by Jehonadab, the Rechabites abstained from drinking wine; they were also forbidden to own fields or vineyards and build houses. God commanded Jeremiah to put them to the test by taking them to one of the chambers of the TEMPLE and serving them wine. However, the Rechabites refused to drink and were rewarded for their faithfulness by a promise of God's favour. When NEBUCHADNEZZAR invaded Israel, they fled to JERUSALEM.

Reconstructionist Judaism

Religious and social movement established by Mordecai KAPLAN. In his view, Jewish theism should be abandoned, and Judaism should be conceived as an evolving religious civilization. Kaplan called for a reconstruction of Judaism in which SYNAGOGUES should serve as centres for all aspects of Jewish culture. His congregation – the Society for the Advancement of Judaism – served as a vehicle for Kaplan's thought. In 1935 he created the Jewish Reconstructionist Foundation in New York and began to publish a magazine, *The Reconstructionist*. In 1954 a congregational organization was established, and the Reconstructionist Rabbinical College opened in 1968.

red heifer

(Hebrew: *parah adummah*)

In accordance with the instructions laid down in Num. 19, a young cow was used for SACRIFICE. The animal should be unblemished and should never have been yoked. Its ashes were mixed with water, forming a substance that would remove impurity created by contact with the dead. When sacrifice was instituted, it occurred outside the Israelite camp. Those who handled the sacrifice required purification. Subsequently the red heifer was sacrificed in JERUSALEM on the Mount of Olives.

redemption of the first-born

(Hebrew: *pidyon ha-ben*)

FAST observed by first-born sons on the day before PASSOVER. It derives from the desire to express gratitutde for the saving of the first-born Israelites during the tenth plague of EGYPT (Exod. 13:1ff).

Subsequently it became a custom to finish the study of a TALMUD tractate on the morning before Passover, when a festive banquet was arranged in the SYNAGOGUE. Since first-born sons were permitted to partake of this meal, they were not obligated to fast.

Reform Judaism

Modern movement established in Europe in the early 19th century; it advocates the harmonization of the Jewish tradition with modern life. It was created initially by lay leaders such as Israel JACOBSON. In the 1840s Reform synods began to formulate the basic principles of the movement. The first Reform congregation in the USA was Beth Elohim in Charleston, South Carolina; its synagogue was built in 1840. Reform Judaism in the USA received its central impetus from Isaac Mayer WISE, who founded the Union of American Hebrew Congregations in 1873, the Hebrew Union College in 1875 and the Central Conference of

Reform Judaism: The West London Synagogue of British Jews, established in 1840, and member of the Reform Synagogues of Great Britain.

American Rabbis in 1889. Reform Judaism has become a central force in Jewish life, with congregations throughout the world.

regard for human life
(Hebrew: *pikkuah nefesh*)

Obligation to save life. *Pikkuah nefesh* is based on the commandment in Lev. 19:16: 'Thou shalt not stand idly by the blood of thy neighbour.' The duty to save life supersedes any other law except those against MURDER, IDOLATRY and INCEST. Further than this, SABBATH laws must be set aside in cases of illness or childbirth. Hence it is permitted to ignite a fire on the Sabbath to keep an ill person warm, or to extinguish a light to help them sleep.

Rehoboam (fl. 10th century BCE)

King of JUDAH (930–908 BCE). He was the son of SOLOMON by Naamah. When he refused to moderate his policy of taxation, the country divided into the kingdoms of ISRAEL and JUDAH. Only the tribes of Judah and Simeon, and most of tribe of Benjamin, remained loyal to Rehoboam. Subsequently Shishak of EGYPT invaded Judah and plundered the TEMPLE (1 Kgs. 11ff).

reincarnation
See METEMPSYCHOSIS.

rejoicing in the law
See SIMHAT TORAH.

remnant of Israel

According to Scripture, even when the nation or its leaders desert the tradition a faithful remnant will remain. The Bible teaches that after God destroys the wicked as a prelude to the DAY OF JUDGEMENT, he will leave a righteous remnant who will serve as his kingdom on earth. The notion is found in the biblical prohetic books from AMOS (eighth century BCE) onwards.

rending of the garments

MOURNING custom, first mentioned in the Bible with regard to JOSEPH (Gen. 37:29,34). Rabbinic law specifies that it is obligatory after the death of a father, mother, son, daughter, brother, sister, wife or husband. The tear should be a hand's-breath wide. When the dead person is a parent, the rent should never be completely resewn. Rending garments is performed before the FUNERAL.

repentance (Hebrew: *teshuvah*)

The renunciation of SIN, appeal for FORGIVENESS and return to God's law. Repentance is a central theme in Scripture, and serves as the motif of the TEN DAYS OF PENITENCE. On the DAY OF ATONEMENT prayers focus on this doctrine. Forgiveness is dependent on true repentance; if another person has been wronged, restitution must also take place. During the middle ages Jewish writers dealt with this subject at length, and in modern times religious leaders created movements (such as the MUSAR MOVEMENT) which stress moral improvement.

resh kallah
(Hebrew, 'head of the *kallah*')

Second in authority to the GAON in the ACADEMIES of BABYLONIA. He was active in the study courses that occurred during the months of Adar and Elul.

responsa
(Hebrew: *she'elot u-teshuvot*)

Replies given to queries on all aspects of Jewish LAW by authorities from the time of the GEONIM to the present. More than a thousand collections of responsa have been written. The influence of responsa is found in codes of Jewish law, in novellae, and in compendia of the tosafists (*see* TOSAFOT).

responsiblity

A person who acts freely and in full knowledge of what he is doing is held responsible for his actions, according to Jewish LAW. However, a person of unsound mind is not responsible for any injuries he inflicts on others; further, he is not obligated to keep Jewish law.

resurrection
(Hebrew: *teḥiyat hametim*)
The raising of the dead. Although there is no developed doctrine of the resurrection of the dead in Scripture, the belief in resurrection became a central principle of the Jewish religion. Although it was never accepted by the SADDUCEES, it was affirmed by the PHARISEES and incoporated into the SYNAGOGUE LITURGY. There is considerable debate in rabbinic sources about the nature of the resurrection; nonetheless, there is general agreement that it will take place during the messianic age. MAIMONIDES included the doctrine in his THIRTEEN PRINCIPLES of the Jewish faith. PROGRESSIVE JUDAISM has largely abandoned this belief, substituting the notion of the IMMORTALITY of the SOUL.

retaliation
Retributive action whereby a wrong is returned in kind. This concept is expressed in the Bible: 'Eye for eye, tooth for tooth, hand for hand, foot for foot, burn for burn, wound for wound, bruise for bruise' (Exod. 21:24–5; Lev. 24: 19–20; Deut. 19:21). In Jewish LAW the person who has inflicted an injury may compensate his victim financially and thereby avert the application of this legislation.

Reuveni, David (fl. 16th century)
Italian adventurer who claimed to be the son of a King Solomon and a brother of a King Joseph (who ruled the lost tribes of Reuben, Gad and half of MANASSEH in the desert of Habor). After travelling to PALESTINE and EGYPT, he appeared in VENICE in 1523. Subsequently he settled in Rome, and Pope Clement VII gave him letters of recommendation. From 1525 to 1527 he lived in Portugal, where he was greeted by MARRANOS (including Solomon Molcho) who regarded him as the herald of the MESSIAH. In 1532 he and Molcho appeared before Charles V. Molcho was burned at the stake, and Reuveni was taken to Spain where he died. He left a diary which records these events.

revelation (Hebrew: *nirah*)
Divine disclosure. According to Scripture, God revealed himself to individuals and on MOUNT SINAI provided the nation with a CODE of LAW. During the middle ages Jewish philosophers discussed the relationship between revelation and human reason. During the modern period REFORM JUDAISM embraced the belief in progressive revelation, maintaining that God's revelation is a continual process throughout history.

revenge
According to Scripture, it is wrong to take revenge: 'Thou shalt not take vengeance, nor bear any grudge against the children of thy people, but thou shalt love thy neighbour as thyself' (Lev. 19:18). Such teaching continued into the rabbinic period and is reflected in the TALMUD and other religious sources.

Revisionism
ZIONIST movement. It was founded in 1925 by Vladimir JABOTINSKY under the name World Union of Zionist Revisionists, or Ha-Tzohar. It pressed for the creation of a Jewish state on both sides of the Jordan. Initially Revisionists were opposed to the official Zionist policy towards British Mandatory rule. In 1935 they seceded from the World Zionist Organization and formed the New Zionist Organization. The IRGUN TZEVAI LEUMI and Loḥame Ḥerut Yisrael originated from the Revisionist section of the HAGANAH.

reward and punishment

Scripture teaches that God rewards the righteous and punishes the wicked. This theme is central to the Jewish tradition and is the basis for the conception of HEAVEN and HELL as formulated in rabbinic sources. According to MAIMONIDES, this belief is one of the central PRINCIPLES of the Jewish faith: 'That He, the exalted one, rewards him who obeys the commands of the TORAH and punishes him who transgresses its prohibitions. That God's greatest reward to man is the World to Come and that his strongest punishment is cutting off of the soul from eternal bliss in the Hereafter.'

righteous stranger

(Hebrew: *ger toshav*)

A person who keeps the laws given to NOAH after the FLOOD. He must not commit the offences of IDOLATRY, MURDER, INCEST, sexual immorality or eating what has been strangled. Such a person will inherit the world to come. Thus Jews feel no obligation to convert other nations to Israel. (*See also* PROSELYTE.)

righteousness

Virtue, honesty, freedom from wickedness. In Jewish teaching a ZADDIK is one who lives according to divine law. Righteousness is a central motif of biblical legislation and prophetic teaching. According to tradition, there are 36 perfectly righteous men in every generation on whose account the world continues to exist. In rabbinic and medieval HEBREW the word *tzedakah* denotes almsgiving and CHARITY. (*See also* LAMED VAV ZADDIKIM.)

rimmonim (Hebrew, 'pomegranates')

Among the SEPHARDIM the term refers to the finial ornaments on the wooden staves on which the SCROLL OF THE LAW is rolled. Originally they were shaped like pomegranates. Subsequently they were in the shape of towers.

Rishon le-Zion

SEPHARDI chief rabbi of the HOLY LAND.

rishonim (Hebrew, 'first ones')

Older authorities. In the TALMUD the term is used to distinguish the earlier from the later PROPHETS as well as the former from the later generations in the talmudic period. In modern times the term is used to refer to all commentators and codifiers of talmudic law of the GAONIC period, up to the time of the compilation of the SHULHAN ARUKH (*c.*600–1300 CE).

ritual slaughter (Hebrew: *shehita*)

Ritual slaughter of animals is performed by a qualified SHOHET using a special knife. Jewish LAW specifies the procedure to be followed.

robbery (Hebrew: *gezelah*)

Unlawful removal of another individual's property. According to Scripture, the penalty for such a crime is restitution of the property or its value. The latter provision pertains if what has been stolen no longer exists, has been seriously altered, has been incorporated in a structure that will have to be demolished if it were removed, or is viewed by its owners as lost.

Rome

Capital of Italy. It has the oldest Jewish community in Europe. The first record of Jewish settlement there dates from the second century BCE. In classical literature there are numerous references to Jews living in Rome. During the middle ages the community dwindled, but in the 13th century the city became a centre for Jewish loan bankers. In Renaissance times Jews were involved in new intellectual and cultural developments. However, the Counter-Reformation initiated anti-Jewish legislation, including the creation of a GHETTO. It was not until 1870 that the Jewish population was fully emancipated.

Rosenzweig, Franz (1886–1929)

German theologian. Born in Kassel, he studied at various universities and eventually resolved to convert to Christianity. However, after attending an ORTHODOX HIGH HOLY DAY service in BERLIN he embraced the Jewish faith. Subsequently he served in the German army and wrote *The Star of Redemption* while in hospital. On his return home, he established an institution for Jewish studies. In 1921 he became partially paralysed, but continued to write. Together with Martin BUBER, he translated the Hebrew Bible into German.

Rosh Ha-Shanah

See NEW YEAR.

Rosh Ḥodesh

Celebration of the appearance of the new moon, marking the beginning of the month. A special SACRIFICE was offered in the TEMPLE on this day, at which the *musaf* (*see* ADDITIONAL SERVICE) was recited (Num. 28:11–15). Scripture lists various observances that should occur on the day of the new moon. During the TALMUDIC period these became more elaborate, including a proclamation of the new moon's appearance which was communicated throughout and beyond PALESTINE. In modern times the celebration is confined to the recital of the half HALLEL and the addition of the *musaf* service to the AMIDAH on the first day of the month.

rosh yeshivah

Originally the title was given to the person who directs an institution for the study of TALMUD. In modern times the title is used not only for the principals of YESHIVOT, but also for the permanent members of the teaching staff.

Rossi, Azariah dei (fl. *c.*1511–78)

Italian scholar. Born in Mantua, he lived in Bologna, Ferrara and Mantua. In his *Meor Enayim*, he illustrates how classical sources cast light on Jewish history and literature. In the third part of this work, he examines ancient Jewish history by comparing Hebrew texts with classical Jewish and non-Jewish sources. He also wrote poetry in Italian, Hebrew and Aramaic.

ruah

See SOUL.

Rubenstein, Richard (b. 1924)

American theologian. Born in New York, he was chaplain to Jewish students at the University of Pittsburgh, and in 1970 became professor of religion at Florida State University. His works include *After Auschwitz*, *The Religious Imagination* and *The Cunning of History*.

Ruth, Book of

One of the FIVE SCROLLS, and part of the HAGIOGRAPHA. It narrates the story of a Moabite woman who makes a LEVIRATE MARRIAGE with her husband's kinsman Boaz. Subsequently she became the ancestress of King DAVID.

S

Saadiah Gaon (882–942 CE)

Babylonian GAON. Born in Pithom in the Faiym district of EGYPT, he settled in BABYLONIA. In 928 he became *gaon* of SURA, but two years later was deposed by the EXILARCH David ben Zakkai. In 936 CE he was reinstated. His earliest work was a polemic against the KARAITE scholar ANAN BEN DAVID. Other writings include a philosophical treatise, a translation of the Bible, Arabic commentaries on biblical books, a HEBREW lexicon and grammar, and a list of biblical *hapax legomena*. He also composed a systematic compilation of the PRAYER BOOK, and wrote liturgical poetry.

Sabbath (Hebrew: *Shabbat*)

Day of rest. It is observed every week from before sunset on Friday until nightfall on Saturday. According to tradition, the Sabbath is celebrated to honour God's day of rest after creation. Its observance was commanded by God in one version of the TEN COMMANDMENTS to commemorate the EXODUS from Egypt. No work should take place on the Sabbath; rabbinic legislation stipulates 39 categories of activity which are forbidden. However, these regulations should be SET ASIDE if human life is in danger. The Sabbath day should be an occasion for PRAYER and study. Readings in the SYNAGOGUE are drawn from the TORAH and the prophetic books. The day ends with HAVDALAH.

Bringing in the Sabbath in Israel: The Sabbath candles are lit and a prayer is being said by a Jew from Bokhara in Central Asia.

Sabbath, Great
(Hebrew: *Shabbat ha-Gadol*)

SABBATH before PASSOVER. A special HAFTARAH (Mal. 3:4–24) is read after the TORAH portions and a rabbinic discourse concerning the laws of the approaching FESTIVAL is delivered. In ASHKENAZI communities part of the Passover HAGGADAH is read during the AFTERNOON SERVICE.

Sabbath, special

Four SABBATHS are named after the special TORAH readings which take the place of the concluding portion of the weekly reading of the law.

Sabbath lamp

Oil lamp lit on Friday night in the home to symbolize the SABBATH light. It was traditionally bowl-shaped, made of brass, copper, pewter or silver, and hung from the ceiling. In modern times CANDLES have been substituted for oil.

Sabbath prayer

On Friday, the *maariv* service is preceded by a special service in the SYNAGOGUE. At home the KIDDUSH prayer is recited before the meal, which concludes with SABBATH songs. Prayers recited on the Sabbath follow the basic structure as on other days. The AMIDAH, however, consists of only seven BENEDICTIONS, and a fourth prayer service is added to the three daily prayers. Many extra psalms and poetic compositions are included in the MORNING SERVICE. At the end of the Sabbath, *maariv* is recited as on weekdays and is followed by HAVDALAH.

sabbatical year

Seventh year when no agricultural work should be done; all crops are therefore the property of the community. The sabbatical year was marked by the rescinding of debts – for this reason it is also referred to as the 'year of release'. The year following seven sabbatical years is the JUBILEE year, when cultivation is prohibited, slaves are freed, and land purchased since the preceding Jubilee reverts to its original owner. Laws relating to sabbatical and Jubilee years are dealt with in the TALMUDIC tractate Sheviit.

sacrifice

Offering to God. In the Jewish tradition sacrifice was made to God to obtain his favour or atone for SIN. According to 2 Kgs. 3:27, the CANAANITES sacrificed human beings. Yet the binding of ISAAC in Gen. 22:1–19 illustrates God's displeasure with this practice. In ancient ISRAEL three types of sacrifice were offered in the TEMPLE: animal sacrifice, meal offerings and libations. The rituals and practices prescribed for Temple sacrifice are outlined in Lev. 2 and 23, and Num. 28–9.

sacrilege

Misuse or desecration of whatever is sacred or worthy of respect. During the biblical period, it was a sacrilege to appropriate TEMPLE property for secular use, to put to secular use the formula for sacrificial INCENSE, and to copy the design of the Temple candelabrum or other vessels for non-cultic purposes. Subsequently, it was sacrilegious to use the SYNAGOGUE improperly, to treat the SCROLL OF THE LAW with disrespect, to imitate Holy Writ for secular purposes, and to recite the SONG OF SONGS as secular poetry.

Sadducees

One of the three main Jewish sects before the destruction of the Jewish state in 70 CE. The others were the PHARISEES and the ESSENES. This group comprised the priestly class who officiated in the TEMPLE. Unlike the Pharisees, the Sadducees did not subscribe to a belief in the RESURRECTION of the dead. Adhering to the WRITTEN LAW, they dispensed with the ORAL tradition.

Safed

Town in Upper GALILEE. Built in 1140, it became the property of the Knights Templar, but was destroyed in 1266. In the 15th century it became a centre of rabbinic and KABBALISTIC activity. Both Isaac LURIA and Joseph CARO lived there.

Salanter, Israel (1810–83)

Lithuanian scholar. Born in Zhagory, he founded the MUSAR MOVEMENT in Lithuania and Russia from 1830 and established *musar* houses for the dissemination of ethical literature. His pupils spread the MUSAR MOVEMENT, particularly among Jewish students in Lithuania.

sale

According to the TALMUD, the sale of property is not legally binding until an act of agreement or possession has been drawn up. An oral agreement is not binding. In the case of movable property, the lender may void the sale even after money has been paid by the buyer as long as a formal agreement has not been exchanged. A sale is effected in cases of movable property by payment of the full cost or by writing an agreement.

salt

Salt is used in the Bible as a symbol of the COVENANT between God and his people (Num. 18:19; 2 Chr. 13:5). All SACRIFICES and meal offerings had to be salted before being placed on the ALTAR in the TEMPLE (Lev. 2:13). After the Temple was destroyed, the meal table in the Jewish home became a symbol of the altar, and salt is placed on it for all meals. Bread is dipped into salt after the *ha-motzi* blessing.

Samael

Prince of demons. He is identified with SATAN, and his wife LILITH is the queen of demons. He appears in MIDRASHIC and KABBALISTIC writings.

Samaria

Capital of the NORTHERN KINGDOM; the term was also used to refer to the Northern Kingdom as a political entity. The city was founded in the ninth century BCE by Omri (1 Kgs. 16:24). In 721 BCE it fell to Sargon II of Assyria. Eventually it became a Macedonian colony in 331 BCE. It was captured by JOHN HYRCANUS at the beginning of the second century BCE, and later rebuilt by Pompey. The city was renamed Sebaste by HEROD the Great. During the Roman period it became an important centre.

Samaritan Pentateuch

Samaritan version of the Five Books of MOSES. The Samaritans maintain that their most ancient scroll dates back to the 13th year of the Israelite settlement of CANAAN.

Samaritans

Ancient people descended from the tribes of EPHRAIM and MANASSEH (Chr. 34:9; Jer. 41:5). They intermarried with non-Israelite colonists (2 Kgs. 17:24–41). Their capital was at SAMARIA.

Sambatyon

Legendary river. The TEN LOST TRIBES of Israel were believed to have been stranded on the other side of the river Sambatyon after the conquest of the NORTHERN KINGDOM by the Assyrians in 721 BCE.

Samson (fl. 12th–11th century BCE)

Israelite JUDGE. A NAZIRITE of great strength, he was tricked by his mistress Delilah into revealing the secret of his strength as lying in his hair. After falling into the hands of the Philistines, his hair was cut and his eyes put out. When he was mocked by the Philistines at a festival, his strength returned and he destroyed the palace, killing all those assembled there.

Samuel (fl. 11th century BCE)

Israelite PROPHET and JUDGE. He was consecrated as a NAZIRITE by his mother before his birth. He served in the SANCTUARY at SHILOH, where he predicted the destruction of the House of Eli. After the death of Eli and his sons and the defeat of the Israelites by the

Philistines, Samuel sought to restore traditional Jewish worship. He lived at Ramah and judged the Israelites at Bethel, Gilgal and Mizpah. Subsequently he acceded to the Israelite wish to have a king and selected SAUL. When Saul lost favour with God, Samuel went to Bethlehem where he anointed DAVID as Saul's successor (1 Sam. 1–16).

Samuel, Book of

Biblical book, one of the FORMER PROPHETS. It relates the history of the Israelite nation from the end of the period of the JUDGES to the last days of DAVID.

sanctification

See KIDDUSH.

sanctuary   (Hebrew: *bet ha-mikdash*)

The most holy part of a place of worship. The term is applied to the TABERNACLE at SHILOH, JERUSALEM and elsewhere. In Shiloh and Jerusalem, it contained the ARK. In the TEMPLE the sanctuary was the HOLY of HOLIES, where the ARK OF THE COVENANT was kept. In modern times the part of the SYNAGOGUE where the ark is kept retains the name 'sanctuary'. The term is also used to refer to a place of refuge for accidental killers. In ancient times, this function was fulfilled by the ALTAR (Exod. 2:14; 1 Kgs. 1:51; 2:28). MOSES set aside six CITIES OF REFUGE where accidental killers could flee. Later the monarchy took over the responsibility of dealing with such cases.

sandak

See CIRCUMCISION.

Sanhedrin   (Hebrew, 'Assembly')

During the rabbinic period the Sanhedrin was an assembly of 71 scholars which acted as a supreme court and legislature. It was headed by the NASI and AV BET DIN. Before 70 CE it convened in the TEMPLE chamber; later it met in various centres. Its duties consisted of proclaming the new moon (ROSH HODESH), declaring leap years, and reaching decisions regarding questions of LAW. It was discontinued before the fourth century. During the 16th century Joseph CARO and Jacob Berab unsuccessfully attempted to revive ordination in PALESTINE and create a new Sanhedrin. The term 'Sanhedrin' also refers to the fourth TRACTATE in the MISHNAH order of NEZIKIN. It deals with courts of justice and judicial procedure; it also contains a list of SINS which exclude a person from entering into the afterlife.

Sanhedrin, Great

Body of 71 members convened by Napoleon in 1807 to confirm the decisions of the Assembly of Jewish Notables.

Saragossa

Spanish city, formerly the capital of Aragon. Jews lived there from the Moorish period (10th–15th centuries). Under Christian rule Saragossa's Jewish community prospered.

Sarah   (fl. ?16th century BCE)

Wife of ABRAHAM. After many years of barrenness, she gave Abraham her maidservant Hagar, who bore him a son, Ishmael. Later Sarah gave birth to ISAAC.

Satan

In Scripture he is referred to as a member of the divine household who functions as God's adversary (Job 1:6). Subsequently he was viewed as an evil spirit. In rabbinic sources, he is identified with the tempter, the accuser, the Angel of Death and the arch-enemy of Israel. In mystical texts other names are used for demonic rulers and princes of evil.

Satmar

HASIDIC sect with centres in Israel and the USA.

Saul (fl. 11th century BCE)

The first King of ISRAEL, selected by SAMUEL in response to the nation's request for a king. He organized the army and waged battles against the Philistines, Moabites, Ammonites and Arameans. Later a rift developed between Saul and Samuel (1 Sam. 13). Saul persecuted DAVID after his victory over Goliath and drove him from the country. Saul fell in battle against the Philistines on Mount Gilboa (1 Sam. 8–12 Sam. 3).

savoraim

BABYLONIAN scholars. They succeeded the AMORAIM in c.500 CE and were eventually succeeded by the GEONIM in c.689 BCE. A number of their decisions were incorporated into the TALMUD.

sayings of the fathers

See AVOT.

scapegoat

Sin offering SACRIFICED on the DAY OF ATONEMENT (Yom Kippur). On Yom Kippur lots were cast between two goats: one was slaughtered and the other, the scapegoat, was dedicated to AZAZEL and released into the wilderness. After the TEMPLE was destroyed in 70 CE, the sacrificial system came to an end and the scapegoat ritual was no longer practised.

Schechter, Solomon (1847–1915)

British rabbinic scholar. Born in Foscani, Romania, he was tutor in rabbinics to Claude MONTEFIORE. In 1890 he became a lecturer in rabbinics at Cambridge University. From 1899 he was professor of Hebrew at University College, London. During this period he discovered the Cairo GENIZAH, the contents of which were taken to Cambridge. In 1901 he became president of the Jewish Theological Seminary in the USA. His writings include *Studies in Judaism* and *Some Aspects of Rabbinic Theology*.

Scholem, Gershom (1897–1982)

Israeli scholar. Born in Berlin, he emigrated to PALESTINE in 1923 where he worked as a librarian in the Judaica collection at the Hebrew University. Later he became professor of Jewish mysticism at the university. His writings include *Major Trends in Jewish Mysticism, The Messianic Idea in Judaism* and *Other Essays in Jewish Spirituality*.

schools

See EDUCATION.

science and religion

The conflict between science and religion that took place in the 19th century had an impact on Jewish thinking. On the basis of the medieval view that faith and reason are compatible, many Jewish writers argued that religion is concerned with transcendent reality and can therefore be harmonized with the scientific world view.

science of Judaism

See WISSENSCHAFT DES JUDENTUMS.

scribe (Hebrew: *sopher*)

Originally one who copies documents, but in later usage a recognized scholar. Under the Judean monarchy the king's scribe held the highest office in his household. EZRA is depicted as the 'scribe' of the law of the God of Heaven (Ezra 7:6). In the Book of ECCLESIASTICUS the scribe is depicted as a literate man, occupied with the study of the law. The New Testament links the scribes and the PHARISEES. In the MISHNAH the phrase 'words of the scribe' refers to post-biblical legislation. In rabbinic sources the term 'scribe' refers to those who write TORAH scrolls and preserve textual traditions. The TRACTATE Sopherim in the TALMUD lists the rules for writing sacred documents.

A Yemeni scribe at work restoring a Torah scroll.

scroll

Length of parchment or vellum on which holy books are written. It is composed of strips which are sewn together to form a roll. Each end is attached to a wooden stave. Scrolls are written by SCRIBES. Today the Five Books of Moses are written on a scroll which is read in the SYNAGOGUE, and several biblical books are customarily written on scrolls. (*See also* SEFER TORAH; FIVE SCROLLS.)

Scrolls, Five

Five books of the HAGIOGRAPHA. They are the SONG OF SONGS (read on PASSOVER), RUTH (read on SHAVUOT), LAMENTATIONS (read on the NINTH OF AV), ECCLESIASTES (read on SUKKOT) and ESTHER (read on PURIM).

Scrolls of the Law

SCROLL of the PENTATEUCH which is kept in the ARK of the SYNAGOGUE. It is read

week by week. (*See also* SCRIBE; SEDARIM; TORAH).

second day of festivals

Second day on which FESTIVALS are celebrated. It became customary to celebrate all festivals except Yom Kippur (the DAY OF ATONEMENT) for two consecutive days in order to ensure they were definitely celebrated on the correct day.

secrets of Enoch

See ENOCH.

secularism

Traditionally Judaism makes a distinction between the secular and the profane; nonetheless, secular life is regarded as good since all things are derived from God. In the modern period, secular Judaism, as represented by the RECONSTRUCTIONIST movement and HUMANISTIC JUDAISM, has fostered a non-supernaturalistic interpretation of the Jewish tradition.

sedarim   (Hebrew, 'orders')

Name given to the six divisions of the MISHNAH.

seder   (Hebrew, 'order')

Home ceremony which occurs on the first night of PASSOVER. The structure of the ritual is based on the MISHNAH. Its essential features include the recitation of the KIDDUSH prayer, the reading of the HAGGADAH, the partaking of BITTER HERBS and UNLEAVENED BREAD, the eating of the festival meal, the drinking of four cups of wine, the recitation of the Hallel, and the singing of songs.

Seder Olam
(Hebrew, 'Order of the World')

Two chronicles. The *Seder Olam Rabbah* is a MIDRASHIC history from creation to the BAR KOKHBA revolt in 132 CE. The

Seder Olam Zuta records the generation from ADAM until the ending of the BABYLONIAN EXILARCHATE.

Sefer Ḥasidim
(Hebrew, 'Book of the Pious')

Medieval German devotional work. The *Sefer Ḥasidim* was influential on the ḤASIDEI ASHKENAZ movement and included the teachings of Samuel ben Kalonymus, Judah ben Samuel and Eleazar ben Judah.

Sefer Ha-Yashar
(Hebrew, 'Book of Jashar')

Ancient book. It is now lost, but is mentioned in the biblical books of JOSHUA, 2 SAMUEL and 1 KINGS.

Sefer Torah
See SCROLLS OF THE LAW.

Sefer Yetzirah

Early BABYLONIAN or PALESTINIAN mystical tract, dating from the third to sixth centuries. According to this text, the cosmos is derived from the HEBREW alphabet and the ten *sefirot* (DIVINE EMANATIONS). Knowledge of these mysteries – including letter combinations – allegedly conferred MAGICAL powers. Hence the GOLEM (an artifical man) was created by means of formulae from this volume. The work influenced later KABBALISTS, and numerous commentaries were written about it.

sefirot
See DIVINE EMANATIONS.

selah

Word found in the Book of PSALMS; its origin and meaning are unknown.

seliḥot
See PENITENTIAL PRAYERS.

semikhah
See ORDINATION.

separating the fat
(Hebrew: *nikkur*)

Removal of the fat from sacrifical animals. According to Lev. 7, fat from the SACRIFICES should not be eaten; rather, it is to be burned on the ALTAR.

Sephardim

One of the two major groups of Jewry. The word comes from the Hebrew Sepharad, originally the name of an area to which Jews were deported after the destruction of the First TEMPLE. It was first used in the middle ages of the Jews of Spain; after the expulsion from Spain in 1492 the Sephardim settled in North Africa, Italy, Egypt, Palestine, Syria, the Balkans and the Turkish Empire. (*See also* ASHKENAZIM.)

Sepphoris

Ancient city in GALILEE, of which it was the capital during the Second TEMPLE period. In 67 CE its inhabitants surrendered to the Romans. It became the seat of the patriarchate from the time of JUDAH HA-NASI until the third century, when the PATRIARCHS moved to TIBERIAS.

Septuagint

Greek translation of the Bible. According to tradition, the PENTATEUCH was translated into Greek at the command of Ptolemy II in the third century BCE. This was undertaken by 70 Jewish scholars, each of whom worked independently.

seraph

Supernatural creature depicted as a winged human or serpent-like figure. In Isa. 6:12 the seraphim are members of a celestial court surrounding the divine throne in the TEMPLE. In medieval sources they comprise one of the 10 classes of ANGELS.

sermon

Address of religious instruction or exhortation. It is normally delivered during the worship service. The institution of the sermon originated during the time of the PROPHETS. In the Second TEMPLE period, there was a need for a system of teaching and preaching: this was accomplished by scholars, who read from the TORAH and the prophetic books on SABBATHS and FESTIVALS. One method of teaching involved the translation of the biblical text into ARAMAIC. After the destruction of the Temple, sermons in the form of MIDRASHIM were delivered in the SYNAGOGUE. In time the sphere of the sermon increased to include discourses for special events. During the medieval period preaching played an important role in Jewish life. In Western Europe the sermon became a central feature of the worship service; however, in Eastern Europe it was increasingly replaced by an ethical discourse. In the modern world, the sermon is a central feature of synagogue worship.

Servant Songs

Poems contained in the Book of ISAIAH. They tell of a faithful servant of God who suffers on behalf of the people. They are found in Isa. 42:1–4; 49:1–6; 50:4–9; 52:13–53:12. They have been interpreted as referring to the Jewish people or to particular historical individuals.

set aside things
(Hebrew: *muktzeh*)

Objects that should not be touched on the SABBATH. The TALMUD decrees that there are four categories of *muktzeh*: objects connected with work, objects not normally used, objects that came into existence on the Sabbath day, and objects which supported objects connected with work.

seudah   (Hebrew, 'meal')

Celebratory meal. A *seudah* is held in conjunction with a CIRCUMCISION,

wedding, FESTIVAL or the SABBATH. It is a religious duty to enjoy such festivities. According to tradition, at the end of time God will give a final *seudah* at which the meat of LEVIATHAN will be consumed. It is meritorious if TORAH is discussed during a *seudah*.

seudah shelishit
(Hebrew, 'third meal')

Third meal eaten in honour of the SABBATH.

seudat havraah
(Hebrew, 'community meal')

Meal provided for MOURNERS.

seudat mafseket
(Hebrew, 'final meal')

Last meal eaten before Yom Kippur (DAY OF ATONEMENT) and Tisha B'Av (the NINTH OF AV).

seudat mitzvah   (Hebrew, 'meal associated with a commandment')

Meal consumed after a religious ceremony or celebration.

seven benedictions
(Hebrew: *sheva berakhot*)

Benedictions recited at a wedding ceremony. The first benediction is said over a cup of wine; the next three praise God; the fifth celebrates the restoration of ZION; the sixth refers to the joy of the first couple in paradise; the seventh thanks God for having created joy and gladness, and for the bride and bridegroom.

Seventeenth of Tammuz

See TAMMUZ, FAST OF

Seville

Port in south-west Spain. Jews lived there during the Roman period. By the 11th century there was an important Jewish community in the town. In 1391 the preaching of Archdeacon Ferrand Martinez of Seville led to a wave of massacres. The INQUISITION began there in 1480, and the town's Jews were expelled in 1483.

severah

See SAVORAIM.

sexual morality

According to the tradition, sexual intercourse may occur only within marriage. Refusal of sexual intercourse within marriage is grounds for DIVORCE. All HOMOSEXUAL activity is forbidden.

Shabbat (Hebrew, 'Sabbath')

First TRACTATE of the MISHNAH and TALMUD. It discusses SABBATH law and outlines the thirty-nine categories of work, forbidden on the Sabbath.

Shabbat ha-Gadol

See SABBATH, GREAT.

Shabbetai Zevi (1626–76)

Turkish scholar and pseudo-MESSIAH. Born in Smyrna, he devoted himself to TALMUDIC and KABBALISTIC study. In 1665 he met NATHAN of GAZA, who proclaimed him the Messiah. As a result, the Jewish world was seized with messianic fervour. In 1666 Shabbetai went to Constantinople, but was arrested and imprisoned by the sultan. Eventually he was brought before the sultan and adopted Islam to save his life. His APOSTASY caused considerable dismay, yet a number of his followers (SHABBETAIANS) remained convinced that he was the long-awaited Messiah.

Shabbetaians

Followers of SHABBETAI ZEVI. After his death in 1676, they believed he would return as the saviour of Israel. Subsequently the Shabbetaians split into various sects.

shabbos goy

(Yiddish, 'Sabbath gentile')

Non-Jewish person who is employed to perform tasks on the SABBATH which are forbidden to Jews.

Shaddai (Hebrew, 'Almighty')

Name of God in the Bible. It later appeared in KABBALISTIC formulae and on AMULETS. It is also frequently inscribed on MEZUZAHS.

shadkhan

See MATCHMAKER.

shaharit

See MORNING SERVICE

shaliah

Emissary. The term applies especially to an emissary sent from Israel to Jewish communities throughout the world.

shalom

Hebrew word which means well-being of different kinds: security, contentment, good health, prosperity, friendship and peace of mind. It is also used in greetings and farewells. (See also PEACE.)

Shalom Aleichem

Greeting meaning 'Peace be with you'.

shalom bayit

(Hebrew, 'domestic peace')

Term used to refer to harmonious relations between husband and wife.

Shammai (fl. first century BCE)

PALESTINIAN rabbi and contemporary of HILLEL; they were the last of the ZUGOT. He was rigorous in moral and religious matters. The School of Shammai later disputed legal issues with the School of Hillel.

shammash (Hebrew, 'beadle')

Caretaker or sexton in the SYNAGOGUE. The term also refers to the CANDLE which is used to kindle the HANUKKAH lights.

shas

Abbreviation of the words *shishah sedarim* (six orders). It refers to the six orders into which the MISHNAH is divided and which form the basis of the TALMUD. From the 16th century the term was used to refer to the Talmud.

shatnes

Forbidden cloth. According to the Bible (Lev. 19:19; Deut. 22:11), it is forbidden to wear clothing woven of linen and wool together.

shaving

Jewish LAW stipulates that men must not shave the corners of the head and beard. Shaving is understood to mean removal of hair with a knife or razor; however, other methods such as depilatories or scissors are not forbidden. Shaving is definitely forbidden on HOLY DAYS, when MOURNING, during the counting of the OMER, and for three weeks before Tisha B'Av (the NINTH OF Av). (*See also* BEARDS; PAIS.)

Shavuot

One of the three PILGRIM FESTIVALS, observed on 6 and 7 Sivan. It commemorates the giving of the law on MOUNT SINAI. It is also known as Pentecost because it commences on the 50th day after the completion of the seven-week period of the counting of the OMER.

Shechem

Ancient town in CANAAN. The PATRIARCHS camped under its walls, and the town was pillaged by Simeon and Levi (Gen. 34). Subsequently it was in the territory of Ephraim, and became the centre of the House of Joseph. The northern tribes who broke away from REHOBOAM camped there when JEROBOAM became king (1 Kgs. 12). Eventually it became secondary in importance to SAMARIA.

shehita

See RITUAL SLAUGHTER.

sheitel

Wig worn by ORTHODOX women. Jewish law decrees that married women cover their hair, and the *sheitel* is used in some traditional circles for this purpose.

shekhinah

Divine presence. The Bible refers to God's dwelling in the midst of the children of Israel (Exod. 13:21–2; 40:34–8). Subsequently the concept of the *shekhinah* embodied God's presence in the world. In KABBALISTIC sources the term *shekhinah* refers to the tenth *sefirah*, representing God's feminine aspect (*see* DIVINE EMANATIONS).

sheliah zibbur (Hebrew, 'emissary of the congregation')

Title given to the person who leads public prayer in a SYNAGOGUE. The term also refers to the HAZZAN.

sheloshim

Thirty-day period of MOURNING which follows the death of a relative. Some of the customs of mourning which are observed during the SHIVAH continue in force for the duration of this period. A public discourse is sometimes delivered at the end of this time.

Shem, Ha-

See HA-SHEM.

shema (Hebrew, 'hear')

Central prayer in the Jewish LITURGY. It is made up of three passages: Deut. 6:4–9; Deut. 11:13–21; and Num. 15: 37–41. It is recited twice every day, once in the morning and once in the evening. It should also be recited before death.

Shemaiah (fl. first century BCE)

Palestinian RABBI. He served as head of the SANHEDRIN in PALESTINE. He and

AVTALYON constituted the fourth of the ZUGOT.

Shemini Atzeret (Hebrew, 'Eighth Day of Solemn Assembly')

Final day of the festival of SUKKOT. Its name is derived from the regulations in Lev. 23:36. It is celebrated for two days, the first day of which is also SIMHAT TORAH. A special prayer for rain is recited during the MUSAF service. In ASHKENAZI communities the YIZKOR prayer is said on this day.

shemoneh esreh

See AMIDAH.

Sheol

Dwelling place of the dead according to the Bible (Gen. 37:35; Isa. 38:10). It is situated beneath the earth (Isa. 57:9).

Sherira Gaon (906–1006)

BABYLONIAN GAON. He served as *gaon* of PUMBEDITA (968–98). Together with his son, Hai Gaon, he maintained contact by means of RESPONSA with Jews in North Africa, Spain and elsewhere. He also wrote commentaries on the Bible and the TALMUD.

shewbread

Twelve loaves which were laid in two roads on the golden tables in the inner shrine of the TEMPLE. They remained there from one SABBATH to the next; they were then divided among the PRIESTS (Lev. 24:1–9).

shiddukh (Hebrew, 'marital match')

Term used in the TALMUD to refer to the conversations between a prospective bridegroom or his parents and a possible bride or her parents, in preparation for BETROTHAL. It has come to mean betrothal or MARRIAGE.

Shiloh

Ancient place in the mountains of the territory of Ephraim. It became the Israelites' first cultic centre after the conquest of CANAAN. During the period of the JUDGES, the ARK OF THE COVENANT and the TABERNACLE were located there.

shirayim (Hebrew, 'leftovers')

Food left by the ZADDIK. It is competed for by the HASIDIM during SABBATH and FESTIVAL meals. According to Hasidic teaching, these remains partake of the same holiness that traditionally resided in the part of the SACRIFICE which was not consumed upon the ALTAR in the TEMPLE.

shivah

Seven-day period of MOURNING which follows the death of a relative. During this period ordinary work is prohibited, and sexual intercourse is forbidden. The mourners sit without shoes on low stools or on the floor – this is referred to as 'sitting *shivah*'. It is usual for friends to make visits to the mourners' home to offer prayers and condolences.

Shneour Zalman (1747–1813)

Russian Hasidic leader, founder of HABAD. The pupil of DOV BAER OF MEZHIRECH, he joined the Hasidim at the age of 20; in 1777 he succeeded Menahem Mendel of Vitebsk as the movement's leader, becoming involved in the controversy with the MITNAGDIM. After his arrest by the Russian authorities, he was imprisoned in St Petersburg. Although he was later released, he was rearrested. In 1804 he settled in Lyady. In his teaching he adopted a rational approach and stressed the significance of study and contemplation. His major work is the *Tanya*.

Shoah

See HOLOCAUST.

shofar

Ceremonial wind instrument, originally made of a ram's horn. Scripture stipulates that it should be sounded on the

NEW YEAR and to announce the Year of Release (Lev. 25:9). It was also blown on FAST days, in the ceremony of EXCOMMUNICATION, before the start of the SABBATH, and at times of famine or plague. The blowing of the *shofar* during SYNAGOGUE services during the month of Elul, on HOSHANAH RABBAH, and at the conclusion of the DAY OF ATONEMENT (Yom Kippur) was introduced later.

The shofar: This is traditionally sounded at the Jewish festivals of Rosh Hoshanah (New Year) and Yom Kippur.

shohet

Ritual slaughterer. According to the TALMUD, any normal person who is not a minor may slaughter animals and poultry, as long as the act is performed in accordance with Jewish LAW. Subsequently a *shohet* had to be trained. During the modern period those who undertake this role must be learned in the HALAKHAH.

shrine

Place of worship. After the conquest of the PROMISED LAND, the Israelites kept the ARK OF THE COVENANT at several locations. Once the TEMPLE in Jerusalem was built, it was felt that the Temple was the proper place for SACRIFICE, even though the HIGH PLACES continued to exist. When the Temple was destroyed in 70 CE, the sacrifical system came to an end and worship took place in SYNAGOGUES.

shroud

Wrapping for the dead. According to the tradition, corpses should be wrapped in plain linen cloth before BURIAL.

shtetl   (Yiddish, 'small town')

Small town in Eastern Europe with a largely Jewish population.

shtibl   (Yiddish)

Small Jewish village in Eastern Europe. The term also refers to a small chapel.

shul

Yiddish term for a SYNAGOGUE.

Shulhan Arukh

See CODES OF JEWISH LAW.

Sicarii   (Latin, 'men with daggers')

Jewish rebels who fought against Rome in the first century.

sick, prayers for the

The eighth benediction of the weekly AMIDAH is a prayer for healing. In addition, any person may offer prayers for sick friends or relatives, which may be added to the eighth or the 16th benediction of the Amidah. Alternatively, they may be offered anywhere at any time. Prayers for the sick may also be made in the SYNAGOGUE after the reading of the law. It is customary to read PSALMS on behalf of the sick. It also became customary for a special form of prayer to be recited by a sick person. (*See also* VISITING THE SICK.)

siddur

See PRAYER BOOK.

sidrah

TORAH portion which is read in the SYN-AGOGUE on the SABBATH. Each *sidrah* has a distinctive name. The PENTATEUCH is divided into 54 *sedarot* so that the entire Torah is read annually.

Sifra

HALAKHIC MIDRASH on the Book of LEVITICUS. It was probably compiled in the fourth century CE.

Sifrei

HALAKHIC MIDRASH on the Books of NUMBERS and DEUTERONOMY. It was probably compiled in the fourth century CE.

Sifrei Zuta

HALAKHIC MIDRASH on the Book of NUMBERS. It probably dates from the fourth century CE.

silent prayer

It is customary for members of a congregation to offer silent prayers at certain points in the SYNAGOGUE LITURGY.

Silver, Abba Hillel (1893–1963)

American REFORM RABBI. Born in Sirvintos, Lithuania, he went to the USA in 1902. He served as a rabbi in Cleveland, Ohio. In 1938 he became chairman of the United Palestine Appeal and joint chairman of the United Jewish Appeal. He led the meetings of the American Zionist Emergency Concil in 1943, and subsequently became chairman of the American section of the Jewish Agency.

Simeon bar Kokhba

See BAR KOKHBA, SIMEON.

Simeon ben Yohai

(fl. second century)

PALESTINIAN TANNA. He was among the five pupils of AKIVA who survived the failure of the BAR KOKHBA revolt in 132–5 CE. When he expressed political views which were regarded by the Romans as seditious, he was forced to flee. According to tradition, he dwelt in a cave for 13 years. He was noted as a MIRACLE worker, and sent on a mission to Rome where he succeeded in obtaining the withdrawal of a decree against the Jewish community. He is traditionally viewed as the author of the ZOHAR.

Simḥat Torah

(Hebrew, 'Rejoicing in the Law')

Holy day on which the completion of the annual reading of the TORAH is celebrated. It is observed on SHEMINI ATZERET. Traditionally it is customary to carry the SCROLLS OF THE LAW round the SYNAGOGUE seven times or more. The last section of DEUTERONOMY is read by the *ḥatan Torah* (BRIDEGROOM OF THE LAW), and the first section of GENESIS is read by the *ḥatan Bereshit* (bridegroom of Genesis).

sin

Violation of God's law. There are three main categories of sin: *ḥet* (sin committed in ignorance); *avon* (sin committed knowingly); and *pesha* (sin committed in a spirit of rebellion). No person is without sin, but REPENTANCE leading to FORGIVENESS cancels sin.

sin offering

See SACRIFICE.

Six Day War

War between ISRAEL and Egypt, Jordan, Syria and Iraq from 5 to 10 June 1967. During the war Israel defeated the armies of its enemies and occupied the Sinai Peninsula, the West Bank and the Golan Heights.

six hundred and thirteen commandments

Laws contained in the PENTATEUCH. There are 248 positive commandments, and 365 negative commandments. The first classification of the 613 commandments was made by Simeon Kayyara, and is listed in the *Halakhot Gedolot*. Subsequently MAIMONIDES classified them in his *Sefer ha-Mitzvot*, and Moses of Coucy made a compliation of them in his *Sefer Mitzvot Gadol*.

siyyum (Hebrew, 'termination')

Term applied to the completion of the copying of a TORAH SCROLL. It also refers to the completion of the study of a TRACTATE of the TALMUD. To celebrate these events a special meal takes place (*seudat mitzvah*), where a concluding lecture is delivered.

skullcap

See YARMULKE.

slander (Hebrew: *leshon ha-ra*)

False report which is uttered maliciously to damage another person. According to tradition, slander is a serious offence, and listening to such a report is also forbidden. Rabbinic courts are empowered to fine offenders and EXCOMMUNICATE them until they apologize. In certain cases FASTING is also imposed as a punishment.

slaughter

See RITUAL SLAUGHTER.

slavery

Condition of a person who is the legal property of another. According to Scripture, an Israelite can become the slave of another Israelite for only a limited period – a manumission must occur in the seventh year of service, or in a JUBILEE year. After the BABYLONIAN exile, the institution of Jewish slavery disappeared, but non-Jewish slaves could be purchased from neighbouring peoples. Male slaves were CIRCUMCISED and all slaves were subject to Jewish law. A slave's marriage was arranged by the owner, and the offspring became his

property. During the middle ages some Jewish merchants engaged in the slave trade. However, Jews were prominent in the struggle for the abolition of slavery.

sod

Esoteric ALLEGORICAL method of Scriptural exegesis. It is based on the belief that the TORAH has several levels of meaning. It was used to interpret the creation account in Genesis 1 and EZEKIEL's vision of the divine CHARIOT in Ezekiel 1.

Sodom

Ancient Israelite city. Lot settled there, but escaped when the city was destroyed because of its inhabitants' wickedness (Gen. 19).

Sofer, Moses (1762–1839)

Hungarian RABBI, HALAKHIC authority and opponent of REFORM JUDAISM. Known as Ḥatam Sofer, he was born in Frankfurt. He later served as a rabbi in Dresnitz and Mattersdorf, becoming rabbi of Pressburg.

Solomon (fl. 10th century BCE)

King of ISRAEL (965–931 BCE), son of DAVID and BATHSHEBA. He became king before his father's death, through the influence of Bathsheba and Nathan. Solomon built the TEMPLE in JERUSALEM, constructed fortresses, store cities and chariot cities, and built a harbour at Elath. He also made administrative innovations, including the division of the country into 12 districts. He is viewed as the author of the SONG OF SONGS and ECCLESIASTES as well as PSALM 72.

Solomon, Psalms of

PSEUDEPIGRAPHIC book, probably composed in PALESTINE after the fall of Pompey in 48 BCE. It contains 18 poems attributed to SOLOMON, which describe the desecration of the TEMPLE by the enemy. It also condemns immorality and looks forward to the coming of the MESSIAH.

Solomon, Song of

See SONG OF SONGS.

Solomon, Wisdom of

APOCRYPHAL book. It is devoted to the promise of wisdom. Chapters 1–5 praise wisdom in human life and emphasize the superiority of the wise over the wicked; chapters 6–9 describe SOLOMON's wisdom; and chapters 10–19 glorify wisdom and its role in history.

Soloveitchik, Joseph B.

(1903–1993)

Amercian talmudic scholar. Born in Pruzhany, Poland, he emigrated to the USA in 1932. He served as a RABBI in Boston, becoming professor of TALMUD at the Isaac Elḥanan Yeshiva in 1941. He was also professor of Jewish philosophy at the university's Bernard Revel Graduate School. His writings include *Ish ha-Halakhah*.

Song of Songs

Biblical book, part of the HAGIOGRAPHA. Attributed to SOLOMON, it consists of a series of love poems. In the TALMUD and medieval Jewish sources, it is interpreted as an ALLEGORY depicting the love between God and Israel.

Song of the Three Children

Addition to the Book of DANIEL. It is now found in the APOCRYPHA. It is dated to *c.*100 BCE and contains the prayer of Azariah, a description of the fiery furnace and the Song of Shadrach, Meshag and Abednego.

Sons of Light

Term in the DEAD SEA SCROLLS, which denotes the godly. In the QUMRAN community, where the scrolls originated, the members of the community and their sympathizers were referred to as 'Sons of Light'.

soul

Spiritual part of human beings. It is viewed as capable of surviving death. In the Bible three words are translated as 'soul': *nefesh*, *ruaḥ* and *neshamah*. The Bible connects the soul and life itself, speaking of the soul as the means by which the body is animated. After death the soul has only a shadow existence in SHEOL. During the HELLENISTIC age the concept of the soul existing independently of the body became a central feature of the Jewish faith. The soul was viewed as originating in HEAVEN and believed to join the body at birth. In KABBALISTIC soures METEMPSYCHOSIS (*gilgul*) was an important doctrine.

Southern Kingdom

Ancient kingdom of JUDAH. After the death of King SOLOMON, the Israelite kingdom was divided into two kingdoms, Israel in the north and Judah in the south. In 586 the Southern Kingdom was conquered by the BABYLONIANS, and the inhabitants were taken into exile. Later the exiles were allowed to return under EZRA and NEHEMIAH, the Temple was rebuilt and the kingdom restored.

spice box

During the HAVDALAH ceremony at the conclusion of the SABBATH, it is traditional to smell spices, and spice boxes are customarily used for this practice.

Spinoza, Baruch (1632–77)

Dutch philosopher. Born in AMSTERDAM, he received a traditional education, but his heretical opinions led to his EXCOMMUNICATION in 1656. From 1660 he lived away from Amsterdam, earning his living as a lens polisher. His *Theologico-Political Treatise* initiated modern biblical criticism. In his *Ethics* he applied Euclidean principles to demonstrate a metaphysical concept of the universe with ethical implications.

Star of David

(Hebrew: *magen David*)

The name given in Judaism to the symbol consisting of two superimposed triangles composing a star. Although it was used in the SYNAGOGUE at Capernaum in the third century, it did not become a Jewish symbol until much later. From the 13th century the name figures in practical KAB-BALAH. The *magen David* also occurs in a Jewish context in PRAGUE in the 17th century. In the 19th century it was adopted by the Zionist Congress, and it appears on the flags of the Zionist Organization and the State of ISRAEL.

Steinheim, Solomon Ludwig

(1789–1866)

German philosopher. Born in Bruch-hausen, Westphalia, he served as a physician in Altona. Later he settled in Rome. His writings include *Revelation According to the Synagogue*.

sterilization

The Bible contains prohibitions against castration and the MARRIAGE of a man 'crushed or maimed in his privy parts' (Deut. 23:2). On the basis of these laws, the rabbis decreed that it is forbidden to impair the reproductive organs in humans, beasts or birds. The use of sterilizing agents is also forbidden, as is the sterilization of females. The marriage ban applies only to those injured by human means rather than through an act of God or illness.

Stern, Avraham (1907–42)

Palestinian underground fighter. Born in Suwalki, Poland, he emigrated to PALESTINE in 1925, becoming active in the IRGUN TZEVAI LEUMI. In 1940 he formed an underground organization, the Stern Gang. He was killed by the British police while being arrested.

stranger

According to Scripture, strangers should be shown consideration and treated like native Israelites (Lev. 19:33–4). The rabbis stressed that in order to qualify for the protection offered by Jewish law, the stranger must adhere to the NOACHIDE LAWS.

streimel

Fur hat worn by the ḤASIDIM.

study

From the early rabbinic period, study of the TORAH was viewed as a religious duty. For this reason Jews have engaged in the study of sacred texts including Scripture, the MISHNAH, the TALMUD, the CODES OF JEWISH LAW, MIDRASHIC LITERA-TURE, KABBALAH, MUSAR and other types of religious literature through the ages.

submission

Obedience to the TORAH or to the teachers of Torah. The Jewish faith demands submission to the will of God and the commandments as prescribed in Scripture and expounded by the rabbis.

suffering

The problem of suffering occupies a central place in both Scripture and the TALMUD. In the Book of JOB, for example, it is stressed that the righteous person may be compelled to undergo suffering in order to demonstrate that he is capable of piety. Other biblical books assume a direct relationship between suffering and SIN. In rabbinic sources, this interconnection was also assumed, yet the rabbis conceded that suffering can occur without explanation. Central to Jewish theology is the belief that the righteous will be rewarded in the AFTERLIFE.

suffering servant

The servant of the Lord as depicted in Isa. 53 as well as Isa. 42:1–4; 49:1–6;

and 52:13–15. In Christianity the suffering servant is identified
with JESUS, but in Jewish sources he
is perceived as representing the Jewish
people.

suicide

In Judaism the taking of one's life is
viewed as a crime equivalent to MURDER.
An individual who has committed suicide is denied normal BURIAL and
MOURNING.

sukkah (Hebrew, 'tabernacle')

Booth erected during the festival of
SUKKOT. Leviticus prescribes that Jews
are to dwell or at least eat in the *sukkah*
for the seven days of this festival (Lev.
23:42). The *sukkah* symbolizes God's
protection in the desert. According to
custom it is decorated with curtains,
fruits and symbols of the holy day. In
modern society the *sukkah* is usually
constructed near the SYNAGOGUE, and a
token meal is eaten there after the service on each day of the festival.

Sukkot (Hebrew, 'Tabernacles')

One of the three PILGRIM FESTIVALS. It
begins on 15 Tishri and lasts for seven
days. The eighth day is a separate holy
day, SHEMINI ATZERET. Work is permitted on the first day of Sukkot, and on
Shemini Atzeret. The festival marks the
end of the agricultural year. Sukkot is
celebrated by taking four species of
plant – palm (*lulav*), citron (ETROG),
myrtle and willow – and carrying them
in procession in the SYNAGOGUE.
According to Lev. 23:42, it is also
required to dwell or at least eat all meals
in the SUKKAH.

Sun, Blessing of the

Blessing which is recited once every 28
years on the first Wednesday of Nisan,
when the sun is believed to be in the
same place in the heavens as at the time
of CREATION.

supercommentary

Commentary on the famous commentaries of the TORAH. They have been
produced on the works of RASHI and
NAHMANIDES.

superstition

Credulity about supernatural beliefs.
Even though the Bible forbids all forms
of MAGIC and later Jewish theologians
condemned such beliefs, many supersti-
tions have persisted in folk belief.

supplication

Liturgical composition, which includes a
wide range of prayers in prose or verse.
Petitionary and abstract in content, they
are used throughout the year. A number
are found in the SEPHARDIC PRAYER BOOK;
they are recited before dawn as a prelude to the regular service.

Sura

Ancient city is southern BABYLONIA. RAV
established an academy there in the early
third century. Here the Babylonian
TALMUD was compiled by Ashi and
Ravina during the fourth and fifth centuries. From the time of Mar bar Huna
in the sixth century the heads of the
ACADEMY were called GAON. The Sura
academy eventually merged with the
academy at PUMBEDITA in about the 11th
century.

Susanna and the Elders

APOCRYPHAL work, which tells the story
of Susanna. It was a popular tale in the
middle ages.

synagogue

House of worship. The institution dates
back to the sixth century BCE. After the
destruction of the Second TEMPLE in 70
CE, the synagogue served as the focus of
Jewish life. Many Temple rituals were
incorporated into the LITURGY, and the
times of the services reflect the pattern of
Temple SACRIFICE. The SCROLLS of the

TORAH are kept in the ARK. Generally a reading desk is located in front of the ark, and the BIMAH is placed in the centre. In ORTHODOX congregations, men and women sit apart; usually the women are behind a MEHIZAH (screen). However, in PROGRESSIVE congregations, men and women sit together. In the USA, REFORM synagogues are known as temples. Officials belonging to the synagogue include the RABBI, HAZZAN and SHAMMASH. Full synagogue services cannot take place unless a full MINYAN of ten adult males are present.

Synagogue, Great

Institution of the Second TEMPLE period. It was probably a body which met periodically to pass legislation. It is believed to have instituted the KIDDUSH and HAVDALAH ceremonies and the FESTIVAL of PURIM.

synod

Religious council. Several synods were held in the past. In 138 CE the Synod of USHA was convened to regulate Jewish life after the Hadrianic persecutions. Local synods were held throughout the middle ages; in the 16th to 18th centuries the Council of the Four Lands was the central governing authority for Polish and Lithuanian Jewry. (*See also* RABBINICAL CONFERENCES.)

Synod of Usha

See USHA, SYNOD OF.

Syria

Eastern Mediterranean country north of ISRAEL. There was continual friction between Syria and the Kingdom of Israel and JUDAH until the eighth century BCE, when Syria was overrun by the Assyrians. During the period of the Seleucids, a large Jewish population was located at Antioch. Few Jews lived in Syria during the TALMUDIC period. However, with the Arab conquest in the seventh century, the population increased. During the middle ages, Jews lived in Aleppo, Damascus and Palmyra. After 1492 their numbers increased. In modern times Syria has been in constant conflict with the State of Israel.

Szold, Henrietta (1860–1945)

American ZIONIST and philanthropist. Born in Baltimore, she was secretary of the Jewish Publication Society. In 1912 she organized HADASSAH, the Women's Zionist Organization of America. She was the first woman to become a member of the executive of the Zionist Organization. Later she worked as a leader of Youth ALIYAH.

Taanit (Hebrew, 'Fast')

Ninth TRACTATE in the MISHNAH order of MOED. It deals with the designation of FAST days during times of drought as well as the prayers for RAIN. Other communal fasts are also discussed.

Tabernacle

Portable habitation used as a sanctuary during the Israelites' wandering in the desert. Set up by MOSES (Exod. 26–7), it was constructed of acacia wood overlaid with gold. It contained layers of curtains and animal skins. Inside the Tabernacle was the HOLY OF HOLIES which contained the ARK OF THE COVENANT, the seven-branched candlestick (MENORAH), the table for SHEWBREAD, and the golden ALTAR for INCENSE.

Tabernacles, feast of

See SUKKOT.

Tablets, feast of

See SUKKOT.

Tablets of the Law

See TEN COMMANDMENTS.

Tadshe

MIDRASH dating from the late second century, dealing with the symbolism of

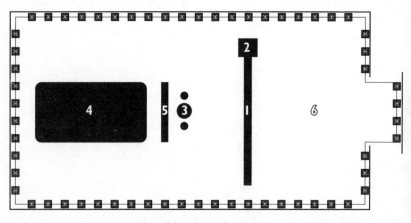

Plan of the tabernacle, showing:
1) sloped ramp; 2) bronze altar; 3) laver; 4) sanctuary of Holy of Holies with a ramskin covering; 5) screen; 6) courtyard.

NUMBERS. It is attributed to Phinehas ben Jair.

tag

Name of a short vertical stroke which is added to the top of various HEBREW letters when they are used in the TORAH and other parts of Scripture. According to the MASORAH, the letters *shin, ayin, tet, nun, zayin, gimel* and *tsadeh* require three such 'crown strokes'. Other letters require one or none. In KABBALISTIC sources the mystical meanings of these crown strokes are discussed.

taḥanun

See SUPPLICATION.

takkanot (Hebrew, 'directives')

Name given to any of the regulations which supplement the law as laid down in the TORAH.

talion

Fitting punishment. Biblical punishments tend to follow the principle of *talion*, (as in 'An eye for an eye . . .'). Later, monetary compensations and fines were substituted.

tallit

Prayer shawl. It is a four-cornered garment, usually made of wool. Fringes are knotted on the corners in accordance with biblical law (Num. 15:37–41). It is worn by adult males during MORNING PRAYER, at the AFTERNOON SERVICE on the NINTH OF AV, and at all services on the DAY OF ATONEMENT.

tallit katan (Hebrew, 'small tallit')

Garment with fringes at each corner. It is worn by ORTHODOX Jews under their clothes, with the fringes visible. This is done out of obedience to the commandment to wear fringes (Num. 15).

talmid hakham
(Hebrew, 'disciple of the wise')

Scholar. A *talmid hakham* should be a pious student of the WRITTEN and ORAL LAW. Traditionally he is viewed as the most desirable type of Jew. According to the rabbis, a *talmid hakham* (even if he is a MAMZER) takes precedence over a HIGH PRIEST who is an ignoramus.

Talmud

Name of the two collections of records of the discussion and administration of Jewish law by scholars in various ACADEMIES from *c.*200 to *c.*500. The PALESTINIAN and BABYLONIAN Talmuds overlap to a considerable degree. Both contain the MISHNAH together with GEMARA (commentary and supplement to the Mishnah text). In addition, both contain AGGADIC digressions. The authorities found in the Palestianian Talmud lived before *c.*400 CE; those referred to in the Babylonian Talmud lived before *c.*500 CE. The Babylonian Talmud contains more material than the Palestinian, and is viewed as more significant.

talmud torah
(Hebrew, 'study of the law')

Religious study. The term was adopted by voluntary associations that encouraged religious education. It was also applied to their schools, and eventually to Jewish religious schools in general. The institution of the talmud torah flourished in Europe and among immigrant communities in Western lands.

talmudic commentaries

The first commentaries on the TALMUD consist of comments found in the works of the later GEONIM. The earliest full commmentaries were by Sherira Gaon, Hai Gaon and Samuel ben Hophni during the 10th and 11th centuries. In the next century Nissim ben Jacob of

Kairouan and Hananel ben Hushiel composed important commentaries. Subsequently the focus of talmudic study moved to Germany and France. The 11th-century commentary by Gershom ben Judah established the foundation for the work of RASHI; he was followed by the *tosafists* (*see* TOSAFOT). Later commentaries were written by NAHMANIDES and Solomon ben ADRET. In the 16th century Solomon Luria, Samuel Edels and Meir Lublin produced significant works. In modern times scientific studies of the Talmud have been produced by various Jewish scholars.

Tam, Jacob ben Meir
(1100–1171)

French *tosafist*, grandson of RASHI. He lived at Ramerupt and Troyes. His *Sefer ha-Yashar* contains many of his TOSAFOT and novellae. He also composed studies of grammar and biblical interpretation and wrote liturgical poetry.

tamid (Hebrew, 'perpetual offering')

Whole offering or SACRIFICE which was made twice daily in the TEMPLE (Num. 28:1–8). The term also refers to the ninth TRACTATE of the MISHNAH order of KODASHIM which deals with the regulations for the daily burnt offerings in the Temple as well as the organization of the Temple cult.

Tammuz, Fast of

FAST which takes place on Tammuz 17. It commemorates the BABYLONIANS breaching the walls of JERUSALEM in 586 BCE and the Romans breaching them in 70 CE.

Tanakh

Hebrew Bible. Tanakh is an acronym for TORAH (LAW), NEVIIM (PROPHETS), and KETUVIM (HAGIOGRAPHA).

Tanhuma

Collection of aggadic MIDRASHIM. It contains many *midrashim* attributed to the fourth-century RABBI Tanhuma bar Abba, but since it also contains anti-KARAITE material it cannot be dated before the ninth century.

tanna

Sage of the first and second centuries CE. Among the *tannaim* are JOHANAN BEN ZAKKAI, AKIVA, ISHMAEL BEN ELISHA and JUDAH HA-NASI. In the TALMUD they are distinguished from the AMORAIM.

Tanya

Code of laws extracted from Zedekiah ben Abraham Anau's *Shibbole ha-Leket*. It was prepared in Italy, probably in the 14th century. The term also applies to a HASIDIC KABBALISTIC work composed by SHNEUR ZALMAN of Lyady.

tappuhim (Hebrew, 'apples')

Fruit-shaped ornaments used to decorate the staves of the TORAH SCROLLS.

targum

ARAMAIC translation of the Bible, or book of the Bible. According to the TALMUD, the custom of adding an Aramaic translation to the reading of Scripture dates from the time of EZRA. The oral *targum* is both a translation and an interpretation of the text. The three *targums* to the PENTATEUCH are: Targum Onkelos; Targum Jonathan; and Targum Yerushalmi. The *targum* to the prophetic books is called after Jonathan ben Uzziel. The *targums* to the HAGIOGRAPHA are MIDRASHIC in character.

taryag mitzvot

See SIX HUNDRED AND THIRTEEN COMMANDMENTS.

tas

Silver plaque which is placed on the TORAH SCROLL to indicate the FESTIVAL for which the scroll has been made ready.

tashlikh (Hebrew, 'thou shalt cast')

Custom which takes place on the first day of the NEW YEAR. Prayers are recited near a stream or body of water. The term derives from Micah 7:19: 'Thou shalt cast all their sins into the depths of the sea.'

taxation

The Book of EXODUS narrates that a poll tax was imposed on the Israelites during their sojourn in the wilderness (Exod. 30:11–16). Subsequently a system of TITHES was employed to maintain the TEMPLE, the priesthood and the poor. After the destruction of the Temple in 70 CE, the Romans imposed the *Fiscus Judaicus* on the Jewish community. This was revived during the middle ages as the *Opferpfennig*. In the 17th to 18th centuries in Italy Jewish communal dues were exacted by a tax on capital. In modern times such special Jewish taxes disappeared, except in some countries where the Jewish community has the right to impose taxes on all its members to sustain communal institutions.

teacher of righteousness

In the DEAD SEA SCROLLS, the title given to the organizer of the sect. The name appears in the Zadokite Fragments and in QUMRAN commentaries on books of the Bible.

tefillin

EXODUS 13 and DEUTERONOMY 6, 11 teach that Jews must bind the commandments upon their hands and between their eyes. This duty is fulfilled by binding special boxes containing biblical passages with leather straps over the forehead and round the arm.

Tel Aviv

City in modern ISRAEL. It was founded near Joppa in 1909. From the founding of the State of Israel in 1948 until the reunification of JERUSALEM in 1967, Tel Aviv served as the nation's capital.

Tel el Amarna

Site of the capital of Pharaoh Amenhotep IV in Middle Egypt. In 1887 cuneiform tablets were discovered there, including letters from CANAANITE kings complaining about disorder in the country caused by the invasions of the HABIRU.

Temple (Hebrew: *Bet ha-Mikdash*)

Principal place of worship of the Jews in JERUSALEM until 70 CE. The first Temple was built by SOLOMON in *c.*950 BCE. It served as a shrine for the ARK OF THE COVENANT and the sacred vessels, as well as a place for the offering of SACRIFICE and PRAYER. Solomon's Temple was destroyed in 586 BCE by the BABYLONIANS. The Temple was rebuilt in the Persian period, and completed and dedicated in 515 BCE. HEROD the Great completely reconstructed the building, beginning in 55 BCE. This Temple was destroyed by the Romans in 70 CE.

Temple Mount

Site of the TEMPLE. The Temple was built on Mount Moriah where ABRAHAM was supposed to have sacrificed ISAAC; later Mohammed is thought to have ascended to HEAVEN from the same spot. ORTHODOX Jews no longer walk over the Temple Mount because the ARK OF THE COVENANT was allegedly buried there in the destruction of 70 CE.

Temple Platform
(Hebrew: *Dukhan*)

According to TALMUDIC literature, the term refers to: the place in the TEMPLE where the LEVITES sang while the SACRIFICES were being offered; the place where the PRIESTS stood when they recited the PRIESTLY BLESSING; the place where the priestly blessing was recited in the SYNAGOGUE after the destruction of the Temple; or the platform where teachers sat while teaching children.

Temple Scroll

One of the DEAD SEA SCROLLS. It dates from the second century CE and includes laws regarding ritual purity and the FESTIVALS.

temple tax

Tax for the maintenance of the sanctuary. The TRACTATE Shekalim in the MISHNAH deals with the laws regarding this tax.

Temunah, Book of

KABBALISTIC text. It was composed in the late 13th century and is attributed to Ishmael the HIGH PRIEST.

Ten Commandments

The laws given to MOSES on MOUNT SINAI as recorded in Exod. 20:2–14 and Deut. 5:6–18. Moses wrote them on two stone tablets; later he broke these in anger when he discovered the Israelites worshipping the golden CALF. He re-ascended Mount Sinai and brought down a second set of tablets inscribed with the Ten Commandments, which were placed in the ARK OF THE COVENANT.

Ten Days of Penitence

First ten days of Tishri, from the beginning of the NEW YEAR to the close of the DAY OF ATONEMENT. According to tradition, individuals are judged at the New Year and the judgement is declared on the Day of Atonement. Clemency may be obtained through REPENTANCE during the Ten Days of Penitence. PENITENTIAL PRAYERS are recited daily, FASTS take place, and there are alterations to the LITURGY which emphasize God's kingship.

ten lost tribes

Ten tribes constituted the population of the NORTHERN KINGDOM of Israel from the time of JACOB until they were led into captivity by the Assyrians in the eighth century. They never re-emerged from this captivity and are assumed to have intermarried with the Assyrians. Those who remained in Israel intermarried with the CANAANITES and became SAMARITANS. It was hoped that the lost tribes would be rediscovered intact. Various travellers reported their discovery: Eldad ha-Dani claimed they were in the mountains of Africa; BENJAMIN OF TUDELA heard a report of them in Central Asia; David REUVENI claimed that he was the brother of one of their rulers in the region of Arabia; Antonio de Montezinos stated that he had found them in South America.

ten martyrs

Ten RABBIS who were executed by the Roman government after the BAR KOKHBA revolt for defying the prohibition against Jewish observances and religious teaching. The following are the names most commonly found in the various sources that list these individuals: AKIVA, ISHMAEL BEN ELISHA, Eleazar ben Dama, Ḥanina ben Teradyon, Judah ben Bava, Ḥutzpit the Interpreter, Yeshevav the Scribe, Eleazar ben Shammua, Ḥanina ben Ḥakhinai, Simeon ben Gamaliel I and Ishmael the HIGH PRIEST.

ten plagues

Afflictions suffered by the Egyptians because of Pharaoh's refusal to permit the Israelites to leave EGYPT (Exod. 7:14–12:34). The waters of the Nile were changed into blood; infestations of frogs, lice and flies took place; the cattle were visited with disease, and both men and animals with boils; a fierce hailstorm was sent; a swarm of locusts devastated the crops; Egypt was blanketed with darkness; and the first-born of the Egyptians died.

tenant

An individual who hires land or property from a landlord. Jewish LAW acknowledges the possibility of paying rent either in produce from the land or in money.

Tent of Meeting

Tent where MOSES encountered God while the Israelites wandered in the desert towards the PROMISED LAND.

terumot

HEAVE OFFERING. The term also refers to the sixth TRACTATE in the MISHNAH order of ZERAIM, which deals with the heave offering due to the PRIEST from the Israelite (Num. 18:8; Deut. 18:4) and the LEVITE (Num. 18:25ff).

teshuvah

See REPENTANCE.

Testament of the Twelve Patriarchs

PSEUDEPIGRAPHIC work, dating from the Second TEMPLE period. It includes the testaments of the sons of JACOB to their descendants. These are modelled on the blessing of Jacob to his sons in the Bible (Gen. 49).

tetragrammaton

The Hebrew name of God written YHWH. Because the Jews would not pronounce the divine name, God was referred to by various other names (*see* GOD, NAMES OF).

Tevet, Fast of

FAST day which commemorates the besieging of JERUSALEM by the BABYLONIAN king NEBUCHADNEZZAR in 586 BCE.

thank offering

SACRIFICE made as an act of gratitude to God. The laws govering such sacrifices are found in Lev. 7:12–15.

Thanksgiving Psalms

One of the DEAD SEA SCROLLS. It dates from the first century BCE and contains a number of psalms.

theatre

Jewish playwrights were active in ALEXANDRIA from the second century BCE. From the medieval period PURIM plays were performed in Central and Western Europe. In the 16th century MARRANO poets composed plays in Spanish, and Portuguese Jews in Italy were active in the theatre. In the 17th century a theatre was established in the GHETTO in Venice. From the 18th century there were outstanding Jewish actors in Western Europe. In eastern Europe and the USA Yiddish theatre played an important role in Jewish life. During the modern period Jews have been involved in drama, film and television.

theft

According to Jewish law, theft is distinguished from ROBBERY. A thief is a person who appropriates another individual's property in secret, while a robber steals without seeking to hide the deed. The thief who is convicted must pay double the value of the stolen goods (Exod. 22:3). It is not permitted to buy stolen property or property which the prospective buyer believes may have been stolen.

Therapeutae (Latin, 'Healers')

Jewish sect in EGYPT in the first century, as described by PHILO. Its members lived in solitude, poverty and celibacy; they spent their time in meditation on sacred texts. Every 50th day they congregated for a meal, spending the night in religious singing and dancing.

thirteen attributes of mercy

Attributes of God, according to EXODUS 34:6–7. Before giving the Law to MOSES a second time, God declared himself the Lord (1), the Lord (2), God (3), merciful (4), gracious (5), long-suffering (6), abundant in loving-kindness (7) and truth (8), keeping mercy unto the thousandth generation (9), forgiving iniquity (10), transgression (11) and sin (12), and able to clear the guilty (13). The 13 attributes are of significance in the LITURGY, particularly in the PENITENTIAL PRAYERS recited on FASTS, in the selihot days before and after the NEW YEAR, and on the DAY OF ATONEMENT.

thirteen principles of the faith

Principles of the Jewish religion as enumerated by MAIMONIDES: (1) God is the Creator; (2) God is one; (3) God is incorporeal; (4) God is eternal; (5) PRAYER is for God alone; (6) the words of the PROPHETS are true; (7) MOSES is the greatest of the prophets; (8) the TORAH was given to Moses; (9) the TORAH is immutable; (10) God is omniscient; (11) divine retribution will take place; (12) the MESSIAH will come; and (13) the dead will be raised.

thirty-two paths of wisdom

Mystical notion, originating in the *Sefer yetsirah*. These paths are used to refer to a system based on the 22 letters of the HEBREW ALPHABET, and the ten primordial NUMBERS that constitute the elements of creation. In KABBALISTIC texts the idea of the 32 paths was reinterpreted in terms of the doctrine of the *sefirot*. The highest *sefirah* emanates into the lower *sefirot* by way of 32 paths or channels (*See* DIVINE EMANATIONS).

three weeks

Period of mourning from 17 Tammuz to 9 Av. The celebration of MARRIAGES, other festive occasions, and cutting of the hair are prohibited during this time. During the latter part of it eating meat and drinking wine are also proscribed, except on the SABBATH.

throne of God

Visions of the throne of God are recounted in various books in the Bible. EZEKIEL's vision gave rise to CHARIOT MYSTICISM; this evoked ecstatic states in which the mystic's soul ascended to HEAVEN.

Tiberias

Israeli town on the western shore of the Sea of GALILEE, founded by Herod Antipas. It was named after the emperor Tiberias. Its inhabitants participated in the war against Rome (66–70 CE). During the third century the PATRIARCHATE was transferred there, and an ACADEMY was founded. Eventually the town became the capital of Jewish PALESTINE until the academy moved to JERUSALEM in the seventh century. It later became a centre of MASORETIC study.

tied woman (Hebrew: *agunah*)

A woman who has been deserted by her husband or whose husband has disappeared. If a married woman has neither a certificate of DIVORCE (GET) nor proof of her husband's death, she cannot remarry for fear of contracting an adulterous relationship. Various solutions have been proposed to alleviate the problems of the *agunah*, yet none has proved satisfactory. The prohibition against remarriage does not apply to deserted husbands since men are permitted to contract a second marriage. Within PROGRESSIVE JUDAISM, the concept of the *agunah* has been abolished. (*See also* ADULTERY; MAMZER.)

tik

SEPHARDI term for the wood or metal case in which the SCROLL OF THE LAW is stored.

tikkun

Any of several collections of biblical, MISHNAIC and KABBALISTIC passages instituted by mystics for reading on special occasions. The term also refers to the concept of cosmic repair in kabbalistic sources.

tikkun soferim

(Hebrew, 'scribal emendations')

Term used to refer to any of the 18 emendations of the Bible attributed to the SCRIBES: they deal largely with pronominal suffixes. The term is also applied to an unpointed copy of the PENTATEUCH, which is used for practice in reading the SCROLL OF THE LAW.

tish (Yiddish, 'table')

Among the ḤASIDIM, a meal taken by the REBBE with his followers. Three such meals are held on SABBATHS, holidays, and the anniversaires of the deaths of ZADDIKIM. During this meal the *rebbe* delivers a discourse, sings hymns and distributes SHIRAYIM. On the Sabbath the meal concludes with dancing.

Tisha B'Av

See NINTH OF AV.

tithes

Tenth part of one's produce, set aside as a religious offering. According to tradition, there are various types. The first tithe (Num. 18:24) was given to the LEVITES after the HEAVE OFFERING for the PRIESTS had been separated from it. During the Second TEMPLE period the first tithe was given as a whole to the priests. The second tithe (Lev. 27:30-1; Deut. 14: 22-6) was a tenth part of the first tithe and was consumed by the owner himself in JERUSALEM. The poor tithe (Deut. 14:28-9; 26:12) was determined in the same way as the second tithe and given to the poor. The tithe of the animal (Lev. 17:32) occurred three times a year when the animals were counted. The Levites also paid a tithe from what they received (Num. 18:26).

Tobit, Book of

APOCRYPHAL book. It depicts how Tobit, a blind exile from NINEVEH, sent his son Tobias to Persia to collect a debt. During his journey, Tobias visited a relative whose daughter had been married seven times; however, each of these bridegrooms had been killed on the wedding night by the demon Ashmedai. With the assistance of the archangel, the demon was exorcized; Tobias then married this woman and Tobit's blindness was cured.

Toledo

City in Castile, central Spain. Jews lived there in Roman times. Under the Visigoths the Jewish community was the most important in Spain. During the seventh century a series of Councils of Toledo formulated legislation designed to extirpate Judaism from Spain. However, under Arab rule from the eighth century the community flourished. After the Christian conquest in 1085 Jewish rights were secured. When the Almohades persecuted Jews in Muslim Spain, the city became the most important centre of Jewry. During the next centuries Jews prospered there, creating a tradition of scholarship. In 1391 massacres took place, and a large number of Jews converted to Christianity. Later it served as the seat of an INQUISITIONAL tribunal.

toledot yeshu

Medieval Hebrew study of the life of JESUS. It depicts Jesus as the illegitimate son of Joseph Pandera. It narrates that he performed MIRACLES but was conquered by an emissary of the rabbis and condemned to death.

Torah

The Five Books of MOSES (GENESIS, EXODUS, LEVITICUS, NUMBERS AND DEUTERONOMY). According to tradition, they were given by God to Moses on MOUNT SINAI. Along with the WRITTEN LAW, God is viewed as having given Moses a detailed explanation of its commandments (the ORAL LAW). Hence in its broadest sense the term 'Torah' refers to both the WRITTEN and the ORAL LAW.

A Torah Scroll from the Great Synagogue of Jerusalem, also showing the Torah Crown, placed on top of the Torah as an expression of reverence, and the pointer which the reader uses.

Torah MiSinai

The doctrine that God gave MOSES both the WRITTEN and the ORAL LAW on MOUNT SINAI. This belief, formulated in MAIMONIDES' THIRTEEN PRINCIPLES OF THE FAITH, is central to Jewish religious understanding.

Torah ornaments

Covering and decorations of the SCROLL OF THE LAW. Special coverings for the scroll are referred to in the TALMUD; they assumed their current form in the middle ages. The binder was used to fasten the scroll, and a mantle was placed over it. The mantle is surmounted with a silver crown.

Torah, reading of the

The practice of reading from the TORAH SCROLL in the SYNAGOGUE. The Torah is divided into 54 sections which are read in the course of a year.

Torah, study of the

TORAH study is a religious duty. The blessing preceding the reading of the SHEMA in the MORNING and EVENING SERVICES asks for grace to perform this act. Rabbinic Judaism emphasizes that when groups engage in such study, the SHEKHINAH dwells among them.

Tortosa

City in northern Spain. Its Jewish community dates from Roman times. The Disputation of Tortosa occurred in 1413–14; it was forced on representatives of Spanish Jewry by Benedict XIII who presided over it. Jewish scholars debated with the Christian convert Geronimo de Santa Fé, who sought to demonstrate the truth of Christianity from the TALMUD and Hebrew literature.

tosafot (Hebrew, 'addenda')

Critical and explanatory notes on the TALMUD. They were composed by French and German scholars from the 12th to the 14th century. Known as *tosafists*, these scholars initially produced supplements to RASHI's commentary on the Talmud. In time they evolved their own method of talmudic study.

Tosefta

TANNAITIC work which parallels and supplements the MISHNAH. Dating from around the second century, it has six orders with the same names as those of the Mishnah. Some of its paragraphs (known as *baraitot*) are alternative versions of mishnaic paragraphs; others supplement the Mishnah or provide elucidation; still others are independent of mishnaic law.

tractate (Hebrew: *massekhet*)

Subdivision of an order (SEDER) of the MISHNAH. Each *seder* is divided into tractates, and each tractate is divided into chapters.

tradition

Teachings and laws passed on from generation to generation. This oral tradition was collected and set down in the MISHNAH and TALMUD and in later rabbinic RESPONSA.

trayf

Food which is not KOSHER; also, an animal which is not slain according to ritual law (*see* RITUAL SLAUGHTER).

tree of life

One of the two trees in the GARDEN OF EDEN (Gen. 2:9). Whoever ate from it lived for ever. Once ADAM and EVE disobeyed God and ate from the second of the trees, the Tree of Knowledge of Good and Evil, they were driven out of the Garden.

trespass offering

SACRIFICE required of a person who has committed certain offences or trespasses. The acts for which such a sacrifice, was to take place were: perjury committed in denying a robbery; profane use of sacred objects; and violation of a betrothed handmaid. In cases of doubt, the offering might be suspended. A trespass offering was also brought by a NAZIRITE after being cleansed from ritual defilement and by a leper after purification. The offering consisted of a two-year-old ram, which was consumed by the PRIESTS.

tsaddik

See ZADDIK.

Tu B'Av

See FIFTEENTH OF AV.

Tu Bi-Shevat

See FIFTEENTH OF SHEVAT.

twelve tribes

According to Scripture, each tribe was descended from one of the sons of JACOB, except for Ephraim and Manasseh. Each tribe except Levi had a particular territory. Reuben, Isaachar, Zebulun, Simeon, Dan, Naphtali, Gad, Asher, Ephraim and Manasseh were in the NORTHERN KINGDOM; Judah and Benjamin were in the SOUTHERN KINGDOM.

tzedakah

See ZEDAKAH.

tzedekah box

See ZEDAKAH BOX.

tzimtzum

See ZIMZUM.

tzitzit (Hebrew, 'fringes')

See ZITZIT.

Ugarit

Ancient CANAANITE city. Archaeological discoveries there have cast light on Canaanite culture and religion in biblical times.

ulpan

Intensive HEBREW course for new immigrants to ISRAEL.

u-netannah tokeph (Hebrew, 'let us declare the importance')

PIYYUT recited on NEW YEAR and the DAY OF ATONEMENT. It was composed in the 11th century and states that PRAYER and CHARITY avert judgement.

Union of American Hebrew Congregations

Association of American REFORM congregations founded in 1873.

Union of Orthodox Jewish Congregations of America

Association of American ORTHODOX congregations founded in 1898.

Union of Sephardic Congregations

Association of American SEPHARDIC congregations founded in 1929.

United Synagogue

Association of British ORTHODOX congregations founded by an Act of Parliament in 1870.

United Synagogues of America

Association of American CONSERVATIVE congregations founded in 1913.

universalism

Doctrine that a religion is true for all human beings. Judaism is a universalist religion in that God is regarded as the ruler for all, and that everyone can have a part in the world to come. Nonetheless, it is particularist in that it teaches that the Jews are the CHOSEN PEOPLE and have greater responsibilities than the other nations of the world.

unleavened bread
(Hebrew: *matzah*)

Unleavened bread is eaten during PASSOVER. According to Exodus 12:39, the ancient Israelites took *matzah* rather than bread with them when they fled from Egypt because they did not have time to wait for the bread to rise. To commemorate this, *matzah* must be eaten on the first night of Passover. For the rest of the Passover season, no leaven may be consumed.

Ur

Ancient city in southern Mesopotamia. ABRAHAM lived there before his family departed for Haran (Gen. 11:29–31).

Uriel

According to mystical texts, he was one of the four ANGELS of the Presence.

Urim and Thummim

Instruments of divination attached to the BREASTPLATE of the HIGH PRIEST. The process of divination involved the use of two stones or tablets by means of which an answer of 'yes' or 'no' could be obtained to important questions (1 Sam. 23:10–12; 30:8).

Usha, Synod of

Convention of scholars in the second century CE. It met after the BAR KOKHBA revolt to re-establish the SANHEDRIN. Simeon ben Gamaliel was appointed NASI. (*See also* TANNAIM.)

ushpuzin (Hebrew, 'visitors')

Seven guests who, in KABBALISTIC literature, visit the SUKKAH of every pious Jew. The idea of the guests is found in the ZOHAR; they are ABRAHAM, ISAAC, JACOB, JOSEPH, AARON, MOSES and DAVID. They are supposed to visit the *sukkah* and share a meal during SUKKOT.

usury

Lending money on interest. According to the Book of DEUTERONOMY, usury is forbidden between Jews. However, it is permitted for Jews to lend money to gentiles. During the middle ages, moneylending became a common means of livelihood among Jews since Christians could not lend money on interest and Jews were excluded from craft and trade guilds.

u-va le Zion (Hebrew, 'And a redeemer shall come to Zion')

Opening words of a prayer in the SYNAGOGUE LITURGY. It is normally recited at the conclusion of the service.

Uzziah (fl. eighth century BCE)

King of JUDAH (c.780–c.740 BCE). He conquered Philistia and led a league of kings opposed to Tiglath-Pileser of Assyria.

va-ani tefillati (Hebrew, 'and as for me may my prayer')

Opening words of a prayer said at the beginning of the SABBATH AFTERNOON SERVICE.

vakhnakht (Yiddish, 'watchnight')

Celebration on the night before a CIRCUMCISION.

va-yekhullu

(Hebrew, 'and they were completed')

Opening words of the final paragraph of the GENESIS narrative concerning the creation of the world. This paragraph (Gen. 2:1–3) is recited after the AMIDAH in the Friday EVENING SERVICE and when making KIDDUSH at home.

vegetarianism

According to tradition, ADAM was a vegetarian; permission was given to consume meat at the time of NOAH. The sages taught that humanity would return to vegetarianism during the messianic age.

vengeance

In general vengeance is viewed as the prerogative of God, and forbearance is to be commended in human beings.

Venice

City in north-east Italy. Jews resided there from the 12th century. In 1509 the German invasion of the Veneto drove many Jewish refugees there. In 1516 they were segregated into the Ghetto Nuovo. During the next century the GHETTO became a centre of Jewish life in Italy. After the French revolutionary forces entered the city in 1797, the ghetto gates were destroyed and the Jews were emancipated.

ve-shameru

(Hebrew, 'and they shall keep')

Opening word of the passage from Exodus 31 recited before the AMIDAH in the Friday EVENING SERVICE. It is also said on the SABBATH during the Amidah in the MORNING SERVICE, and the KIDDUSH after the service.

vessels, sacred

Vessels and other implements and furnishings used in the TABERNACLE during the wilderness years and in the TEMPLE. They included the ARK, seven-branched candelabrum (MENORAH), veil, table, LAVER, altar, coal shovels and large shovel.

viddui (Hebrew, 'confession of sin')

Special confession which is recited at death.

Vienna

Capital of Austria. Jews lived there from the 10th century. During the middle ages the community was a major centre of Jewish scholarship. In the 13th century a GHETTO was introduced, and in the 14th century the Jewish population was devastated by anti-Semitic unrest. The Jewish community was re-established at the beginning of the 17th century, but expelled in 1670. The Jews of Vienna participated in the Revolution of 1848, and in 1867 were granted equal rights. In the 19th and 20th centuries Jews played an important role in the life of the city until the Jewish community came under attack by the Nazis during the HOLOCAUST.

Vilna

Capital of Lithuania. Jews lived there from the 15th century, but were banished in 1527. However, they were permitted to return later in the 16th century. In the next century they were allowed to engage in various trades. In 1655 the Jews of Vilna were massacred by the Cossacks. From the 18th century the city became a centre of rabbinical scholarship, and of the HASKALAH movement. It was also a centre of ZIONISM.

Vilna Gaon

See ELIJAH BEN SOLOMON ZALMAN.

vimpel

Fabric strip which is used as a binder around a SCROLL OF THE LAW.

visiting the sick
(Hebrew, *bikkur ḥolim*)

In the Jewish tradition, visiting those who are ill is an important duty. According to the rabbis, this obligation derives its importance from God's visit to ABRAHAM during his illness which was caused by CIRCUMCISION (Gen. 18:1).

Vital, Ḥayyim

PALESTINIAN KABBALIST. A student of Moses CORDOVERO and Moses Alshekh, he was associated with Isaac LURIA in SAFED. After Luria's death, he claimed that he alone had an accurate account of Luria's teaching. From 1590 he lived in Damascus where he composed kabbalistic works and preached the coming of the MESSIAH.

vocalization

Indication of vowel sounds in HEBREW by means of marks or points placed above or below consonants. Initially Hebrew was written only with consonants; these were 'vocalized' to show where vowel sounds occured and what vowels should be sounded. At the end of the TALMUDIC period a system of distinctive signs to indicate vowels began to develop; eventually three so-called punctuation systems evolved: Babylonian, Palestinian and Tiberian. The Tiberian system became fixed in two different forms associated with the MASORETIC schools of Ben Asher and Ben Naphtali. The Ben Asher system passed into common use and is found in printed Bibles. (*See also* ALPHABET.)

vow

Solemn pledge, binding on the person making it. According to tradition, it was common to make religious vows undertaking to perform a specific act or behave in a certain fashion. In TALMUDIC law there are two types of vow: (1) a promise to provide TEMPLE SACRIFICES or make gifts of property to the Temple or to CHARITY; (2) a commitment to abstain from eating specified food or from financial exploitation of specified property.

wages

The Bible specifies that an employer must pay wages without delay (Lev. 19:13). The TALMUD explains that a person hired for the day should be paid not later than the next morning. One hired for the night must be paid by the following evening. Whoever withholds payment violates several biblical prohibitions.

Wailing Wall

Western wall of the JERUSALEM TEMPLE. The Wailing Wall was all that remained after the destruction of the Temple in 70 CE.

Wandering Jew

Image of the Jew in medieval Christian legends. The story concerns a Jewish cobbler, Ahasuerus, who was condemned to wander eternally for taunting JESUS on his way to the crucifixion.

war

Settlement of disputes through armed force. The Israelites participated in wars against their neighbours from the time of the conquest of CANAAN. Since modern ISRAEL was founded in 1948, the Israeli army has fought to defend the Jewish state.

War of Independence

War for Israeli independence fought during 1947–9. After the United Nations resolution passed on 29 November 1947 to partition Palestine into Jewish and Arab states, Palestinian Arabs began hostilities against the Jewish population. They were eventually joined by volunteers from Arab states. Jewish forces were organized in the HAGANAH. In May 1948 the forces of the Arab League invaded the country. From February to July 1949, Israel signed armistice agreements with Egypt, Jordan, Lebanon and Syria.

war scroll

One of the DEAD SEA SCROLLS. It describes the war at the end of time between the Sons of Light and the Sons of Darkness.

watcher

Heavenly being in the Book of DANIEL.

water

See ABLUTION.

wedding

See MARRIAGE.

weekday of the festival

Intermediate days of PASSOVER and SUKKOT. The first and last days are holy days; however, normal work may be carried out on the intervening days. Nonetheless, MOURNING is forbidden and no MARRIAGES should be celebrated.

weeks, feast of

See SHAVUOT.

Weizmann, Chaim (1874–1952)

ZIONIST leader and Israeli statesman. Born at Motel near Pinsk, he settled in England and became a lecturer in chemistry at Manchester University. He was a major influence on the BALFOUR DECLARATION. At the Paris Peace Conference of 1919 Weizmann represented the ZIONIST movement, and in the same year he became president of the World Zionist Organization. He subsequently retired to Reḥovot to work at the Weizmann Institute. In 1948 he became the first president of the State of ISRAEL.

whole offering

Term used with reference to a TEMPLE offering which was consumed entirely when burned. Specifically it is used of the meal offering (Lev. 6:15–16). In this more limited sense, 'whole offering' is parallel to a 'burnt offering', the one referring to a SACRIFICE of a meal and the other to an animal sacrifice.

widow

According to Scripture, a widow is to be protected and maintained (Exod. 22:21; Deut. 27:19). She is entitled to payment of the sum stipulated by her husband in the MARRIAGE contract. Alternatively, she is to be supported by her husband's descendants.

Wiesel, Elie (b. 1928)

American author. Born in Sighet, Romania, he was a survivor of the concentration camps. He lived in Paris and New York, becoming a correspondent for an Israeli newspaper. From 1957 he worked for the Jewish daily, *Forward*; later he was appointed a professor at Boston University. In 1986 he was awarded the Nobel Peace Prize.

wig

See SHEITEL.

The Wailing Wall: An Israeli soldier still carries his gun while he prays at the Wailing Wall wearing his phylacteries and prayer shawl.

willow

See FOUR SPICES.

wine

In ancient times wine was drunk at meals. In the TEMPLE it was poured on the ALTAR with the SACRIFICES. Wine also played a role in later rituals, such as KIDDUSH, HAVDALAH and the PASSOVER SEDER. A special BENEDICTION is recited beore and after drinking it. At the festival of PURIM and on SIMḤAT TORAH over-indulgence in wine is encouraged as part of the celebration. Wine made for gentiles is forbidden according to Jewish LAW.

wisdom

According to Scripture, wisdom results from education and experience, and is a gift from God. It is not viewed as existing only in Israel; rather, it is found among the nations as well. The Book of PROVERBS stresses its significance. During the post-exilic period, wisdom was identified with knowledge of the TORAH and the law.

wisdom literature

Biblical and APOCRYPHAL literature in which wisdom is presented as based on fear of God and knowledge of the commandments. The works concerned are the Books of PROVERBS, JOB and ECCLESIASTES, PSALMS 37, 49 and 73, and the apocryphal books of ECCLESIASTICUS, Wisdom of Solomon and 4 MACCABEES.

Wise, Isaac Mayer (1819–1900)

American REFORM RABBI. Born in Steingrub, Bohemia, he served as a rabbi in Albany, New York. Later he moved to Cincinnati, Ohio where he founded the German-language weekly, *Die Deborah*. He also published an American Reform PRAYER BOOK, *Minhag America*. In 1855 he attempted to establish a rabbinical seminary; subsequently he was instrumental in creating the Hebrew Union College. He summoned reform rabbinical conferences, and helped form the UNION OF AMERICAN HEBREW CONGREGATIONS. In 1889 he founded the Central Conference of American Rabbis.

Wissenschaft des Judentums

(German, 'science of Judaism')

Scientific study of Jewish history, literature and religion. The methodology developed in Europe in the 19th century as a result of the HASKALAH and the rise of REFORM JUDAISM.

witness

According to Jewish LAW, a person who has evidence concerning an event is under an obligation to testify before a court. In civil cases the testimony of a single witness obligates the accused to take an OATH that he is not liable for the claim against him. Similarly, with regard to religious law concerning things permitted or prohibited, the testimony of

one witness is valid. In all other cases, two witnesses are needed.

Wolffsohn, David (1856–1914)

German Zionist leader. Born in Dorbiany, Lithuania, he lived in Cologne. He served as co-founder of a society to promote Jewish agricultural work and handicrafts in PALESTINE. Subsequently he became an assistant to Theodor HERZL. Wolffsohn succeeded Herzl as president of the World Zionist Organization in 1905.

woman of valour

(Hebrew: *eshet ḥayil*)

The phrase occurs in Prov. 31 in a passage praising women. The whole passage is recited by the householder before KID-DUSH on Friday evenings. The SABBATH CANDLES are lit, and before the meal the wife is praised and the children blessed.

worlds, four

Kabbalistic doctrine. According to kabbalists, the four worlds of creation correspond with the letters of the TETRAGRAMMATON. The worlds are the source of all being, creation, formation and the angelic realm.

worship

see BENEDICTION; FASTING; FESTIVAL; KID-DUSH; KIDDUSH HA-SHEM; LITURGY; PRAYER BOOK; SABBATH; SACRIFICE; SYNA-GOGUE; TABERNACLE; TEFILLIN; TEMPLE.

Writings

See HAGIOGRAPHA.

written law

Law given by God to MOSES on MOUNT SINAI. According to tradition, it consists of GENESIS, EXODUS, LEVITICUS, NUMBERS and DEUTERONOMY. By extension the term is also used for the prophetic books and the HAGIOGRAPHA. The written law is complemented by the ORAL LAW, which is viewed as originating in God's revelation to Moses.

Y

yaaleh ('may it arise')

Opening word and the name of a hymn sung in the SYNAGOGUE during the EVENING SERVICE on the DAY OF ATONEMENT.

yaaleh ve-yavo

('may it arise and come')

Opening words of a paragraph added to the AMIDAH and GRACE AFTER MEALS at NEW YEAR and FESTIVALS.

yad (Hebrew, 'hand')

Pointer used in the SYNAGOGUE to indicate the place during the reading of the TORAH SCROLL.

Yah

See GOD, NAMES OF.

yah ribbon olam

('God, master of the universe')

Opening words and title of an ARAMAIC hymn which is generally sung at the table during the SABBATH meal.

yaḥad (Hebrew, 'unity')

Term used in the DEAD SEA SCROLLS to describe the unifying spirit of the sect that produced the scrolls.

yahrzeit

Anniversary of the death of a relative. It is observed by kindling a light and reciting the KADDISH.

Yahweh

God's sacred name which is never pronounced.

Yahwist

Editor of one of the sources of the PENTATEUCH. According to biblical scholars, the Pentateuch was compiled from four different sources. The Yahwist (J) Source is distinctive because God is referred to as the TETRAGRAMMATON. It is thought to have originated in the ninth century BCE.

Yalkut (Hebrew, 'Compilation')

Title of several anthologies of MIDRASH. These include the *Yalkut Reuveni*, the *Yalkut Shimoni* and the *Yalkut ha-Meiri*.

yamin noraim

(Hebrew, 'days of awe')

Rosh Ha-Shanah (NEW YEAR), Yom Kippur (DAY OF ATONEMENT) and the TEN DAYS OF REPENTANCE. According to rabbinic teaching, humanity stands before God for judgement on Rosh Ha-Shanah; judgement is finally pronounced on the Day of Atonement.

yarmulke

Skullcap worn by religious Jewish men. The practice of wearing a *yarmulke* goes back to around the 12th century. It is worn at all times by the ORTHODOX, while the less observant cover their heads only for prayer. An alternative Hebrew term is *kipah*.

year, Jewish

See CALENDAR.

year of release

See SABBATICAL YEAR.

yekum purkan

(Aramaic, 'may redemption come')

Aramaic prayers which are recited after the reading of the TORAH SCROLL. They date from the GAONIC period.

Yelammedenu

(Aramaic, 'Let Him Pronounce')

Alternative title for the TANḤUMA.

yeshivah

Jewish rabbinical academy devoted to the study of the TALMUD and other rabbinic sources. The institution of the *yeshivah* is a continuation of the ACADEMIES in BABYLONIA and PALESTINE during the talmudic and GAONIC periods. Many modern *yeshivot* teach a programme of secular studies to complement traditional talmudic learning.

yetzer ha-ra

See EVIL INCLINATION.

yetzer ha-tov

See GOOD INCLINATION.

Yetzirah, Sefer

See SEFER YETZIRAH.

YHWH

See TETRAGRAMMATON.

Yiddish

Language spoken by ASHKENAZI Jews from the middle ages. It is derived from Hebrew, Loez, German and Slavic. Since its formation in *c.*1000–1250, it has undergone constant development. It can be classified into Old Yiddish (1250–1500), Middle Yiddish (1500–1750), and Modern Yiddish (1750–20th century).

yiddishkeit

Jewish culture.

yigdal

(Hebrew, 'may he be magnified')

Opening word and title of a liturgical hymn. It is based on MAIMONIDES' THIRTEEN PRINCIPLES OF THE FAITH. It originated in Italy *c.*1300; its author may have been Daniel bar Judah. It is recited on the SABBATH eve in the SEPHARDI and Italian rites; among ASHKENAZIM it is used as an opening hymn for the daily MORNING SERVICE. On HIGH HOLY DAYS it is chanted to a special melody.

yiḥus

Distinguished ancestral descent.

yishtabbaḥ

(Hebrew, 'may his name be praised')

Opening word and title of the concluding blessing of the *pesuke de-zimra*. It contains terms of praise and adoration, and in some rites is recited while standing.

yizkor (Hebrew, 'he shall remember')

Opening word and title of the prayer in commemoration of the dead. It is recited in ASHKENAZI communities on the last days of PASSOVER, SHAVUOT and SUKKOT, and on the DAY OF ATONEMENT. The term also refers to the memorial service held on each of those days, at which the members of the congregation remember their relatives who have died.

Yom Atzmaut

Israeli Independence Day. It is the anniversary of ISRAEL's Declaration of Independence made on 14 May 1948 (5 Iyyar 5708). It is observed as a public holiday in Israel.

Yom Kippur

See DAY OF ATONEMENT.

Yom Kippur Katan

(Hebrew, 'Minor Day of Atonement')

FAST observed on the day before the NEW MOON. The custom of fasting on this day existed in PALESTINE in the 16th century. It was brought from there to Italy by Moses CORDOVERO; eventually it spread to Germany. The day is commemorated by a special order of prayer.

yom tov (Hebrew, 'a good day')

Term applied to all festivals, signifying joy and festivity.

yontif

Holiday or celebration.

Yoreh Deah

Laws of KASHRUT as delinineated by JACOB BEN ASHER in his CODE, the ARBAAH TURIM. It also forms a major part of the SHULḤAN ARUKH.

yotzer (Hebrew, 'He createth')

Name derived from the opening word of the first of the blessings that frame the SHEMA; it is applied to various elements of the LITURGY. In some rites it is used of the service of morning prayer. It is also applied to a hymn preceding the Shema. More generally it refers to all the special hymns added to the blessings of the Shema on SABBATHS and FESTIVALS. The term is used in the plural to refer to the entire group of liturgical hymns added at various points in the MORNING SERVICE.

Z

zaddik (Hebrew, 'righteous man')

Term used to describe a person of faith and piety. It is found in both the Bible and the TALMUD. In ḤASIDISM the concept of the *zaddik* was developed by DOV BAER of MEZHIRECH and JACOB JOSEPH OF POLONNOYE as one of a spiritual leader. The *zaddik* is viewed as the intermediary between God and human beings. Individuals frequently visited the *zaddik* for advice; on SABBATH and FESTIVALS multitudes of Ḥasidim gathered at his festival table for a meal known as a TISH.

Zadok (fl. 11th century BCE)

Israelite priest. A descendant of AARON, he went to DAVID at HEBRON after SAUL's death and became David's chief priest. He remained loyal to David during Absalom's rebellion, and at David's request he anointed SOLOMON king. Solomon later appointed Zadok's son HIGH PRIEST in the TEMPLE. From that time onward the high priesthood remained in the Zadokite family.

Zadokite Fragments

Name of two manuscripts found in the Cairo GENIZA. In 1952 fragments of other copies of the same documents were found in a cave near Khirbet Qumran. All the manuscripts form part of the literature to which the DEAD SEA SCROLLS belong.

Zadokites

Self-designation of the members of the QUMRAN sect. The high priesthood was no longer held by members of the Zadokite family when the DEAD SEA SCROLLS were composed. The members of the sect viewed themselves as the remaining faithful of Israel. In their MANUAL OF DISCIPLINE, it is recorded how new initiates placed themselves under the authority of the sons of Zadok.

zayde

Old man, grandfather.

Zealots

Jewish rebels who participated in the war against Rome in 66–73 CE. The activities of the Zealots are recorded by JOSEPHUS in *The Jewish War*.

Zechariah, Book of

Biblical book, one of the books of the 12 MINOR PROPHETS. It recounts the prophecies of the Israelite prophet Zechariah, who lived during the sixth century BCE. He predicted material prosperity, the ingathering of the EXILES, liberation from foreign rule and the expansion of JERUSALEM. In addition, he encouraged the people to rebuild the TEMPLE.

zedakah (Hebrew, 'charity')

CHARITY, philanthropy. The rabbis encouraged *zedakah* and particularly praised charity which was done secretly.

zedakah box

(Hebrew, 'charity box')

Charity box. It is located in Jewish homes to encourage philanthropy.

zekhor berit

(Hebrew, 'remember the covenant')

Penitential hymn recited on the eve of Rosh Ha-Shanah (NEW YEAR) and during the concluding service of Yom Kippur (DAY OF ATONEMENT).

zekhut avot

See MERITS OF THE FATHERS.

Zelophehad's daughters

Biblical characters in Num. 26. Because of the legal precedent of their case, women could inherit their father's property provided they were married to men of the same tribe.

zemirot   (Hebrew, 'songs')

Psalms and hymns. Among the SEPHARDIM the term refers to the psalms recited before the main part of the MORNING SERVICE. The ASHKENAZIM use the term for the hymns sung during and after the SABBATH meal.

Zephaniah, Book of

Biblical book, one of the books of the 12 MINOR PROPHETS. It contains an acount of the seventh-century BCE prophet Zephaniah who described the DAY OF THE LORD, when the wicked will be punished, the poor will inherit the land and the Lord will be universally acknowledged.

Zeraim   (Hebrew, 'Seeds')

First order of the MISHNAH; it deals with agricultural laws and laws of prayer.

Zerubbabel   (fl. sixth-century BCE)

Israelite leader. With the consent of King CYRUS of Persia, he returned to JUDAH from BABYLON to help rebuild the TEMPLE. With Joshua the priest, he set up an altar, re-established the FESTIVALS, and commenced the rebuilding of the Temple.

zikhrono li-verakhah   (Hebrew, 'may his memory be for a blessing')

Expression of respect and blessing. It is uttered when mentioning someone who has died.

zikhronot

(Hebrew, 'remembrances')

Name of the second of the three sections in the additional AMIDAH service on Rosh Ha-Shanah (NEW YEAR). It contains ten biblical verses with an introductory paragraph and concluding blessing.

zimzum

(Hebrew, 'divine contraction')

KABBALISTIC doctrine which teaches that God makes a space in which the process of creation can occur.

Zion

Jeubusite stronghold in JERUSALEM which was captured by DAVID and became part of the City of David (2 Sam. 5:6–7). During the MACCABEAN period, Mount Zion was identified with the TEMPLE MOUNT and the City of David to the south-east. The name is used in poetic and prophetic language to refer to Jerusalem as a whole. It symbolizes the spiritual capital of the world, and the messianic city of God.

Zionism

International political and ideological movement devoted to securing the return of the Jewish people to ISRAEL. Modern political Zionism was initiated by Theodor HERZL and launched at the first Zionist Congress in 1897. As an ideology Zionism was initially opposed by ORTHODOX Jews who claimed that divine intervention in history should not be usurped by human action. After the creation of a Jewish state in 1948 the Zionist movement continued its activities, raising money to support settlement in Israel and encouraging immigration.

zitzit (Hebrew, 'fringes')

The Bible commands the wearing of fringes on the corners of garments (Num. 15:37–41). Initially all garments had fringes; later an undergarment with fringes on the corners was devised for daily use.

zogerin

Title given to the woman who recites the prayers in the vernacular in the SYNAGOGUE for those women who are unable to read HEBREW.

Zohar

Mystical commentary on the PENTATEUCH and parts of the HAGIOGRAPHA. According to tradition, it was composed in the second century by SIMEON BEN YOHAI. It was first published in the 13th century by Moses de Leon in Spain. The work is in HEBREW and ARAMAIC; it consists of HOMILETICAL passages alternating with short discourses and PARABLES.

zugot

Term designating pairs of PALESTINIAN sages who for five generations led the rabbinic tradition of Judaism (second century BCE to first century CE). According to tradition, one was president of the SANHEDRIN (NASI) and the other the head judge of the BET DIN (AV BET DIN).

Zunz, Leopold (1794–1886)

German historian. Born in Detmold, his work laid the foundations for the scientific study of Jewish history. From 1840 to 1850 he was principal of the Berlin Teachers' Seminary. His early writings include a biography of RASHI and a history of Jewish HOMILETICS. Among his later publications are a history of Jewish geographical literature, a history of Jewish liturgy, studies of medieval PIYYUTIM and their authors, and Bible studies.

Chronology

c. 200–600	Talmudic period
c. 5th century	Jerusalem Talmud
c. 6th century	Babylonian Talmud
600–700	End of the Academies
700–800	Rise of Karaism
800–900	Conversion of the Khazars to Judaism, Era of Karaite biblical scholarship
c. 8th century	Messianic Jewish movements
882–942	Saadiah Gaon
900–1000	Golden age of Spain
1021–1056	Solomon ibn Gabirol
1040–1105	Rashi
1078–1141	Judah Halevi
1096	First Crusade
1100–1200	First example of blood libel, Era of the Ḥasidei Ashkenaz, Kabbalistic study in Provence
1135–1204	Moses Maimonides
1145–1147	Second Crusade
1182–1198	Expulsion of French Jews
1189–1190	Third Crusade
1194–1270	Naḥmanides
c. 1230	Establishment of the Inquisition
1240	Disputation of Paris
1263	Disputation of Barcelona
c. 1286	Zohar
1288–1344	Gersonides
1290	Expulsion of Jews from England
1340–1412	Ḥasdai Crescas
1380–1445	Joseph Albo
1413–1415	Disputation of Tortosa
1437–1508	Isaac Abrabanel
1492	Expulsion of Jews from Spain
1500–1600	Era of Safed mystics, Council of the Four Lands
1534–1572	Isaac Luria
1542–1620	Ḥayyim Vital
1555	Ghetto in Italy
1600–1700	Chmielnicki massacres, Shabbetai Zevi proclaimed Messiah
1626–1676	Shabbetai Zevi
1650–1700	Golden age of Dutch Jewry
1700–1800	Rise of Ḥasidism, Opposition of Mitnagdim
1700–1760	Baal Shem Tov
1707–1747	Moses Ḥayyim Luzzatto
1710–1772	Dov Baer of Mezhirech
1726–1791	Jacob Frank
1729–1786	Moses Mendelssohn
1750–1800	Beginning of the Haskalah
1772–1811	Naḥman of Bratslav

1795–1874	Zevi Hirsch Kalischer
1798–1878	Yehuda Ḥai Alkalai
1808–1874	Samson Raphael Hirsch
1810–1875	Abraham Geiger
1812–1875	Moses Hess
1821–1891	Leon Pinsker
1842–1918	Hermann Cohen
c. 1850	Reform Judaism founded
1856–1922	Aaron David Gordon
1860–1904	Theodor Herzl
1865–1935	Abraham Isaac Kook
1873–1956	Leo Baeck
1878–1965	Martin Buber
1880–1940	Vladimir Jabotinsky
1880–1900	Pogroms in Russia, Dreyfus case, mass emigration to the USA
1881–1983	Mordecai Kaplan
c. 1895	Conservative Judaism founded
1897	First Zionist Congress
1900–1920	Pogroms in Russia, mass emigration from Eastern Europe, Jewish settlement in Palestine
1902–1944	Menahem Mendel Schneerson
c. 1905	Modern Orthodoxy founded
1907–1972	Abraham Joshua Heschel
1920–40	Emigration restrictions to Palestine, Western Europe and the USA, Rise of Nazism
1930–40	Nuremburg Laws, Kristallnacht
c. 1935	Reconstructionist Judaism founded
1942–5	Holocaust
1948	Founding of the State of Israel
1965	Humanistic Judaism founded
1967	Six Day War
1973	Yom Kippur War
1982	Israeli advance into Southern Lebanon

Thematic Bibliography

General

Abramson, G. (ed.), *The Blackwell Companion to Jewish Culture*. Oxford, Blackwell, 1989

Baeck, L., *The Essence of Judaism*. New York, Schocken, 1948

Baron, S.W., *A Social and Religious History of the Jews*. New York, Columbia University Press, 1952–76

Cohn-Sherbok, D., *The Blackwell Dictionary of Judaica*. Oxford, Blackwell, 1992

Cohn-Sherbok, L. and D., *A Short History of Judaism*. Oxford, Oneworld Publications, 1994

Cohn-Sherbok, L. and D., *A Short Reader of Judaism*. Oxford, Oneworld Publications, 1996

Cohn-Sherbok, L. and D., *A Short Introduction to Judaism*. Oxford, Oneworld Publications, 1997

De Lange, N., *Judaism*. Oxford, Oxford University Press, 1986

Encyclopedia Judaica. Jerusalem, Keter Publishing House, 1972

Epstein, I., *Judaism*. London, Penguin, 1975

Gilbert, M., *Jewish History Atlas*. London, Weidenfeld & Nicolson, 1988

Jacobs, L., *A Jewish Theology*. London, Darton, Longman & Todd, 1973

Jacobs, L., *The Book of Jewish Belief*. New York, Behrman House, 1984

Jacobs, L., *The Book of Jewish Practice*. New York, Behrman House, 1987

Jacobs, L., *The Jewish Religion*. Oxford, Oxford University Press, 1995

Katz, S.T., *Jewish Ideas and Concepts*. New York, Schocken, 1977

Margolis, M.L. and Marx, A., *A History of the Jewish People*. New York, Harper & Row, 1965

Neusner, J., *The Way of Torah: An Introduction to Judaism*. Dickenson, 1974

Roth, C., *A History of the Jews*. New York, Schocken, 1973

Sachar, A.L., *History of the Jews*. New York, Knopf, 1973

Seltzer, R., *Jewish People, Jewish Thought*. Hemel Hempstead, Collier Macmillan, 1980

Siegel, R., Strassfield, M. and Strassfield, S. (eds), *The Jewish Catalogue*. Jewish Publication Society of America, 1973

Strassfield, S. and Strassfield, M. (eds), *The Second Jewish Catalogue*. Jewish Publication Society of America, 1976

Strassfield, S. and Strassfield, M. (eds), *The Third Jewish Catalogue*. Jewish Publication Society of America, 1980

Trepp, L., *A History of the Jewish Experience*. New York, Behrman House, 1973

Werblowsky, R.J. and Wigoder, G. (eds), *The Oxford Dictionary of the Jewish Religion*. Oxford, Oxford University Press, 1997

Wigoder, G., *The Encyclopedia of Judaism*. London, Macmillan, 1989

Wouk, H., *This is My God*. New York, Doubleday, 1968

Ancient Near Eastern Background

Beyerlin, W. (ed.), *Near Eastern Texts Relating to the Old Testament*. London, SCM Press, 1978

Frankfort, H. (ed.), *Before Philosophy*. London, Penguin, 1964

Hooke, S.H., *Middle Eastern Mythology*. London, Penguin, 1981

Pritchard, J. (ed.), *The Ancient Near East: An Anthology of Texts and Pictures*, Princeton, Princeton University Press (Vol. 1, 1958; Vol. 2, 1975)

Winton Thomas, D., *Documents from Old Testament Times*. New York, Harper & Row, 1976

Patriarchy to Monarchy

Anderson, G.W., *The History and Religion of Israel*. Oxford, Oxford University Press, 1966

Bright, J., *A History of Israel*. London, Westminster Press, 1972

Drane, J., *The Old Testament Story*. Oxford, Lion, 1983

Grant, M., *The History of Ancient Israel*. New York, Scribner's, 1984

Kenyon, K.M., *The Bible and Recent Archaeology*. John Knox Press, 1978

Kings and Prophets

Anderson, B.W., *The Eighth Century Prophets*. London, SPCK, 1979

Gray, J., *The Biblical Doctrine of the Reign of God*. Edinburgh, T. and T. Clark, 1979

Lindblom, J., *Prophecy in Ancient Israel*. Oxford, Blackwell, 1962

Vawter, B., *The Conscience of Israel*. London, Sheed & Ward, 1961

Von Rad, G., *The Message of the Prophets*. London, SCM Press, 1968

Captivity and Return

Ackroyd, P.R., *Exile and Restoration*. London, SCM Press, 1968

Ackroyd, P.R., *Israel under Babylon and Persia*. Oxford, Oxford University Press, 1970

Blenkinsopp, J., *Prophecy and Canon: A Contribution to the Study of Jewish Origins*. London, University of Notre Dame Press, 1977

Hengel, M., *Judaism and Hellenism: Studies in their Encounter in Palestine during the Early Hellenic Period*. Nornstown, PA, Fortress Press, 1974

Kaufmann, Y., *The Babylonian Captivity and Deutero-Isaiah*. Union of American Hebrew Congregations, 1970

Rebellion and Dispersion

Dodd, C.H., *The Bible and the Greeks*. London, Hodder & Stoughton, 1935
Sandmel, S., *Judaism and Christian Beginnings*. Oxford, Oxford University Press, 1978
Schurer, E., *The History of the Jewish People in the Age of Jesus Christ*. Edinburgh, T. & T. Clark, 1973
Tcherikover, V., *Hellenistic Civilization and the Jews*. Jewish Publication Society of America, 1962–8

The Emergence of Medieval Jewry

Abrahams, I., *Jewish Life in the Middle Ages*. London, Athenaeum, 1969
Marcus, J.R. (ed.), *The Jew in the Medieval World*. New York, Harper & Row, 1965
Parkes, J., *The Jew in the Medieval Community: A Study of His Political and Economic Situation*. Harmon Press, 1976
Sharf, A., *Byzantine Jewry: From Justinian to the Fourth Crusade*. London, Routledge & Kegan Paul, 1971
Trachtenberg, J., *Jewish Magic and Superstition*. Jewish Publication Society of America, 1961

Medieval Jewish Philosophy and Theology

Agus, J.B., *The Evolution of Jewish Thought: From Biblical Times to the Opening of the Modern Era*. Manchester, NH, Abelard-Schuman, 1959
Blau, J.L., *The Story of Jewish Philosophy*. London, Random House, 1962
Cohn-Sherbok, D., *Medieval Jewish Philosophy*. Richmond, Curzon, 1996
Husik, I., *A History of Medieval Jewish Philosophy*. Jewish Publication Society of America, 1958
Sirat, C., *A History of Jewish Philosophy in the Middle Ages*. Cambridge, 1995

Medieval Jewish Mysticism

Abelson, I., *Jewish Mysticism*. Harmon Press, 1969
Dan, J., *Jewish Mysticism and Jewish Ethics*. Washington, Washington University Press, 1986
Dan J. and Talmage, F. (eds), *Studies in Jewish Mysticism*. Association for Jewish Studies, 1982
Scholem, G., *Kabbalah*. Quadrangle, 1974
Scholem, G., *Major Trends in Jewish Mysticism*. New York, Schocken, 1954

Judaism in the Early Modern Period

Katz, J., *Tradition and Crisis: Jewish Society at the End of the Middle Ages*. New York, Free Press, 1961
Roth, C., *The Spanish Inquisition*. London, Norton, 1964
Soholem, G., *Sabbatai Sevi: The Mystical Messiah 1626–1676*. Princeton, Princeton University Press, 1973

Stern, S., *The Court Jew: A Contribution to the History of the Period of Absolutism in Central Europe.* Jewish Publication Society of America, 1950

Weinryb, B., *The Jews of Poland: A Social and Economic History of the Jewish Community of Poland from 1100 to 1800.* Jewish Publication Society of America, 1973

From Hasidism to the Enlightenment

Ben-Amos, D. and Mintz, J.R. (eds), *In Praise of the Baal Shem Tov: The Earliest Collection of Legends about the Founder of Hasidism.* Bloomington, Indiana University Press, 1970

Dawidowicz, L.S., *The Golden Tradition: Jewish Life and Thought in Eastern Europe.* London, Holt, Rinehart & Winston, 1966

Dubnow, S., *History of the Jews in Russia and Poland.* Hoboken, NJ, Ktav, 1973

Hertzberg, A., *The French Enlightenment and the Jews.* New York, Columbia University Press, 1968

Katz, J., *Out of the Ghetto: The Social Background of Jewish Emancipation 1770–1870.* Harvard, Harvard University Press, 1973

The Rise of Reform Judaism

Jacob. W. (ed.), *American Reform Responsa.* Central Conference of American Rabbis, 1983

Marmur, D. (ed.), *Reform Judaism.* Reform Synagogues of Great Britain, 1973

Meyer, M., *Response to Modernity: A History of the Reform Movement in Judaism.* Oxford, Oxford University Press, 1988

Plaut, G.W. (ed.), *The Rise of Reform Judaism.* World Union of Progressive Judaism, 1963

Plaut, G.W. (ed.), *The Growth of Reform Judaism.* World Union of Progressive Judaism, 1965

Jewish Life in the Nineteenth and Early Twentieth Centuries

Glazer, N., *American Judaism.* Chicago, University of Chicago Press, 1972

Laqueur, W., *A History of Zionism.* New York, Schocken, 1976

Poliakov, L., *The History of Anti-Semitism*, 3 vols. New York, Vanguard Press, 1965–76

Reinharz, J., *Fatherland or Promised Land: The Dilemma of the German Jew, 1893–1914.* Michigan, University of Michigan Press, 1975

Sachar, H.M., *The Course of Modern Jewish History.* New York, Delta, 1958

Holocaust and Aftermath

Dawidowicz, L.S., *The War Against the Jews, 1937–1945.* London, Holt, Rinehart & Winston, 1975

Dawidowicz, L.S. (ed.), *A Holocaust Reader.* New York, Behrman House, 1976

De Lange, N., *Atlas of the Jewish World.* London, Phaidon, 1985

Levin, N., *The Holocaust: The Destruction of European Jewry 1933–1945.* New York, Schocken, 1973

O'Brien, C.C., *The Siege: The Saga of Israel and Zionism.* London, Weidenfeld & Nicholson, 1986

Modern Jewish Thought

Agus, J.B., *Modern Philosophies of Judaism*. New York, Behrman House, 1971

Bergman, S.H., *An Introduction to Modern Jewish Thought*. New York, Schocken, 1963

Kaufman, W., *Contemporary Jewish Philosophies*. New York, Behrman House, 1976

Rotenstreich, N., *Jewish Philosophy in Modern Times: From Mendelssohn to Rosensweig*. London, Holt, Rinehart & Winston, 1968

Rubenstein, R.L. and Roth, J.K., *Approaches to Auschwitz*. London, SCM Press, 1987

Thematic Index

Within this index, note that some entries appear under more than one theme.

Beliefs

afterlife
angel
Ani Maamin
anthropomorphism
apikoros
apocalypse
apologetics
asceticism
atonement
Baal
bat kol
cherub
chosen people
covenant
creation
Day of Judgement
Day of the Lord
death
devil
dream
faith
Fall
fear of God
forgiveness
free will
Gabriel
geullah
glory
ḥasidei ummot ha-olam
heaven
hell
heresy

holiness
Holy Spirit
image of God
kingdom of heaven
merits of the fathers
messiah
metempsychosis
miracle
name, change of
neshamah yeterah
original sin
pantheism
procreation
providence
reincarnation
remnant of Israel
resurrection
revelation
Sheol
superstition
thirteen attributes of mercy
Torah MiSinai
zimzum

Codes

Alfasi, Isaac ben Jacob
Arbaah Turim
Caro, Joseph
codes of Jewish law
Isserles, Moses
Jacob ben Asher
Kol Bo
law

Mishneh Torah
Mishpat Ivri
oral law
responsa
Shulḥan Arukh
six hundred and thirteen commandments
Yoreh Deah

Concepts

afterlife
allegory
am ha-aretz
amulet
angel
anthropomorphism
anti-Semitism
apikoros
apostasy
asceticism
assimilation
astrology
atonement
badge, Jewish
ban
bat kol
blasphemy
Book of Life
celibacy
charity
chastity
chosen people
covenant
cruelty
curse
danger to life
death
derekh eretz
devekut
devotion
dibbuk
din Torah
dina de-malkuta dina
ecstasy
education
emanation
epitropos

eshet ḥayil
evil eye
evil inclination
excommunication
exiles, ingathering of
faith
Fall
fathers, merits of
fear of God
fence around the law
forgiveness
free will
geullah
giving of the law
glory
goyim
ḥakham
Ha-Shem
ḥasidei ummot ha-olam
ḥaver
heaven
hell
heresy
holiness
Holy Spirit
homosexuality
hospitality
ḥukkat ha-goy
iconography
idolatry
illegitimacy
image of God
imitation of God
incest
ingathering of the exiles
insanity
intermarriage
Jew
Judaism
judge
judgement
judgement of the law
justice
justification
kabbalah
kal va-ḥomer
keneset Israel
keter malkut

war
watcher
wisdom
witness
Yahweh
Yahwist
yiddishkeit
yiḥus
zaddik
zayde
zikhrono li-verakhah
Zion

Ethics

abortion
adoption
adultery
animals
Avot
birth control
capital punishment
charity
chastity
compassion
corporal punishment
cruelty
derekh eretz
duty
entertaining travellers
euthanasia
evil inclination
false witness
Fathers, Sayings of
fine
gambling
giving of kindness
good inclination
halakhah
Ḥasidim, Sefer
hekdesh
holiness code
homosexuality
hospitality
illegitimacy
imitation of God
incest
justice

kidnapping
lamed vav zaddikim
love of neighbour
mitzvah
murder
musar
Musar movement
orphan
peace
Pirke Avot
punishment
rape
rebuke
regard for human life
repentance
retaliation
revenge
reward and punishment
righteous stranger
righteousness
robbery
sexual morality
shalom bayit
sick, visiting the
sin
slander
suicide
theft
zedakah
zedakah box

Festivals

Adloyada
afikoman
al ḥet
Ashamnu
Avinu Malkenu
Avodah
Azazel
binding
bitter herbs
bridegroom of the law
calendar
cup of Elijah
Day of Atonement
Days of Awe
dayyenu

Groups

Aaronides
Abrahamites
Aḥaronim
Amalekites
amoraim
anusim
Ashkenazim
Bene Israel
Bet Hillel, Bet Shammai
black Jews
Bnai Brith
Boethusians
Bratslav Ḥasidim
Canaanites
Conservative Judaism
Donmeh
Ebionites
Essenes
Falashas
Hasmoneans
Ḥibbat Zion
Humanistic Judaism
Irgun Tzevai Leumi
Karaites
Khazars
Levite
Love of Zion
marranos
maskilim
mitnagdim
Mizraḥi
monasticism
Mourners for Zion
Musar movement
nakdanim
nazirite
neo-Orthodoxy
Neturei Karta
Orthodoxy
Pharisees
pioneer
Poale Zion
posekim
Progressive Judaism
Rabbinites
Rechabites

Reconstructionist Judaism
Reform Judaism
Revisionism
Sadducees
Samaritans
Satmar
savoraim
Sephardim
Shabbetaians
Sicarii
Sons of Light
ten lost tribes
ten martyrs
Therapeutae
Zadokites
Zealots

History

Abrahamites
academy
anti-Semitism
anusim
apostasy
Ashkenazim
assimilation
Auschwitz
Babylonia
badge, Jewish
Balfour Declaration
Bet Hillel, Bet Shammai
blood libel
calf, golden
Chmielnicki massacres
Conservative Judaism
consistory
Copper Scroll
court Jews
crypto-Jews
Damascus affair
Dead Sea Scrolls
decree
desecration of the host
dialogue
diaspora
Discipline, Manual of
dress
Ebionites

Institutions

darshan
elder
emissary
epitropos
exilarch
family
Great Assembly
ḥeder
High Priest
home
judge
kabronim
kallah
kehillah
kibbutz
kingship
Knesset
kollel
Liberal Judaism
mahamad
marshalik
matchmaker
melammed
meturgeman
mezumman
minyan
mohel
nagid
nasi
oleh
oneg shabbat
ordination
parents
parnas
polygamy
priest
prostitution, sacred
rabbi
rabbinical conferences
rabbinical seminaries
rav
rebbe
resh kallah
Rishon Le-Zion
Rishonim
rosh yeshivah
Sabbatical year
Sanhedrin

Sanhedrin, Great
scribe
seudah
shaliaḥ
shammash
shiddukh
sick, visiting the
slavery
Synagogue, Great
synod
Tabernacle
tanna
taxation
Temple
temple tax
theatre
tish
ulpan
Union of American Hebrew
    Congregations
Union of Orthodox Jewish
    Congregations of America
Union of Sephardic Congregations
United Synagogue
United Synagogues of America
Usha, Synod of
usury
yeshivah
Zionism
zugot

Liturgy

additional service
Adon Olam
afternoon service
Akdamut
al het
Alenu
aliyah
amen
amidah
Ani Maamin
Ashamnu
Ashrei
av ha-raḥamin
Avinu Malkenu
Avodah

Literature

Shulḥan Arukh
Tanya
Temple Scroll
Temunah, Book of
Thanksgiving Psalms
toledot yeshu
Tosefta
vocalization
war scroll
wisdom literature
yaḥad
yiddish
Zadokite fragments
Zohar

Apocrypha and Pseudepigrapha:
Abraham, Apocalypse of
Abraham, Testament of
Adam, Book of
apocalypse
Apocrypha
Asmodeus
Baruch, Apocalypse of
Bel and the Dragon
Ecclesiasticus
Elijah, Apocalypse of
Enoch, Book of
Esdras
Jeremy, Epistle of
Jubilees, Book of
Judith, Book of
Moses, Assumption of
Pseudepigrapha
Solomon, Psalms of
Song of the Three Children
Susanna and the Elders
tetragrammaton
Tobit, Book of

Midrash:
aggadah
Aggadat Bereshit
Hekhalot, Books of
mekhilta
midrash
Midrash Rabbah
midrashic literature
Pirke De-Rabbi Eliezer

Seder Olam
Sifra
Sifrei
Sifrei Zuta
Tadshe
Yalkut
Yelammedenu

Mishnah:
Avodah Zarah
Avot
Fathers, Sayings of
Gemara
ḥallah
Judah Ha-Nasi
Meir
Mishnah
Moed
nashim
nezikin
niddah
Pirke Avot
sedarim
shas
Taanit
tamid
temple tax
terumot
tractate
Zeraim

Talmud:
Avodah Zarah
Babylonian Talmud
Berakhot
Gemara
matmid
shas
siyyum
talmid hakham
Talmud
talmudic commentaries
tosafot

Mysticism:
Abulafia, Abraham ben
alphabet
amulet
angel

People

Places

Egypt
Elephantine
Fez
Fostat
Galilee
Hebron
Holy Land
holy places
Israel, Land of
Israel, State of
Jabneh
Jericho
Jerusalem
Judah, Kingdom of
Judea
Kairouan
Leontopolis
Liubavich
Machpelah
Mari
Masada
Mezhirech
Mount Carmel
Mount Gerizim
Mount Sinai
Nehardea
New York
Nineveh
Northern Kingdom
Nuzi
Palestine
Paris
Prague
promised land
Pumbedita
Qumran
Ras Shamra
Rome
Safed
Samaria
Sambatyon
Saragossa
Sepphoris
Seville
Shechem
Shiloh
shtetl
shtibl

Sodom
Southern Kingdom
Sura
Syria
Tel Aviv
Tel el Amarna
Temple Mount
Temple Platform
Tent of Meeting
Tiberias
Toledo
Tortosa
Ugarit
Ur
Venice
Vienna
Vilna

Prayer

Adon Olam
al ḥet
Alenu
amen
amidah
Ani Maamin
av ha-raḥamin
Avinu Malkenu
Barekhu
barukh ha-shem
benediction
bensh
birkat ha-minim
blessing
daily prayer
daven
dayyenu
dead, prayers for the
early rising
el male raḥamim
gartel
government, prayer for the
grace after meals
grace before meals
Haggadah
hallel ha-gadol
hallelujah
hashkivenu

Ritual

fish
fromm
genizah
get
gleanings
going up (1)
gown
hakhel
hakhnasat kallah
halakhah
ḥallah
hands, laying on of
hands, washing of
Ha-Shem
havdalah
heave offering
hekdesh
high places
holiness code
idolatry
immersion
incense
inheritance
insanity
intermarriage
isser ve-hetter
Jubilee
justification
kaddish
kapparah
karet
keter torah
kiddush
korban
kosher
kuppah
lamps
laver
leprosy
levirate marriage
levitical cities
libation
loans
maggid
Mah Nishtannah
maot ḥittim
Maoz Tzur

maphtir
marriage
marriage canopy
marriage contract
marriages, forbidden
mazevah
meḥitzah
melavveh malkah
mezuzah
mikveh
milk
mitzvah
mohel
mourning
name, change of
nesekh
ohel
oil
omer
omer, counting of the
ownerless property
parveh
peace offering
peah
peot
profanation
prosbul
proselyte
prostration
punishment
purification after childbirth
purity
ransom
red heifer
redemption of the first-born
rending of the garments
repentance
reward and punishment
ritual slaughter
Sabbath lamp
sacrifice
sacrilege
sale
salt
seder
separating the fat
set aside things
seudat havraah

Scripture

Gog and Magog
Habakkuk, Book of
haftarah
Haggai, Book of
Hagiographa
hakhel
ḥallah
Haman
Hexateuch
Hezekiah
high places
holiness code
Hosea, Book of
image of God
incense
ingathering of the exiles
Isaac
Isaiah, Book of
Jacob
Jeremiah, Book of
Jeroboam
Jezebel
Job, Book of
Joel, Book of
Jonah, Book of
Joseph
Joshua, Book of
Jubilee
Judah
judge
Judges, Book of
Ketuvim
kidnapping
Kings, Books of
kingship
Lamentations, Book of
latter prophets
laver
law
leku nerananah
Levi
Leviathan
Levite
levitical cities
libation
Maarekhet Ha-Elohut
Maaseh Book
Maccabees

major prophets
Malachi, Book of
Manasseh, Prayer of
Manual of Discipline
marriages, forbidden
masorah
matriarchs
megillah
Melchizedek
Micah, Book of
Michael
minor prophets
Miriam
Moses
Moses, Blessing of
Nahum, Book of
nazirite
Nehemiah, Book of
Noah
Numbers, Book of
Obadiah, Book of
onanism
orphan
parokhet
patriarchs
peace offering
peah
Pentateuch
polygamy
priest
priestly blessing
procreation
promised land
prophet
Proverbs, Book of
Psalms, Book of
Rebekah
Rechabites
red heifer
Rehoboam
Ruth, Book of
sacrifice
Samson
Samuel
Samuel, Book of
Sarah
Satan
Saul

Synagogue